100+ VOICES FOR MISS LOU

100+ Voices for Miss Lou

Poetry, Tributes, Interviews, Essays

Edited by

Opal Palmer Adisa

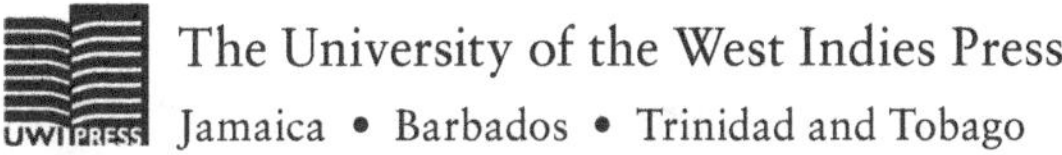

The University of the West Indies Press

Jamaica • Barbados • Trinidad and Tobago

The University of the West Indies Press
7A Gibraltar Hall Road, Mona
Kingston 7, Jamaica
www.uwipress.com

© 2021 by Opal Palmer Adisa
All rights reserved. Published 2021

A catalogue record of this book is available from the National Library of Jamaica.

ISBN: 978-976-640-887-9 (print)
978-976-640-888-6 (mobi)
978-976-640-889-3 (ePub)

Cover image: Tommy Ricketts, *Writes of Passage*.
Cover and book design by Robert Harris
Set in Scala 11/14 x 24

The University of the West Indies Press has no responsibility for the persistence or accuracy of URLs for external or third-party Internet websites referred to in this publication and does not guarantee that any content on such websites is, or will remain, accurate or appropriate.

Supported by the CHASE Fund, Jamaica CHASE Culture · Health · Arts · Sports · Education Fund Working for you

Printed in the United States of America

This book is dedicated to my late mother, Catherine James Palmer, and to all Jamaicans, especially the post–Covid-19 generation, who I hope will still be able to appreciate and recite Miss Lou's poetry with more diversity of interpretation, and thus more depth, and really understand Louise Bennett's legacy and immense cultural contribution.

Contents

SECTION 2. REAFFIRMING OUR CULTURE

SECTION 3. AUNTY ROACHY SEH

FOREWORD

Simply Love

LORNA GOODISON

Thus it was that little Louise Simone Bennett said to herself, "These people are good people, so they cannot talk bad. These are nice people; they are kind people, so the way they talk cannot be bad." And just like that, Louise Simone Bennett found her purpose in life. The good people, many of them women, would come to Louise's house to see her mother, Kerene Robinson, a dressmaker, whom Louise called Love. She called her maternal grandmother Mimi. Her father, Cornelius, a baker, died when Louise was a small girl, but all her life she would remember the stories he told her.

These good people would sit around and talk as they waited on her mother to finish sewing a baby's christening gown, or a school uniform, or a dress for work or church, or sometimes a wedding dress, and sometimes a shroud, because the job of dressmakers is to keep you well outfitted from you come into this world till you leave. Louise Simone would have observed all the people coming and going to her home on North Street in Kingston, then later in Spanish Town, and she would have listened to them telling their stories, in what she'd later call her Jamma language, which linguists call Creole. This was a language forged over hundreds of years from African languages like Akan and Twi, spoken by a great number of the enslaved Africans from whom many of us are descended, and mixed with a variety of the languages spoken by the English, Scottish, Irish and Welsh functionaries who conducted the day-to-day running of sugar estates. Some Portuguese, French, German and other words were also thrown in too.

This is not unlike the English language itself, which has drawn from Saxon and Norse languages, Celtic and Latin, North Sea German dialects and the French language.

So, Louise Simone looked upon and loved these people around her, some of whom had relatives old enough to remember working as unpaid labourers on Jamaica's sugar estates and who had been emancipated. Emancipation came to them in 1838, largely through their own stubborn efforts never to accept the abomination that was plantation slavery, but who had not received even one shilling in payment for their part in creating the enormous wealth of the British Empire.

Notwithstanding the fact that, in 1833, the British government used twenty million pounds, sixteen billion pounds in today's money and forty per cent of their then national budget, as they put it, to "buy freedom for all the slaves in the empire". The amount of money borrowed for the Slavery Abolition Act was so large that it was not paid off until 2015. All of it was given to forty-six thousand British slave owners as recompense for loss of property, their "property" being the former enslaved African people.

The people waited for Miss Lou's mother, whom they called Miss Rob, to finish sewing a garment or stitching in a zip, or running the pinking shears down the side of a seam and snipping off a thread-end and say, "See it here, it finish." Some would say, "Thank you. How much I owe you?" And she would tell them, and they would pay. But some would lower their voices and say something like, "I will send that thing fi yu tomorrow."

Louise Simone learned early what that meant. It meant trust or credit. Credit, as my husband, Ted Chamberlin, likes to remind us, means he or she believes. And she believed in her people. For these were the people who were given nothing, but who built post-slavery Jamaica with their network of friendly societies, lodges and burial scheme societies, leaders' meetings, prayer meetings, diggings, and "day-fi-day" groups.

The people who created the "su-su" or "partner" were thus able to pay the school fees of many of the first Jamaicans to become doctors and lawyers and teachers, nurses and such. It was these people, according to another great Jamaican, Philip Sherlock, who created the social and economic linkages that encouraged social cohesion and built a tradition of social responsibility, of caring, of sisterhood and brotherhood.

Louise Simone made up her mind from early that she would be their champion to the end of her days. From them she learned to trust her instincts, her feelings, her mind. As Jamaican people say, "Yu must follow yu mind."

And so when she started to learn, maybe at school, or at church, or from some smaddy about how some people were better than others because of how they spoke, she refused to believe them. In those days, every single one of us, as Miss Lou's dear friend Rex Nettleford would say, we were all just a few steps behind or ahead of each other out of the cane piece.

If one of those people began to go on about how some people talk bad, Louise Simone would just laugh. And so, in the tradition of great poets and writers like Chaucer, Shakespeare, Dante, and Walt Whitman, she set out to honour her people by writing them into literature as rightful human beings, not as Quashies, but as thinking, feeling human beings with hearts and minds and ambition.

Maybe writers and artists are born that way. This little girl from North Street was a born poet, a born entertainer. There is a powerful scene from an interview with Miss Lou where she describes how, as a young girl, she was moved to wish upon a star for the gift of poetry. And just like in a storybook, that wish came true; but as always, with any wish granted, there would be responsibilities.

She once told me about what was perhaps her earliest public performance. She said that one day, no doubt influenced by the city of Kingston's strolling balladeers and entertainers like Slim and Sam, she just decided to perform in a public space. In this case, I believe it was actually near the Ward Theatre where she, accompanied by her cousin, stood on the sidewalk and started performing right there, reciting poems and singing songs she'd learned at school. Soon people gathered and began to enjoy the show. "Mi sey the likkle gyal good so till. Clap her!"

And clap her they did; and they did something else. Some threw pennies and ha'pennies and maybe even a quattie,[1] or a threepence, and Louise

1. "Quattie" was the Jamaican term for the monetary amount of penny half-penny.

Simone's cousin, Dainty, who had managerial instincts, proceeded to lift up her dress hem and collect the money off the sidewalk. So they came away from her first public performance with a clear profit, because they didn't have to pay for the venue, and there were no overheads.

Louise Simone was granted the gift of poetry and with it came the additional role of freedom fighter; for just as Nanny of the Maroons had to bounce bullets off her body, Louise would have to spend years "chucking" off the wrath and condemnation of the gatekeepers of society, including many of the people she was defending, who brutally attacked her for championing Jamaican speech.

"Ah dat yu madda sen yu go a school fah?" bawled a dissenting voice from the back of an audience during one of Miss Lou's performances.

Her detractors excluded her from anthologies, but she found sponsorship and published and sold her poems herself. She was not invited to their exclusive poetry gatherings yet she ended up performing to tens of thousands. School children recited her poems but were not encouraged to regard her work as real poetry – not like, say, the dialect poetry of Robbie Burns – but her work eventually found its way into the *Norton Anthology of Modern and Contemporary Poetry.*

Louise Bennett was the right woman for the job of freedom fighter for the Jamaican language, for she armed herself with knowledge of the way languages develop. She knew how some people believe that language itself may have begun with gestures, so that there was sign language before spoken language. She knew which language sprung from what branch, and that English is identified as being from the West Germanic family of Indo-European languages. She made herself fully acquainted with her subject.

And so she could, and did, in the words of the prophet Isaiah, confound every tongue raised against her in judgement, as she eloquently defended her Jamma language. She could hold her own with anybody in academia because, among other things, she knew that the first professor of English at Harvard University, in 1876, was Francis James Child, editor of the famous collection *English and Scottish Popular Ballads,* often referred to as the *Child Ballads.* She knew that folk songs and folk tales are at the heart of what is known and taught in the academies as literature, and that folk songs and folk tales come from ordinary people. Often she routed her critics by laughing at them. Her poem "Bans a Killing" is one of the funniest, wickedest, smartest defences ever crafted.

And speaking of crafted, her poems are wonderfully well crafted. For one thing, Miss Lou chose to write them, for the most part, in conventional four line quatrains, so that the reader is drawn in by what looks like a regular poem. Once you are drawn in, the defamiliarizing begins, and you realize you are reading a poem written in Jamaican speech. You realize that the speaker is not some important philosopher or poet located atop a lofty mountain, but a higgler who is selling hairnets and fine-tooth combs downtown, and being harassed by the police for vending illegally.

Miss Lou made brilliant use of the ballad form and the dramatic monologue, and she scored some wicked political points with her deft turns of phrase like in her poem "Pass fi White", but her poetry never served just as a vehicle for her progressive political point of view. She was, in the opinion of no less a critic than Jahan Ramazani, the editor of the *Norton Anthology of Modern and Contemporary Verse*, always a poet. She was a poet whose talent and gifts were wholly Jamaican, and every Jamaican writer since owes her a huge debt for being the model of how to be a Jamaican writer and artist.

Her work took its shape and character from everything Jamaican, the best and worst of us, but mostly the humour and the heartbreak of us, and it excluded absolutely no one. She was a brilliant performer who charmed and captivated audiences all over the world. If you are ever in danger of forgetting what joy and wonder look like, just watch a video of one of her charismatic performances, where everyone in the audience becomes innocent again as they sing along with her and laugh and, as she would say, "Tek kin teeth kibba heart bun."

She was the most Jamaican of Jamaicans, but she was also totally at home in the wider world. She lived and worked in Britain and the United States and she spent the last years of her life living in Ontario, Canada, but her Jamaicanness never diminished. If anything, it was a light that burned brighter and steadier as she grew older. Her Jamaicanness was a powerful magnetic force that drew people to her everywhere she went.

She was always a great encourager to me. She always wanted to know how my writing was going, and if nothing much was happening she'd always say, "Lorna, tek wey you get, so till yu get wey you want."

Miss Lou was a do-good woman. She believed in the power of goodness, kindness, mercy and generosity. She believed that, as it says in the book of Revelations, "The dwelling of God is with people", and she surrounded herself with people at her Enfield great house in Gordon Town – her mother; her mother-in-law; her dear step-son, Fabian; her wards, Christine, Odette and Simone; and what seemed like countless other children whom she took care of. I believe her religion was kindness.

If we were talking with her and someone said something bad, something unkind, she immediately said something good so we would never come away from a conversation with her feeling out of balance. And I know for a fact that this was something that she worked hard to maintain. She taught me that you have to do the work to maintain balance.

It is not an accident that she liked to end her performances by singing "Walk Good". She tried never to leave any encounter on a negative note. "Walk good and good duppy walk with you", she would say.

Something else I learned from her: money and things serve you, you do not serve them. When Miss Lou's beloved Rico, as she called her husband, Eric Coverley, began to have health problems, she sold off all their houses in Gordon Town and moved into an apartment in Canada, where Eric was able to get the excellent health care that added decades to his life. She did this because she loved and valued her husband above all else; and she trusted her instincts, because, at the time, few people thought she was making a wise move.

She told me at the time she was making that decision, that she kept dreaming of losing her handbag; and ladies, we all know what that means. Your handbag has your keys, your wallet, the one lipstick that really suits your complexion, that pack of water crackers, your various ladies' private business. Miss Lou did not want to lose her handbag. Her Rico.

Acknowledgements

Thanks to Dr Rachel Mosley-Wood – head of the Department of Literatures in English of the University of the West Indies (UWI) – who was the first person on the campus whom I approached with this idea of the UWI celebrating Miss Lou, and who immediately said "Yes." Thanks for inviting Dr Isis Semaj-Hall, who simplified the title of the series of events to "Miss Lou 100" and agreed to teach a seminar on Louise Bennett's work. And of course, I want to thank my other colleagues for their tremendous support, particularly Professor Hubert Devonish for his relentless championing of the Jamaican language, and for bringing the Jamaican Language Unit on board. Dr Joseph Farquharson, current head of the unit, hosted part of the one hundred days of celebration. Thanks to the Institute of Caribbean Studies and Dr Sonja Stanley Niaah, and to Michael Holgate from the Philip Sherlock Centre. Thanks to the Mona Library for the amazing exhibition they put on, and to Jessica Lewis, Bernadette Worrell-Johnson and Karen Levy, who actively participated in the planning of the events.

Special thanks to Principal Dale Webber of the university's Mona campus, MultiLink, Irie FM, the Jamaica National Group, the National Housing Trust, and the CHASE Fund, who sponsored the gala event which was held on 6 September 2019 at the UWI Undercroft. Thanks to all of the performers and to Lorna Gordon, who coordinated the gala and helped with public relations.

I am grateful to the administrative staff of the Institute for Gender and Development Studies – Regional Coordinating Office. Bronty Williams-Liverpool worked hard from the very beginning. Kudos to Kadine Marshall-Williams, who assisted with the collation of the book and helped tremendously in contacting contributors and overseeing the management for this anthology. Thanks to Margaret Rowe-Hunter, who transcribed numerous interviews. "Big up" to Sean Mock Yen at the UWI Archives, who recorded some of the interviews, and thanks to Imani Tafari-Ama, who brought an important sponsorship through Irie FM for the gala event at the UWI, Mona.

A special thanks to Minister Olivia Grange, who endorsed this programme and expanded it by bringing embassies, the National Library and schools on board. Thanks to Beverley Lashley, Vivian Crawford, Jo-Anne Archibald, and the other members of the Miss Lou Committee.

Special thanks, too, to Tommy Ricketts and the Poetry Society of Jamaica for organizing readings, producing videos and for creating an exhibition of Miss Lou's life and work.

Finally, thanks to all those who submitted work for the anthology, including those whose works are not included, and special thanks to Isis Semaj-Hall and Lisa Tomlinson who, along with me, read through all the submissions and helped in the selections. Thanks to Juleus Ghunta for his support with editing some of the interviews and essays, and Berl Francis, who assisted with copy editing and working with me to bring this anthology together.

Miss Lou's poems included in this volume are reproduced here as they appeared in the first edition of *Jamaica Labrish* (Kingston: Sangster's, 1966).

If I have failed to mention any of the amazing individuals who supported this venture, please forgive me, and accept my sincerest thanks.

Walk good and may good duppy walk with you.

Louise Bennett-Coverley

A Cultural Icon

Louise Bennett-Coverley, popularly known as Miss Lou, is a household name in Jamaica, a legend and a cultural icon. Born in Kingston, Jamaica, on 7 September 1919, Louise Simone Bennett was the daughter of Kerene Robinson, a seamstress, and Cornelius Bennett, a baker. Her father died when she was seven years old. She attended Calabar Elementary School, St Simon's College and Excelsior High School. She also studied social work at Friends' College in Highgate, St Mary.

In 1945, Louise Bennett was awarded a scholarship to study at the Royal Academy of Dramatic Arts in London. While in England, she had her own radio programme, *Caribbean Carnival*, on the BBC. After returning to Jamaica in 1947, she taught at Excelsior. In 1950, she was back in England where she again worked for the BBC on *West Indian Guest Night* and with various repertory companies. In 1953, she moved to New York and co-directed *Day in Jamaica*, a folk musical at the St Martin's Little Theatre in Harlem. On 30 May 1954, she married actor, radio personality and calligrapher Eric Winston Coverley. She had first met him in 1938 when he invited her to perform at a Christmas concert, where she made her professional debut.

The Coverleys returned to Jamaica in 1955 and Miss Lou joined the Jamaica Social Welfare Commission as a drama officer, a position she held until 1959. Pursuing her studies of Jamaican folklore, she wrote poetry and stories, often in Patwa, had a weekly column in the *Daily Gleaner*, was a fixture in the annual National Pantomime until 1971, and performed on radio in the popular *Lou and Ranny Show*, with Ranny Williams. She pioneered the television programme *Ring Ding*, a children's show, which ran from 1970 to 1982. In 1986, she acted in the American comedy film *Club Paradise*. Shot in Portland, the movie featured Robin Williams, Twiggy, Peter O'Toole and Jimmy Cliff.

She was the author of many books, including *Jamaican Dialect Verses*, *Jamaican Humour in Dialect* and *Anancy Stories and Poems in Dialect*. Her most notable book is *Jamaica Labrish*, which was published in 1966. She also recorded many albums, such as *Jamaican Folk Songs* and *Children's Jamaican Songs and Games*.

Louise Bennett received many awards and honours: MBE (1960); the Silver and Gold Musgrave Medals (1965, 1978); the Norman Manley Award for Excellence in the Arts (1972); the Order of Jamaica (1974); the National Black Arts Festival's Living Legend Award (1992); the Gabriela Mistral Commemorative Award from the Chilean Government (1996); Hon. Doctor of Letters from the University of the West Indies (1983) and York University (1998), and the Jamaican Order of Merit (2001). In 1990, she was appointed cultural ambassador at large by the Jamaican government. Louise Bennett-Coverley died on 26 July 2006 at the Scarborough Grace Hospital in Toronto. Although she and her husband had moved to Canada in 1987, she never forgot her homeland. Their bodies were interred together in Kingston, Jamaica, on 9 August 2006.

INTRODUCTION

Promise Fulfilled

OPAL PALMER ADISA

FIRST ENCOUNTER

My mother would call my sister and me to come and listen whenever Miss Lou came on the radio. If we talked, she would shush us, putting her index finger up to her mouth for emphasis, insisting we listen. She would be completely attentive to every word and pause, laughing at expressions I did not understand. Sometimes my mother would burst into tears and, at the end of the programme, she would shake her head and declare, "That Miss Lou is something else! She sure is something else."

My mother loved laughter and that was perhaps why she loved Miss Lou and never missed a pantomime, always taking my sister and me to see Miss Lou and Maas Ranny, the duo team that had the entire Ward Theatre in stitches. Although I was too young to catch the jokes, I noticed that everyone in the theatre seemed as awestruck as my mother and, as we left the theatre, I overheard various people discussing what aspect of the show they liked. On the drive home to Caymanas Estates, my mother would relive the show, and the car would be filled with laughter. Days after, if a neighbour or relative came to visit, my mother would engage them about Miss Lou, and if they said they had not seen the pantomime, she would insist that they go.

When my mother formed a theatre company for the children of the neighbourhood, she had us do riddles, proverbs, comedic pieces and, of course, Miss Lou's poems. One of the older girls was assigned "Me Bredda", and she stole the show as I looked on enviously. However, I can still see myself being taken in by the poem, and the wonderful surprise ending:

You would like fe know me bredda?
Me kean help you eena dat
Me hooda like know him meself,
For is me one me parents got!

The audience roared and, weeks later, I heard two women arguing and one shouted, "Oonu call me bredda fah me, is not only Miss Lou who ave bredda." This was but one indication of how Miss Lou crept into the life of the people, and how she echoed their voice and how they, in turn, echoed her voice in a symbiotic call-and-response mode, in keeping with our African Jamaican cosmology. Working-class Jamaicans loved Miss Lou because she saw them and gave them a space on the national platform. For the same reason, I suspect my mother, one step removed from the rural agrarian life of her family in Flamstead, St James, had also heard and recognized the voice and the story. Ironically, she had worked hard to ensure that my sister and I, students of St Andrew High School and Wolmer's Girls' School, did not speak that way, as doing so in school would earn us detentions.

But we spoke that way because many of our friends in the community spoke that way. I must admit that I did not then understand the politics of language or the whole colonial process of denigrating what is native.

SECOND ENCOUNTER

When I began writing poetry and publishing, I wrote in standard English, as was expected, but I felt that did not do justice to the Jamaican circumstances that I was exploring. After I entered Hunter College in New York, at seventeen years old, I stepped into my feminist shoes and realized that the market women of my childhood were the first feminists I knew, next to my mother. They were feminists on the basis that they were fiercely independent, had economic viability, were free to move about and, most importantly, exhibited a sense of self-confidence and pride, which is what I believed feminism to be about. Similarly, Miss Lou, taking the brave stance to write in Jamaican nation language, to celebrate our people in such a way, had taken a fierce feminist stance.

Returning home at age twenty, and writing more consciously, with the intention of portraying the lived experiences of working-class Jamaicans, I decided to follow in Miss Lou's footsteps and integrate Jamaican nation language with standard English in my work. Miss Lou paved the way for me and all dub poets who followed.

I first read Louise Bennett's poetry while studying in New York and it was only after my undergraduate degree that I began to study her work seriously. My mother applauded this approach and remarked, "I see you find your way home." My mother typed all of my poems that were published in the *Sunday Gleaner* at that time. Her love and praise for Miss Lou never waned.

Later, when I moved to California to pursue graduate studies, she brought me an eight-track tape of Miss Lou's performances. I think it is fair to say my love for Miss Lou was nurtured by my mother, who raised us on proverbs, which is perhaps why one of her favourite Miss Lou poems is called "Proverbs". She often quoted the third stanza:

> Me know plenty o'dem noh like me,
> An doah de time so hard,
> Me kip fur fram dem far – cock-roach
> Noh biniz in a fowl yard.

In 1987, when I entered the doctoral programme at the University of California, Berkeley, I had intended to write my dissertation on Louise Bennett, by way of a biography. Consequently, I came home and did the first of two interviews with her before she left Gordon Town for Canada, due to her husband's ill health.

Although I ended up not writing Miss Lou's biography, the first essay I wrote in graduate school was based on the interviews; an excerpt of the first interview is published in this anthology. Doing this publication feels like the fulfilment of the promise I made to Miss Lou when I interviewed her more than thirty years ago.

For me, Miss Lou epitomized the spirit of her feminist poem "Jamaican Oman". When I asked her about this poem in 1987, she was reluctant to identify herself as a feminist. However, she did emphasize that she was concerned about women's issues and women's place in the society. Laughing – which was both her joy as well as her mask – she recited verses eight and nine of the poem:

Jamaica oman know she strong,
She know she tallawah,
But she no want her pickney-dem
Fi start call her "Puppa",

So de cunny Jamma oman
Gwan like pants-suit is a style,
An Jamaican man no know she wear
De trousiz all de while!

It was clear to me, and to anyone who knew and worked with Louise Bennett, that she was a strong, determined woman, who was adept at getting her way by being "cunny". The triumphant tone of this narrative poem does not downplay the challenges that women had to navigate or what was perceived to be a woman's place, as is evident in the penultimate stanza:

For "Oman luck deh a dungle",
Some rooted more than some,
But as long as fowl a scratch dungle heap
Oman luck mus come!

This poem, like some others, effectively demonstrates Bennett's socio-historical narrative style. Her poems provide a vivid picture of what was happening in Jamaica and with Jamaicans during her era. More importantly, Bennett's work portrays her love for working-class Jamaicans, who she saw and elevated, not as perfect beings but as incredible, dogged and resourceful people, with magnanimity as well as foibles, as is depicted in the poem "Walk Bout":

Jamaica people walk bout, sah!
Dem get around fi true.
Any part a worl yuh go, yuh
Boun fi meet up one or two.

The first stanza serves as a preamble to the persona's shameful surprise to encounter a "mouti-mouti" Jamaican in France who sees her walking the streets barefoot, not knowing that her shoes were hurting her feet so much she had to take them off. As is customary with the majority of Bennett's poems, the movement is captured in humour.

THIRD ENCOUNTER

My first interview with Miss Lou confirmed her to be the jolly, vibrant person whom I had experienced through hearing her on the radio and seeing her on stage and on television. She spoke fluently, sliding with ease between standard English and nation language. Her experience was vast. She had travelled, she had accomplished a great deal, but there were no airs about her.

I met up with her at Oxford Pharmacy, and then we travelled in my mother's car to Gordon Town. Once home, she called Eric to come and meet me, and she gave instructions to various personnel in the house before settling on the patio off her bedroom.

She talked and laughed, sometimes at herself, and kept asking what I was going to do with the interview. She made me promise that I would send her copies because many had come to interview her but never sent her anything. I assured her that I would, and I did send her copies of both tapes. I also told her I wanted to write her biography, and she was happy about that, but remarked that another woman had started such a project and had been interviewing her, so perhaps I should contact her so there wouldn't be any duplication.

By my second interview in 1988, Miss Lou had already relocated to Canada for Eric's health. She did not want to leave Jamaica, but she didn't want Eric to die either. She was still inviting and welcoming, but tinges of disappointment at the current affairs of her life emerged ever so often. However, she tried to keep positive and in that I realized that controlling her disappointments had been a good part of her life; she was able to keep ahead of disillusionment. If she had not managed this throughout her life, she would not have become what she represents today for Jamaica and Jamaicans.

The guidance and support of her mother and grandmother were important aspects of her foundation, which allowed her to embark on this brave walk. And I suppose, and Miss Lou intimated as much when we talked, that once she decided to pursue a goal, she would not turn back. The further she explored, the more compelling and rich was the material that she unearthed. She learned about the richness and dynamism of the Jamaican folk culture that the people had preserved, without even being consciously aware of her African retention work.

In 2018, when I realized that Miss Lou would have been one hundred years old the following year, I decided to have an event as my personal way to say thanks and pay tribute. Then I had to face the fact that Miss Lou belonged to all of Jamaica and it would take all of Jamaica to honour her. My initial thought was to have a conference at the University of the West Indies (UWI), but again that seemed too limiting. I later decided, as the university director of the Institute for Gender and Development Studies, to use my platform to create a UWI-wide event and get buy-in from colleagues across the different disciplines.

As the idea of a big celebration began to take shape, I realized that it was really bigger than me and the university. I felt that it was Jamaica that should celebrate her, so I knew I had to speak to the minister of culture, gender, entertainment and sport, Olivia "Babsy" Grange, not only because of her portfolio, but also because of her unabashed celebration of our culture, and I knew that she was also an admirer of Louise Bennett.

I am grateful to have lived to see this moment. This anthology is an acknowledgement of the work of Miss Lou. She stepped out on a limb at a time when it was not easy to do so as a woman, as someone from the working class. When I interviewed her, this was one of the things I tried to get at but never quite managed to do. I guess some people are just born where they are born, some to be leaders; they hear the calling and they move with it and Louise Bennett did just that.

She had so much gumption and an unflagging belief in the Jamaican people and the Jamaican language that she spent her entire life researching and showcasing our language and culture.

I saw her perform when I was a child and I have seen videos of her performing. She was an amazing performer and, as other people who have worked with her have said, she had such a strong sense of extemporaneousness, such a sense of pacing, such a sense of command of a situation that she took over wherever she went, without overshadowing or undershadowing others.

She was a social commentator and a culture critic. This latter term has more credence now, but when you look carefully at her work, not just her Aunty Roachy or Anancy stories and her poetry, you will understand how keenly and how acutely she had her finger on the pulse of the people and the society.

This anthology of 100+ voices, in recognition of Louise Bennett's one hundredth birthday, is our tribute to a woman who helped to give many of us the voices we have today; who helped to make us proud as Jamaicans; who has made us see how glorious a people we are, flaws and all; and who has taught us most profoundly about resilience, fortitude and advocacy. She said, "Chat what you have fi chat and no worry bout wha nobody have fi sey."

Tenk you, Miss Lou, for your determination to celebrate the best of who we are. Tenk you too to all those who answered the call and sent in poems, reflections, interviews and essays.

An Outstanding Cultural Influencer

OLIVIA GRANGE

It is a unique honour and privilege for me to contribute to this very significant homage to the Honourable Louise Bennett-Coverley, OM, OJ, MBE, our beloved mother of Jamaican culture, to mark the centenary of her birth. This publication *100+ Voices for Miss Lou* is a tour de force which fittingly locates Miss Lou among the cultural and literary giants of the Caribbean. Miss Lou captured the imagination and hearts of Jamaicans and others everywhere.

Miss Lou's work may be seen as the catalyst that took our culture to the world, in writing, speech and song. She became our chief folklorist, progressed from leading actress in the National Pantomime to one of the chief architects who transformed its format, utilizing the people's language and telling their stories. Taking the stage with the likes of Ranny "Maas Ran" Williams, Lois Kelly-Miller, Leonie Forbes, Bobby Ghisays, and a host of other stars and upcoming artistes, she used her talent as an entertainer and performer to engage the Jamaican children and adults who flocked to the Ward Theatre in their thousands. It was a euphoric experience to see ourselves on stage, and we reveled in it.

I met Miss Lou while growing up in West Kingston. Our first meeting was through her characters, as our teachers and elders took us through her works. Among my favourites was the one about "Mary dry foot bwoy", the migrant Jamaican of humble stock, who returned to the island with a foreign accent after a stint abroad, seeming not to remember his heritage.

Jamaicans love to find humour in our idiosyncrasies; we can get on a plane, return immediately, and end up with a foreign accent overnight. Miss Lou captured that perfectly! So I immediately identified with the female character who decided to give Miss Mary's bwoy less than subtle reminders of his origins – with fun, humour and undistilled mockery. Consider these verses from "Dry Foot Bwoy":

Wha wrong wid Mary dry-foot bwoy?
Dem gal got him fi mock,
An when me meet him tarra night
De bwoy gi me a shock!

Me tell him seh him auntie an
Him cousin dem sen howdy
An ask him how him gettin' awn,
Him seh, "Oh, jolly, jolly!"
Me start fi feel so sorry fi
De po bad-lucky soul,
Me tink him come a foreign lan
Come ketch bad foreign cole!

Similar to the first three stanzas that narrate the pretentiousness of the dry foot bwoy, the last three stanzas expose him as a sham whose disdain for the sweet Jamaican language makes him the laughing stock of the community.

An now all yuh can seh is "actually"
Bwoy, but tap!
Wha happen to dem sweet Jamaica
Joke yuh use fi pop?

Him get bex and walk tru de door,
Him head eena de air;
De gal-dem bawl out affa him,
"Not going? What! Oh deah!"

An from dat night till tedeh, mah,
Dem all got him fi mock.
Miss Mary dry-foot bwoy!
Cyaan get over de shock!

Among the challenges of being Jamaican is the chance that somebody "remember who you be" and where you come from and could trace your lineage, or measure your pedigree, using that knowledge. Miss Lou's lessons in self-identification became a basis for cultural identity formation.

Miss Lou's work also tackled the social and economic power play between men and women, offering much to the discourse on gender politics and gender relations in Jamaica. This focus on the role of women as guardians and bearers of our culture and heritage is seminal to Miss Lou's work. She lived through the turmoil of the 1930s and must have witnessed and been inspired by the activism of such women as Aggie Bernard, Lady Bustamante, Edna Manley, Amy Jacques Garvey, and others who struggled for better working conditions for working-class Jamaicans. Also worthy of mention is the indomitable role played by women working in Jamaican households.

When Miss Lou performed live, she often quipped that her legendary Aunty Roachy said of the "Jamaica Oman": "Dem cyan gwaan sing bout oman a hebby load", as she explains in the poem:

Jamaica oman cunny, sah!
Is how dem jinnal so?
Look how long dem liberated
An de man dem never know!

Look how long Jamaica oman
– Modder, sister, wife, sweetheart –
Outa road, an eena yaad, deh pon
A dominate her part

From Maroon Nanny teck her body
Bounce bullet back pon man
To when nowadays gal-pickney tun
Spellin-Bee champion

From de grass root to de hill-top
In profession, skill, an trade,
Jamaica oman teck her time
Dah mount an mek de grade.

Some backa man a push, some side-ah
Man a hole him han,
Some a lick sense eena man head,
Some a guide him pon him plan!

Neck an neck an foot an foot wid man
She buckle hole her own;
While man a call her "so-so rib"
Oman a tun backbone!

But de cunny Jamma oman
Ban her belly, bite her tongue,
Ketch water, put pot pon fire
An jus dig her toe a grung.

For "Oman luck deh a dungle"
Some rooted more dan some,
But as long as fowl a scratch dungle heap
Oman luck mus come!

Lickle by lickle man start praise her,
Day by day de praises a grow;
So him praise her, so it sweet her,
For she wonder if him know!

The "report" ends with Auntie Roachy no longer singing "Oman a hebby load" but rather "Oman a bread winna, oman stamina, oman tallahwah, oman a man mooma!"

I finally met Miss Lou and interacted with her in my role as community organizer in West Kingston and then as a politician focused on Jamaican culture, heritage and tradition through the Ministry of Culture and the Jamaica Cultural Development Commission. What struck me was that Miss Lou's expressed mission and purpose was to proclaim and celebrate the dignity and pride of the ordinary Jamaican who suffered discrimination and various indignities in post-slavery, pre-independence Jamaica. In her own words, "When I was a child, nearly everything about us was bad, you know; they would tell yu seh yu have bad hair, that black people bad . . . and that the language yu talk was bad. And I know that a lot of people I knew were not bad at all; they were nice people and they talked this language."

As a result, often dressed in the bandana of the people, she lived and carved out her destiny among us, absorbing the rhythm of our language, culture and heritage; cataloguing, portraying and promoting Jamaicans as we are, with our proverbial wit and humour, dignity and self-respect.

Miss Lou immersed herself in the Jamaican character and allowed us to see ourselves in ways that caused us to love, challenge and appreciate who we were. For her, the ordinary Jamaican was the embodiment of the true Jamaican spirit – feisty, fractious and forward, never backing down in the face of challenges. It was this rambunctiousness that we took with us whenever we had situations that needed those extra bouts of assertiveness.

It was the spirit found in our street peddlers, many of whom I got to know as I grew up in Kingston; like the "South Parade Peddler" who had to navigate the streets of downtown Kingston and simultaneously negotiate with potential customers in an undesignated area, with a seeming I-don't-really-need-your-money attitude, while looking around regularly for the approaching "corpie", aka Babylon. At the sight of the police, vendors would "pick up (dem) foot inna (dem) han'", while still touting their wares:

> Ef dah police ever ketch we Lize
> We peddla career dun.
> Pick up yu foot eena yuh han'
> Hair pin! Hair curler! Run!

Interacting with Miss Lou helped me to understand and appreciate the various movements I witnessed in West Kingston, as I noticed the many regular people who gathered at places like Chocomo Lawn and Orange Street (now Beat Street) "holding a rhythm", as they created a new brand of music that took on the world.

Encouraged by the vision of Miss Lou, I was able to appreciate how the hustlers and inventors used their creativity to hone new skills in their quest to overcome poverty and achieve recognition. These were the guardians of the culture, determined never to bow to domination, but rather to engage their history, heritage and culture to position themselves for global acclaim.

It was for me an eye-opening experience to discover how Miss Lou had succeeded in transforming everyday people into folk heroes. She was able to create scenes that mirrored the real experiences of our people and convert them into stories of bold adventures and acts of heroism. We knew them. We met them every day. Our lives were filled with their escapades. They spoke the language we spoke – the Jamaican language.

Vendors on the streets found space in her stories as she famously portrayed their braggadocio and belligerence as they peddled their wares. There were dressmakers, policemen, preachers, census takers, politicians – every character of note was given pride of place and, on a whim, could irreverently be brought low. Not to mention snippets we get of everyday life, such as in the excitement of passengers riding on the tramcar. With the tram arriving late, as it often did, Miss Lou captured the fast-paced changes a passenger could experience in a "Rough Riding Tram":

> Hi, sah, me deh pon hase. Ah beg
> Yuh lif up fas. Yes bwoy!
> Dis is de way tram-car fi drive,
> Yuh feel de cool breeze? Whai!
>
> Me nearly drop offa de seat!
> All right, sah, dat wi do!
> Me pan a bickle tun over!
> Tap! Man wha wrong wid yuh

And then at the end of the journey the passenger leaves the tram cursing out the driver:

> Ah gwine mark yuh buck-buck forehead,
> An yuh kooroo-kooroo face!
> Ah gwine beat me mumma grave fi yuh
> An put yuh to disgrace!
>
> Ah gwine fi meck yuh swell an bus
> Like Sam craven goat-kid!
> Me is de las smaddy yuh gwine
> Teck tram-car run weh wid.

It was real. It was fun. It was engaging. It positioned the ordinary Jamaican people as literary figures deserving of recognition and investigation and elevated their character, behaviour and language to academic discourse, social documentation and commentary.

Miss Lou's insight and indelible influence have made a long-term impression on me, deepening my understanding and determination of self, while reinforcing my confidence in the limitless capacity of the Jamaican people to entertain and do just about anything. It was a signal honour and a prized opportunity to be mentored by our matriarch, a certain preparation for my current role.

She recognized in calloused hands the proof of a hard life endured for the benefit of our children. She saw in our faces the hope for prosperity and a brighter future, and in our eyes the determination to let nothing impede our progress. It was always obvious that she had an undying love and appreciation for the Jamaican people, the heroes who triumphed over slavery, whose independence of spirit was the backdrop of the national independence movement, as she penned in the poem "Independence":

Independance is we nature
Born an bred in all we do,
An she glad fe see dat Govament
Tun independant to.

Through the social commentaries and depictions in Miss Lou's writings, Jamaicans came to understand and affirm their identity and appreciate their heritage. She challenged education policy by creating *Ring Ding*, a television programme for children aired on the Jamaica Broadcasting Corporation. Together with Marjorie Whylie and other artistes, she set out to instill in the children of Jamaica pride in their language, heritage and culture. With riddles, poetry, songs and dances, she stood up to the critics and naysayers and ensured that a generation of young people would grow up having a more respectful approach to the nation's language and, by extension, the people whose creation it was. There has not been any other programme on national television to rival the influence that *Ring Ding* had on children across Jamaica.

Her tireless efforts to liberate the people's language from the prejudicial clutches of those who would use it to devalue them are a lasting legacy. To her credit and, in response to her influence, I was part of the decision that ensured that poetry in dialect became a signal element of the repertoire of the Jamaica Cultural Development Commission's National Festival of the Arts.

Miss Lou loved to laugh and I loved it when she laughed. Hers was a contagious, full-belly, unbridled, passionate laughter that filled her eyes. And because she loved the people, all her characters were touched with that freedom to be who they were, whether in the intemperate scoldings of Uriah when he substituted for the pastor "when rain fall hard" in "Uriah Preach", or Winjy who was the source of "Cass Cass".

Another dimension of my experience with Miss Lou was in Toronto, Canada. These were emotionally charged and fulfilling moments in my long-standing relationship with her. The group of us included Judge Pam Appelt, executor to Miss Lou's estate, my late mother, and a host of supporters, who rallied around her on every occasion. The group has managed to keep her image and memory alive over the years since her death, including the designation of a space in her honour and the proclamation of Miss Lou Day in Toronto. It was there that she made the utterance that became the mantra of our Jamaican diaspora. In her words: "Any whe mi deh, a Jamaica me deh", a statement that captures the truism that every Jamaican in the diaspora carries the country in his or her "lion heart", faithfully committed to the Black, Green and Gold.

Miss Lou has left the physical realm, but her life's work lives on in each of us, and I am honoured to have my voice counted among the 100+ voices in this anthology paying homage to her. In recognition of her monumental influence on the culture and people of Jamaica, the government has erected a statue of her in the Gordon Town Square, now renamed the Miss Lou Square. May Jamaican people now, and those yet unborn, always gaze up at the monument and remember her as one of the greatest influencers on the culture of the Jamaican people. Walk good, Miss Lou!

A Formidable Woman

PERCIVAL J. PATTERSON

Interview with Opal Palmer Adisa

Opal Palmer Adisa: When did you first hear of Miss Lou?

Percival James Patterson: I heard of Miss Lou when I was attending Somerton Elementary School in St James. We had a headmaster who was preparing us for independence, and Miss Lou was a source of inspiration for that new Jamaica. From Mondays to Thursdays, we were taught the syllabus. As far as literature was concerned, it was largely English-based. For our headmaster, that was not good enough. So on Fridays he exposed us to things Jamaican and that was where Miss Lou came in.

We were encouraged to recite some of her poems. The poem that was assigned to me was "Miss Mary's Turkey Dead". So we began to get a taste of Jamaica, and the significance of it was that her poetry was in the language of the people. I think everybody should understand that, when it came to an understanding of English grammar and English literature, there was hardly anybody that could beat Miss Lou. So her choice in writing in Jamaican dialect was a deliberate decision to express herself in the manner in which we speak from day to day.

I think we also have to appreciate her seminal influence at that time. She wanted to celebrate Jamaican grammar, and once Miss Lou said it, that was it. Miss Lou is responsible for the spelling of most Jamaican words because, although we spoke in dialect in our homes and in the villages, there was no dictionary to which one could refer to find out how a word was properly spelled, and so how Miss Lou spelt it became the authority on the subject.

I moved to Kingston to attend Calabar High School, where we continued to recite poems done by Miss Lou, but I didn't meet her until much later on. She was very close to Norman Manley and his wife Edna and, on occasions when I visited them at their home, Drumblair, I would see Miss Lou there.

OPA: Can you reflect a bit on what your first meeting was like?

PJP: Drumblair was a place where those who were involved in the field of culture would gather from time to time, particularly to meet with Edna Manley, who I think is one of the mothers of Jamaican culture. Whether you were a poet, a potter, a painter or a playwright, there was always a special place for you at Drumblair. I had seen Miss Lou's photograph in the *Gleaner* before I met her in the flesh at Drumblair. In that first meeting, she was sharing some of her most recent poetry.

Miss Lou was very caring and patient, particularly towards younger people, but she hated formalities and did not entertain anybody who was pompous or who pretended to be other than they were. I was very comfortable in her presence. She told us stories about her childhood and her time in the United Kingdom on a scholarship which was awarded by the British Council.

When she returned to Jamaica, she became Pantomime Queen and Ranny Williams was the Pantomime King. They brought laughter and a certain quality to pantomime which, at that time, was a must-see for families. Miss Lou had a very sharp intellect and there was no subject that could be raised in which she couldn't bring a point of view in her own inimitable way.

After that meeting, we crossed paths frequently. Jamaican culture meant a great deal to her and she wasn't selfish about it. She shared her skills and knowledge with any young person who was interested in learning.

OPA: Did you, at any point, have a one-to-one conversation with her about her work?

PJP: No, I never had an occasion when we met one-to-one. I met her mostly at Drumblair and sometimes at her theatrical presentations, when I went backstage to talk with some of the actors.

After she decided with her husband to move to Canada for health reasons we spoke very frequently on the telephone and, whenever I visited Toronto, I always made sure to find some time to look for them. I would always call her on her birthday. I once sang the popular happy birthday song for her and she stopped me and told me to sing the Jamaican version. We sang together but she was a much better singer than I was.

By then we had conferred on her all the medals that were possible, including the Musgrave Gold Medal from the Institute of Jamaica, the doctor of letters from the UWI [University of the West Indies], the Order of Jamaica, and the Order of Merit which is reserved for persons who have made excellent contributions at the international level.

OPA: Tell us about your decision to bring her home to Jamaica in 2003.

PJP: I decided to bring her home for several reasons. I thought younger Jamaicans should see her live and that she should see Jamaica as it was developing. I didn't have any difficulty in persuading the cabinet that she should be invited home as the guest of the Government of Jamaica. The main thing we wanted to do was to allow the younger generation who had heard and read about her, who had listened to her when they were growing up, to meet her in person. We wanted to have her back and to show our gratitude for her distinctive contribution to the country.

She was always yearning to be home and she had made it very clear that she wanted to be buried here. We were happy to do that for her. She earned the recognition that she got all over the world. She had a way with words, so even those who were not familiar with the Jamaican dialect could understand her. When she said "boonoonoonoos", you understood that this was something nice, something very special.

OPA: Talk a bit more about some of the other activities she had engaged in during her state visit and about her wanting to be buried here and how you helped to make that happen.

PJP: We arranged groups from the theatre and creative-writing fields to meet with her informally. These groups included very young children. I'll never forget going to Vale Royal with her for a special function arranged in her honour. I had taken my eldest granddaughter with me and Miss Lou held her spellbound for the whole time. My granddaughter was twelve then. Miss Lou had an encyclopaedic memory. She had met my granddaughter when she was much younger and had mentioned her grandmother who was a minister of government in Guyana, and who had been responsible for arranging a production of CARIFESTA in Georgetown which Miss Lou had attended as a featured artiste.

At the time, we brought her home we had just gone through an exercise of returning Emancipation Day to its rightful place in our national life, and we had also ordered, based on the recommendations of our committee, that the black on the Jamaican flag would not mean hardships, but would mean resilience. We saw Miss Lou as a critical figure who could help us to express these sentiments.

When Eric died in 2002, I spoke to her to convey my sympathy and best regards and she said to me in very clear terms that she wanted to be buried in Jamaica and she insisted that in death, as in life, they should be together. When she passed I was no longer in government, but the cabinet records reflected that intention and so we were able to celebrate her life and to ensure that she was reunited with Eric in death. Theirs was a union which always reflected the values of self-worth and of excellence in whatever one was asked to do.

OPA: What do you think Miss Lou's legacy will mean for future generations of Jamaicans?

PJP: I think she will forever remain an icon for her creative skills. She was a heroine for what she did to build the confidence of the Jamaican people. Particularly at this time, as we are passing through the challenges of Covid-19, something she wrote as an early poem should be a source of inspirational comfort for us:

> Sun a shine but things no bright
> Pot a boil but bickle no nuff
> River flood but water scarce ya
> Rain a fall but dutty tough.

I mentioned earlier that she was part of the nationalist movement that helped us, as a people, to achieve sovereign status and to be in charge of our own destiny. When the independence observance took place on the sixth of August, 1962, she wrote in "Independence":

Independance wid a vengeance!
Independance raisin' cane!
Jamaica start grow beard, ah hope
We chin can stan' de strain.

And then she went on in another poem, "Jamaica Elevate", with:

We defence is not defenceless
For we got half o' brick
We got we broken bottle
An we Cookoomacka stick.

That was Miss Lou – formidable. I think I can say that without any chance of being successfully challenged. We will remember her for her vibrant life, for the very sharp intellect and the genius of imagination which were her hallmarks during her rich and glorious life.

SECTION 1

ONE BIG FAMILY

This section records the love and regard held for Miss Lou by her family, close friends and those she mentored. As is evident in her poem "Love Letta", Miss Lou had no inhibitions when it came to expressing her love. She was generous to a fault with both her possessions and her time, as she said once: "Sometimes, I'm in the middle of mi work and a whole heap a pickney just arrive and I seh Lord have mercy, I have plenty things to do, but I tell dem to come in and sit and talk. Sometimes dem hiking and somebody tell dem seh Miss Lou live up there so, so dem come look for me. I would say I can't stay too long and we sit and talk for a little while. I like that, mi just like people."

Love Letta

LOUISE BENNETT

Me darlin Love, me lickle Dove,
Me dumplin, me gizada,
Me Sweety Sue, I goes for you
Like how flies goes for sugar.

As ah puts me pen to paper
An me pen nib start to fly,
Me remembrance remember
De fus day you ketch me y'eye!

You did jus come off o' tram-car,
A bus was to you right,
A car swips pass you lef-aise,
An you stan up stiff wid fright!

You jaw drop, you mout open,
Jus like wen jackass start yawn,
Me heart go boogoo-boogoo,
An ah know wha meck ah born!

Noh scorn me lickle letter Love,
Noh laugh after me yaw,
Me larnin not too good, but wat
Me kean spell, me wi draw!

De ting eena de corner wid
De freckles is me heart,
An de plate o' yam an salfish mean
Dat we can never part.

See how me draw de two face dem
Dah-look pon one anada
Well one is you an one is me,
Teck anyone you rada!

Is not a cockroach foot dis, is
A finger wid a ring,
An it mean ah want to married you
Dis line is piece o' string.

Teck it put roun de wedden-finger
A you wedden-han,
Careful fi get de right size, an
Den gi it to dis man.

De man is me. Now sweet-rice,
Keep swell til ah see you nex'
Accep me young heart wile ah close
Wid love and bans o' X.

My Mother, My Friend

FABIAN COVERLEY

Interview with Opal Palmer Adisa

Opal Palmer Adisa: You are here for the one hundred days celebrations. How do you feel to be a part of this, and what do you think Miss Lou would be thinking if she were alive today?

Fabian Coverley: This is a big programme. Miss Lou would have called it "a boonoonoonoos task". You and your team will go down in history for having done it. Miss Lou was appreciative of people, and they gave her inspiration, and knowledge for most of her poems and verses.

OPA: Yes, perhaps Miss Lou would have said that, but I think it is a small way to recognize her for celebrating and preserving our culture, and for putting our nation language on the world map. There was a young man at one of our events who asked, "Who is Miss Lou?" I was shocked that there could be someone who is not familiar with Louise Bennett's work.

FC: Yes, many young people do not know about Miss Lou. This is why the work we are doing at the Miss Lou Estate and at the Foundation is so important. We have to maintain her legacy. My family and I understand this, and so we have decided to raise awareness in schools. Miss Lou's work should be on schools' curricula. When I was going to Jamaica College, I learned so many things that were not relevant to my history and me. Louise Bennett-Coverley is relevant to Jamaica. She did her work from her heart. People sometimes say to me, "Your mother was an activist". I didn't really see my mother that way, but if you think about what she did, what she was up against, you can see why that designation makes sense.

OPA: Absolutely. One of our presenters said she was a social commentator. Her work was rich with references to Jamaica's history, with what was happening with soldiers in England, and what was happening in Jamaica during the turbulent 1970s and 1980s. She captured the experiences of ordinary people.

FC: Many of her poems that were written thirty, forty years ago are still relevant today; for example, "Colonization in Reverse" and "Dutty Tuff". The more things change the more they remain the same. When she was writing those poems, I don't think she was thinking they would be relevant in 2020.

OPA: Most people knew Miss Lou as a cultural activist and as a performer. What was she like as a mother?

FC: Well, I didn't think of her as a celebrity. I thought of her as my mother, as Aunt Louise, as the person I looked to for guidance, the person who – along with my father, Eric Coverley – provided me with food and shelter, knowledge, and a sense of purpose. So my perception of Miss Lou was different from the perception that the public had. I accompanied her on many of her projects, and we developed a very strong bond.

OPA: How did it affect you when she was flocked by supporters while you were with her in public?

FC: At first, I wondered why people did that, but after a while, I began to understand what she meant to Jamaica, to Jamaicans. And, of course, being Miss Lou's son meant that I was able to access certain resources, enjoy certain privileges, and "get a spot in the line". I eventually realized that she was special, because she was surrounded by people who were always hailing her, and she always had a kind word for everyone she met, regardless of their status in life.

OPA: What was it like to accompany her on her research projects? That must have been an incredible learning experience for you.

FC: Well, at that time, I didn't really know what was happening. She would come home, pick me up, and say, "We going to country." She did not like to travel on her own. So we would travel together and talk about all kinds of things that were pertinent at the time. When I got my licence, we both drove. We would go to a village and people would crowd around. Hol Plummer from RJR and I would deal with the technical aspects of the meetings, such as recording the interactions between her and the people she was teaching and learning from.

OPA: Everybody talks about how Miss Lou was this remarkable person, but her struggle was extremely hard at times. She had to fight because she insisted on writing in the Jamaican language, and people in power didn't see any academic value in her work.

FC: She did not necessarily want this battle. It was forced on her by people who believed in the superiority of the Queen's English. Miss Lou knew English better than most because she had to understand it to know how to depart from it properly. She researched African languages to understand her roots, and certain people started to put her down. "Is dat yuh sen yuh chile go learn a school?" This is one of the questions they asked my grandmother. At that time, some upper-class Jamaicans were more English than the English. Miss Lou kept going. After a while, people began to accept her.

OPA: Talk about your grandmother.

FC: Her name was Kerene Robinson. I called her Miss Rob, and Miss Lou called her Mother Love. While I was growing up, Miss Lou and my father were always busy working, and so Miss Rob was the one who ran the house. Miss Lou provided funds and Miss Rob looked after us.

OPA: As a young poet writing poems in nation language, I often wondered where Miss Lou got the bravery and stamina from to do her work. The colonial spirit was so strong. While I was in school, students were not allowed to talk Jamaican. Where did she find the strength to push back against people who were telling her "no"?

FC: A lot of it came from her mother and her grandmother, Meme. They told her, "If you want to do something, do it". As a seamstress, Miss Rob made the best dresses for the "hoity toities" of the day. So, Miss Lou was brought up to take note of the little details, and to be best at whatever she put her mind to.

OPA: I was told that Miss Lou's mother made the first bandana outfit in Jamaica. Is this true?

FC: I'm not sure. Bandana came from India and was quite popular among higglers. Higglers in those days always wore a big bandana skirt to hold their goods and money. Miss Lou brought bandana to the stage, and it became very popular.

OPA: And "the stage" includes pantomime. What was pantomime like in the early days?

FC: Pantomime began as a show for middle- and upper-class Jamaicans. The content of the productions was similar to what was popular in the 1940s in England. Local producers quickly learned that most Jamaicans were not interested in the style or content of those productions. With the introduction of local talents such as Miss Lou, Ranny Williams, Lois Kelly-Barrow-Miller, Oliver Samuels, Rex Nettleford, and Noel Vaz, Henry and Greta Fowler, who were the original pantomime producers, realized they had to change the format in order to appeal to a wider cross-section of the population. Initially, English themes and stories were Jamaicanized. After a while, the productions became fully Jamaican. Back in those days the principals were barely paid, and entire casts worked as volunteers. We should be grateful to them for doing it because they built a tradition. I used to look forward to the season, because it drew me closer to my mother. It also gave me opportunities to enjoy my passion for driving and to develop my technical skills.

OPA: Did Miss Lou talk with you about her writing process?

FC: I was more interested in the technical side of things. However, Miss Lou had stations throughout the house where she created her work. These included her bedside table; her favourite red couch in the living room; the chair in front of her bureau mirror in her bedroom, which was eventually moved to her personal patio that my father built. The patio became her extended office. There was always a notebook at the dining table in the kitchen. At the time, I didn't realize what was happening.

OPA: Tell us about the relationship and partnership between Miss Lou and Eric Coverley. What pushed them to move from Jamaica to Canada?

FC: Miss Lou and my father bought ten acres of land in Gordon Town. They renovated an old estate house that was on the property and, even after they moved in, there was no road to drive up to the house. So they had to park the car at the bottom and walk up the hill. My father and I would literally push Miss Lou up. Later, a road was cut and we were able to drive to the house. The property had a servants' cottage that they rented out, and after a while they started to build houses on the property to help supplement their pension. My father did the design and construction management, while Miss Lou provided administrative support, inspiration, imagination, and "backative". They worked well together and complemented each other.

Leaving Jamaica was not in the game plan. However, my father became ill, and Jamaica wasn't prepared at that time to provide the heart surgery he needed. By moving to Canada he gained seventeen more years of life. By that time, I was already living in Canada, and my wife and I prepared the way for them. After a while, they became citizens. They died in Canada and were buried in Jamaica.

OPA: Tell us about *Ring Ding*.

FC: I believe *Ring Ding* was inspired by *Sesame Street*. When television came to Jamaica many foreign programmes came in, and *Sesame Street* was very popular among children. Barry Johnson from JBC [the Jamaica Broadcasting Corporation], Miss Lou, and others got together and decided to create a Jamaican kids' show. This is how *Ring Ding* came about. They did a test run, with back-up music by Fab 5, and it took off. It was Marjorie Whylie, though, who became the staple musician for the show, and she and Miss Lou developed a strong relationship. I was studying radio and TV overseas at the time. When I returned, I became the driver for the show and helped with the technical challenges as an employee at JBC. There was a set format, but a lot of improvs took place. Children would come from all over to show their talents. The island tuned in on Saturday mornings to watch the show. It became an institution. There are lots of *Ring Ding* children out there.

OPA: Yes there are. What would you say has been Miss Lou's greatest contribution to Jamaican culture?

FC: She made people conscious of who they are, conscious of their Jamaicanness. She made people realize that "wi likle but we tallawah", and inspired them to promote our culture and heritage, to understand the importance of preservation. She is an important figure in Jamaican and world history. She probably has more prominence overseas than in Jamaica.

OPA: Yes, I know that many groups in Canada have recognized her work.

FC: Shortly after Miss Lou died, the Ontario government dedicated a room at Harbourfront Centre in her memory. The Miss Lou Room can hold about 250 people. Visitors get to see photographs of her on the wall and to listen to her recordings. Some people go there to tell their stories. All of her work from the twenty-odd years she had lived in Canada is being digitized and stored at McMaster University, in Hamilton, Ontario. Dr Tony McFarlane was the one who encouraged me and my co-executor, Pam Appelt, to contact McMaster, which is well known for digitizing works of famous people. Before she came to Canada, Miss Lou gave her collection to the Institute of Jamaica, which turned it over to the National Library of Jamaica. They are collaborating with McMaster so that researchers will be able to access the files on the internet.

OPA: Miss Lou always seemed happy even when things were not going right. Was this her personality at home?

FC: Yes, it took a lot for someone to get Miss Lou upset. She gave a lot and expected a lot too, and she was usually happy. There were times, though, when her Aunty Roachy side came out. Aunty Roachy would fix you up! Miss Lou was able to cut to the chase without using curse words. She simply spoke the truth.

A Strict but Wonderful Mother

CHRISTINE SWABY

Interview with Opal Palmer Adisa

Opal Palmer Adisa: Tell us about your relationship with Miss Lou.

Christine Swaby: I grew up with Louise Bennett. You could say I am her daughter. I started living with her at six months old. There was a problem in my mother's marriage, so Aunt Louise's mother, Miss Rob, who lived with Aunt Louise at the time, said she wanted to keep me. Aunt Louise loved Miss Rob so much that she gave her whatever she wanted. That's how my mother and I ended up living with her. Aunt Louise was a wonderful mother to me – strict but wonderful. When I was bad, I got a good whipping, but other than that, things were fine. Mr Coverley was a great stepdad. I got the best of both worlds.

OPA: In what ways was Miss Lou strict?

CS: In good ways. She never let any of us get away with anything bad. We had to tell the truth, get home on time if she was not able to pick us up from school, and so on. She didn't spare the rod when we misbehaved. She taught us to be respectful. Whenever people visited her, we made sure they had a refreshing drink. I remember a couple of times when Edna and Norman Manley, and others like Lois Kelly-Barrow came to the house and it was my job to make sure everyone was comfortable.

OPA: What are some specific things Miss Lou taught you?

CS: I learned to use the typewriter at age eight. When she handwrote her scripts, I had to type them up for her. I learned a few of her poems from doing this. I also worked as her assistant at *Ring Ding* on Saturday mornings. I can't remember how old I was when I started doing that. I remember doing a lot of behind-the-scenes work, though. I followed her to pantomime and to JBC Radio as well. My main role was to type her scripts.

OPA: As you got older how did your relationship with Miss Lou change? Were you given more responsibilities?

CS: I just continued doing whatever she needed. She was very independent, so she didn't really ask much of me. However, she made sure I and my sisters had a good life. She sent all four of us to Holy Childhood High School. After high school, she allowed me to take my own path. Unlike my sisters, I didn't go to college. I regret that now and I'm drilling the importance of higher education into my kids.

OPA: Did your sisters live with her as well, or just you?

CS: Yes, they came to live with us when I was about twelve. Before that, we would visit each other. Education was a big thing for her. When we got bad grades, we were punished. She kind of spoiled me; she was a bit tougher on my three sisters.

OPA: Give some examples of how she spoiled you.

CS: I remember getting bad grades one year and she said, "Oh, that's my baby. Don't worry, she'll do better next time." Well, that didn't happen frequently, now that I'm thinking of it. When it was time for me to go to high school, I had to repeat the fifth grade and she punished me by ending my dancing lessons. That was hard, because dancing was my passion. I also attended piano lessons with Lois Kelly-Barrow. She stopped that too, after she was told that I kept picking the chips off the piano. She promised to let me dance in high school if I got better grades. I never went back to dance class; I wasn't the brilliant type.

OPA: As a mother, how did Miss Lou encourage you? How did she talk to you about womanhood?

CS: Truthfully, she didn't say much. I remember when I got my period and thought I was dying, she said, "Now you are a woman and you have to watch out for boys. If you play with them you will get pregnant." She really didn't explain how I would get pregnant. But whenever I had it real bad, she was always there. A couple of times, I was so sick that she had to leave what she was doing just to pick me up from school. She would drop everything and come.

OPA: Tell us about "family time".

CS: When we didn't have light we would play games. There was a running joke that daddy wasn't the disciplinarian in the family, and sometimes when we got into trouble, Aunt Louise would mock him, and daddy would say, "I don't get any respect around here." He got respect, of course. Sometimes, during blackouts, Aunt Louise encouraged us to perform. I remember doing a Donna Summer song once and she just cracked up. We ate together, recited her poetry, played dominoes or cards.

OPA: Did Miss Lou cook or was there someone who did that?

CS: We had a cook, and we had a woman who did house cleaning three times a week, but the cleaning was limited to Aunt Louise's room, the living room, daddy's man cave and grandma's room. They would not touch our area. We had our area and chores to do.

OPA: Did you ever accompany Miss Lou when she went to interview people about Jamaican culture?

CS: Yes, but I usually waited in the car. I went to Jamaica House with her to see Michael Manley and to support Jimmy Cliff when he got his Order of Jamaica. When I was twelve she took me to England for two months where she was doing a movie. I enjoyed it. We went to Buckingham Palace and Windsor Castle and spent time with family.

OPA: What was Miss Lou Like in those settings?

CS: She was humble. She did her job. I was always by her side. Whoever was with her, she made sure we were taken care of. She was very kind and I believe some people abused that.

OPA: That's what everybody says – that she was very generous.

CS: Yes, people in our neighbourhood would come to the house and get a day job or a job for a week, if something was broken. We had mangoes and pears on the property, and people came and reaped, but they did not share whatever profits they made.

OPA: How did you feel when you saw her on stage and all of the children clamouring to get her attention?

CS: I was really proud, but to me she was just Aunt Louise. They didn't know the true person; they only saw the person on the screen or on the stage. I got more love than she gave to other people. I would hate when she came to pick me up at school, because the kids would crowd the car, trying to get *Ring Ding* tickets. When I was in high school, a girl said to me, "Why you trying to go in her car? You are not her child!" My friends dealt with her for disrespect. I wasn't trying to say, "Oh, I'm her child, you better move!"

OPA: Did she show affection easily at home?

CS: Oh yeah, she would give us hugs. She made us feel wanted and special.

OPA: Talk a bit more about the relationship with Miss Lou and her mother.

CS: She was the love of Aunt Louise's life. She loved her husband, but grandma was everything. Whenever she returned from a trip, the first person she checked on was her mother. When grandma died, Aunt Louise was doing a show in Spanish Town. We got a call from home after the show telling her she should come home immediately. She said, "My mom is gone." I said, "No, no. They probably just want to make sure that you are there." When we got home, grandma was gone. She took it really hard for a long time. She didn't participate in the pantomime that immediately followed grandma's death.

OPA: When did you leave Miss Lou's house?

CS: I left in '82. I was kind of a rebel and she was very strict. In hindsight, I can see that she meant well. If I wanted to go out, she'd give me chores to do. After I did them and went about by business I'd get into trouble – even though I was twenty-one! I moved out when I was twenty-one. This really hurt her, because I was her baby.

When the opportunity came for me to move to Chicago she signed the paper right away. By then we had made up. The move made me grow up because I no longer had helpers to do everything for me.

OPA: When I interviewed her in 1988, she went into her bedroom. It seemed like her bedroom was where she kept court. What do you remember about her bedroom?

CS: She had a big dresser in there where she would put on her makeup and get dressed, and that's where the TV was. It was her sanctuary. What I loved about her bedroom was that it led onto the enclosed patio. Before she had that enclosed patio she would sit at the table and do her work then give it to me through the window. Eventually she started going from her bedroom to the patio where she had her coffee in the morning. She and Lois Kelly-Barrow would talk on the patio for hours. Lois would come up for Christmas breakfast each year.

OPA: What was the Christmas breakfast like?

CS: We had a big ham, ackee and salt fish, fried dumplings, orange juice, bammy. Everyone would hang till dinnertime. Then we served the ham with rice and peas, salad, roast pork. It was a feast. One or two other friends would come. When she became really popular people would spill out onto the patio. She had a gathering every New Year's Eve. People came for the curried goat, roast pork, jerked chicken. When we got older we were able to invite our friends; no one paid. It was just a big old house party.

Tenky Miss Lou, Tenky

JOAN ANDREA HUTCHINSON

Mi is a born Jamaican, an mi proud
An yuh fi feel proud to
Fi walk roun an big up yuh chest
An say t'anks to Miss Lou

When she did start, she neva know
A how it woulda go
An nuff nuff people wen da laugh
An a call har poppyshow

But she galang strong an stick it out
For she know say she did right
Inna har belly battam she did know one day
Dem mus an bound fi see di light

En time trouble teck wi, a Miss Lou wen put
Wi good name pan di map
An wen dah push Jamaica heritage
An Lawd, she wouldn stap

She say, "Teck kin teet kibba heart bun"
When time neva so sweet
"Good luck will come as lang as fowl
A scratch up dungle heap"

Nuff a dem did tink say she crazy
An nuff meck up dem face
How she a chat dis buguyaga Patwa sinting
All ova di place

For dem did tink Patwa was bad English
Dem neva know, poor ting
Wouldn tell dem pikni 'Nancy story
An folk song, dem wouldn sing

But a di jackass wid him lang tail
Bag a coco comin down
An di peel head jankro pon tree tap
Jus meck dem head spin roun

An lickle by lickle, dem start fi back har
Start fi fan har flame
An see it deh, afta all dese year
Miss Lou a one household name

Now wi nuh shame fi chat wi owna language
An wi dah tank yuh fi it Miss Lou
Dem a teach it clear up a university
An ongle sake a yuh

Dem a meck flim, dem a write book
Dem a sing wole heap a song
An a say "Oh Patwa a one good language"
But yuh wen know dat all along

So now wi tan up proud fi be Jamaican
An wi waan di whole world fi hear
Miss Lou, nuff tanks fi howdy an tenky
Neva bruck no square

Together for Life*

Louise and Eric Coverley

MERVYN MORRIS

When Eric "Chalk Talk" Coverley, a well-known figure in Jamaican show business, attended an Excelsior High School prize-giving ceremony at which Louise Bennett performed, she asked for his autograph. Mr Coverley expressed pleasure in Louise's talent and encouraged her to develop it. (He was aware of her work before that day; he had been shown some of her dialect poems left by mistake in a car she had travelled in.)

An impresario, he asked her mother's permission for Louise to take part in the popular Christmas morning concert he organized. After he had visited three or four times, Louise was persuaded by her mother to accept the invitation. Seventeen years old, she took part in the 1936 edition of the Christmas morning concert at Coke Memorial Hall in downtown Kingston. She pleased the audience and did three encores. Eric Coverley's cheque was her first professional fee: one guinea (twenty-one shillings – more than enough, she often said, for a pair of wedge-heel shoes).

She continued to perform, and her first book, *(Jamaica) Dialect Verses,* came out in 1942. In May 1943 when the *Gleaner* began to publish Louise Bennett's poems, "Jamaica in Dialect", each Sunday (paying her half a guinea a column), her work became widely known. She was often invited to perform at churches, for women's clubs and at drama festivals. Sometimes she was asked to come and see, and comment on, dramatizations of her poems.

---

*Adapted from Mervyn Morris, *Miss Lou: Louise Bennett and Jamaican Culture* (Kingston: Ian Randle, 2014).

She found herself increasingly involved in assessing performances, and began to feel the need for formal training. She thought of studying in the United States where her father's sister, Aunt Florence, lived; but while doing promotional work for the Jamaica Federation of Women, she was told of another possibility and encouraged to apply. She was awarded a 1945 British Council scholarship to the Royal Academy of Dramatic Arts (RADA), the famous drama school in London.

Three months after she arrived in England, when she went with others to record Christmas messages, she was offered a contract to host a radio programme on the BBC Overseas Service. Called *Caribbean Carnival*, it was recorded each week before a live audience and transmitted worldwide.

In 1947, after RADA, she rejected opportunities to remain in Britain as a professional actress and returned to work in Jamaica. She taught speech and drama at Excelsior High School and continued to write and perform. Then, in 1950, she was appointed island supervisor of the Women's Federation; but, finding it difficult to make ends meet, she went back to England and the BBC. She hosted an hour-long weekly radio show, *West Indian Guest Night* (recorded on Tuesday evenings for broadcast to the West Indies the following day), did television work as a storyteller, and acted with some repertory companies.

Urged by her Aunt Florence, Louise moved to New York in February, 1953. In spite of her experience, it was not easy to get a job. After a while, she did some radio broadcasting at WWRL with Alma John, and sang folksongs at the Village Vanguard in Greenwich Village. She taught folksongs to various people, including Irving Burgie and Harry Belafonte.

When Eric Coverley came to New York in September 1953, on assignment with the Jamaican delegation to the United Nations, he phoned Louise on her birthday. She was delighted to hear from him, and they got together immediately. They co-directed a folk musical called *Day in Jamaica*, which included folksongs, Anancy stories, Bennett poems and *Chalk Talk* routines by Eric. The show began at St Martin's Little Theatre in Harlem and, by request, moved around Episcopalian church halls in New York, New Jersey and Connecticut.

As they were often invited to the same parties, they spent a lot of time together. After seeing her safely home, Eric would often be hurrying to catch a late train back from Brooklyn to where he was staying in Manhattan. Sometimes he was so tired that he fell asleep and missed his stop. According to them both, before rushing to catch his train late one night he said, "It looks like I'll have to marry you", and she said, "Coverley! That could never be a proposal!" They were married on 30 May 1954, at St Martin's Episcopal Church in Harlem, in the presence of Eric's mother and Louise's Aunt Florence, both resident in the United States. Eric was forty-two, Louise thirty-five.

They returned to Jamaica in 1955. Looking for somewhere to make their home, they bought a neglected stone building on a hill beside the river in Gordon Town and transformed it into a haven. Eric had had a son, Fabian, before he married Louise. For the next quarter of a century, their well-staffed household absorbed a steady stream of other people's children, who they brought up with Fabian, some staying a few months or a few years, and some longer.

Louise and Eric were based in Gordon Town until after *Ring Ding* and *Miss Lou's Views* (called *Smile Jamaica* at that time) were cancelled by the Jamaica Broadcasting Corporation in 1982. They moved for a while to Fort Lauderdale, Florida, from where it was easy to travel to engagements in North America and the United Kingdom.

Eric's health became a serious problem while they were in Florida. To get medical care they might afford, they returned to Jamaica and were advised that he needed heart bypass surgery. Fabian, who was now a Canadian citizen, suggested they come to him in Toronto, and he sponsored their admission in 1987. After a while, they were able to get an apartment for themselves in Scarborough in a building for senior citizens. When Miss Lou performed in Jamaica on World Theatre Day in March 1990, she sang (to the tune of *Come back, Liza*):

> Nuff Jamaica sinting mi miss,
> Nuff foreign tings sweet mi too,
> Mi nah tell yuh no lie,
> But when mi memba sweet Jamaica
> Water come a mi yeye.

And she also declared, "Any which part mi live – Toronto-o! London-o! Florida-o! – a Jamaica mi deh!" As many people noticed, in Jamaica as in Canada, Louise and Eric were a very loving couple.

Their happiness together is celebrated in an anniversary poem written by Louise in May 2000.

Forty-six-'ear-ole today
De jokify ole-oman an
De boasify ole-man
Got wedden annivers'ry
Forty-six-'ear-ole today!
Dem a memba one-anada
Bout de bright an sunny wedda
Pon dat happy married Sunday
Forty-six-'ear ole today
An de jokify ole-oman laugh an sey
"Ole-age meck de body shaky,
But de spirit strong wid love"
An de boasify ole-man sey
"Spirit strong wid love same way!"
Den dem hug up one-anada
An w'isper to one-anada
"Happy Lovin' Annivers'ry
Forty-six-'ear-ole today."

They were residing in Toronto when they died, Eric in 2002, Louise in 2006. Her body was flown to Kingston, accompanied by Eric's remains, which were reinterred in National Heroes Park next to where Louise would be buried. In the eulogy at the official funeral, Rex Nettleford said, "Dear Miss Lou, just walk good yuh hear, along with Maas Eric (or Coverley as you affectionately called him), who is waiting for you at Heroes Park. Just remember us back here. We remain your faithful friends and admirers."

One of the Great Joys of My Life

EASTON LEE

Interview with Opal Palmer Adisa

Opal Palmer Adisa: When and in what capacity did you work with Miss Lou?

Easton Lee: At age fifteen, while I was a student at Windsor High School, I was invited to participate in the annual pantomime. This was in the '50s, when being invited to play in pantomime was the ultimate achievement. I met Miss Lou at one of my rehearsals. After I performed, she called me to give me some tips.

Miss Lou always did that with the younger performers. That was her way of coaching us.

When we were performing at the Ward Theatre, for instance, she would call us quietly to a seat when we were not on stage and were required to sit in the audience and watch. One of the things I remembered her telling me was, "When you talk, people must hear you; and if it is possible at all, dem must see you mouth moving. Dem must see you face."

Working with her was one of the great joys of my life and our bond grew when I was appointed the drama officer for the whole island of Jamaica. She was the drama officer for Jamaica Welfare, now the Social Development Commission, and when she resigned and moved to England, she recommended that I take her place. This was in the '60s and it changed my life.

OPA: Tell us how it changed your life.

EL: There were a lot of welfare drama groups in Jamaica then and I went across the country to help them perform their plays. It changed my life because I hadn't done anything like that before. I was working in commerce. Before Louise left, she would invite me to join her on her trips to places like rural St Thomas. If she was working with a group of forty people, she would give me half of them. She was prepping me to replace her.

When she retired, she told the commission that I was the only person in drama that she knew who could do what she was doing and I did that for five years. I learned so much from the people I met as well.

OPA: What other interactions did you have with Miss Lou and can you tell me about some memorable incidents, anecdotes?

EL: One Chinese New Year, when we had our family dinner, I saved a serving of pork and took it to Louise. After that, no New Year don't come when she don't invite us to her house. We had to bring pork, of course. Once when I was in Canada, my daughter had arranged for me to see her. On our way we stopped at a Chinese restaurant and we got her a dish of pork. She loved pork.

OPA: Talk about Miss Lou as a cultural icon and her significance to Jamaica.

EL: We were not permitted to speak Patwa in school; wi would get wi head lick off when wi spoke dialect. So when she started speaking dialect, some people gwaan bad, saying it is low class and this and that. When I was in high school we went on a trip out in the country and when I came back I wrote a poem in dialect and performed it for the students and dem nearly tear down di place.

After that, I would go to see Miss Lou perform. Young actors and students who were into drama looked forward to her performances. There was always something new to learn and she was always open to teaching others. She treated others like royalty. She made sure to see all the high school performances and would be frank but kind with her advice. When I was appointed to go around Jamaica and help groups do their drama, I remembered what and how she had taught me. She never called me out; she always talked to me quietly.

OPA: Did Miss Lou ever share anything about her childhood with you?

EL: Yes. She told us that she was born on North Street, downtown Kingston, near Public Hospital, and that she went to a nearby school. She talked about her mother a lot but didn't say much about her father, only that he used to walk with her from where they lived on North Street to the Roman Catholic Cathedral. She said they both enjoyed listening to worshippers preaching in the Jamaican language and singing Jamaican spirituals in a nearby Seventh-Day Adventist church.

OPA: Did she tell you why it was important for her to collect folklore?

EL: She didn't tell us why she was doing it, but she said that the stories of the "real Jamaican people" are important. I think her greatest contribution was getting others to see that the Jamaican language is legitimate. She made people acknowledge that all Jamaicans, no matter how poor, no matter what they did for a living, were important and worthy of respect.

She wrote a poem called "Strike", about the protest action of managers and workers at Appleton sugar factories. It was published in the *Sunday Gleaner* and drew attention to their plight. At the time, the factories were owned by British companies. Her poem made the strike public. She gave people a voice.

Conversation, Consultation, Communication, Celebration

MARJORIE WHYLIE

Ah . . . Jamaica, land of wood and water, and so much more. Island of contrasts, soaring undulating mountains, lush green valleys, colourful tropical blooms, climbing vines and lianas, birds of vibrant colours, darting, flying and perching in the forest canopy, chattering, singing and whistling, and the blending of the sounds of nature.

Conversations are a suite of speech patterns that are musical, melodic, with rising and falling tones, the percussive rhythm of consonants and the pitch of vowels, accompanied by gesture and movement. All this in the conversation and interactions of our people "pon de corner" becomes a dramatic scene, a presentation of mood, emotion and apparent meaning being conveyed unaware and out of earshot. Perhaps, if our hands were tied, we would not be able to express ourselves successfully or succinctly.

A male friend, in one of our conversations about the culture and habits of Jamaicans, spoke of the enticing rhythm of the swinging arms and circling hips of women as they walk, making men pause their usually assertive strides, stopping to lean against a wall or a pole, rubbing the chin to admire and appreciate the passing parade with winks and catcalls.

These rural and urban settings inspired Miss Lou to document her observations of the life and lifestyle of the several layers of colonial Jamaica and the use of the challenges as stepping stones in a movement towards political independence, and the establishment of full self-government.

Her work, which is unique, documents the situational dramas and social interaction in verse, in the language of the people. Many of these poems are of priceless historical value, as they tell his story and her story, so true to life with serious intent, but couched in humour, which is, more often than not, sidesplitting.

In my earliest years, I listened to Miss Lou on radio. Her programme was a mixture of poems and depictions of life and traditional songs, music that accompanied the stages of life, from the cradle to the grave, from lullabies to ring games, work songs that take on the rhythm of the task, almost turning a work gang into a well-oiled machine.

Add to the mix songs of praise and derision. Commenting on the social environment, the domestic dramas of "man and woman story" and family life, the topic of the day and socio-religious activities – worship to the beat of the drum, and death celebrations, which in today's observance, are accompanied by "duppy bands".

I met Miss Lou's songs on radio, sang them to myself and accompanied myself for my ears only. All that changed when I was nearly six years old; I was asked to play the piano at Miss Amy Bailey's Housecraft Training Centre. Miss Lou was the main performer, but was a little disturbed that the person who was to accompany her was nowhere to be seen. I offered to play for her. Her doubt at my ability showed on her face, but she was gracious, and we did three songs together, the most successful being "Banana, Banana, Banana".

Banana, banana, banana!
In the island of Jamaica
The food we eat so very nice
Especially in the parish of Hanover!
The food we eat so very nice.
Banana, banana, banana.
Ripe an green, banana,
Roas' an bwile, banana,
Gros Michel, banana,
Eat wid ile, banana . . .

When it was finished she said to me, "But chile, yuh can play!" I smiled for many days after that. That was to be the first of many occasions that my piano was heard supplying accompaniment for her, being ever mindful of the appropriate harmonic chord progressions and providing a hint of the rhythms that would be played on hand drums.

My next meeting with Miss Lou was at a variety concert at the church hall of St Luke's Anglican Church in Cross Roads. This was an extremely popular type of function which could, and often did, include a great variety of presentations from singers, ballet dancers, violinists and guitarists, classical and popular musicians, magicians, elocutionists, and often, the Frats Quintet, members of the Langley family, Marse Ran (Ranny Williams) with his jokes, and from time to time Miss Lou. On those occasions in my childhood and teenage years, I played a classical piece chosen by my piano teacher, Miss Ena Helps, or a popular song of the day.

Just to be in the company of Miss Lou was a joy. Louise had been to Friends' College, a Quaker institution in Highgate, St Mary, at the same time as my older cousin Marilyn from Detroit, Michigan, and she was known by my mother.

After my graduation from the University of the West Indies with an honours degree in Spanish and while I was employed at Kingston College, note of my musical activities seemed to have gone before me, and I was given the task of teaching singing and musical appreciation to forms one and two. I was absorbed into the Kingston College Chapel Choir as an accompanist and assistant to the choirmaster, with responsibility for working with the trebles and altos. This was a learning experience for me, although I had been a singer and accompanist with the University Singers. The skills learned at Kingston College were exceedingly useful, as I was invited by Greta Fowler to be rehearsal pianist for the Little Theatre Movement's National Pantomime in 1966. I think she was aware that I had been a member of the orchestra for Roots and Rhythms, a dance show in celebration of independence in 1962.

There I met Miss Lou again and this time, she was on stage and I was in the orchestra pit. I was only to be involved in rehearsals, but it turned out that the music was written by the late Sonny Bradshaw, and I was given the task of leading the orchestra. I had some experience, as I had been the pianist for the National Dance Theatre Company (NDTC) from 1963, so there was some confidence. Happily, the chorus rehearsed at different times to the "stars", so I worked closely with Miss Lou, and had to transpose some of her songs to keys that were more comfortable. As she often said, "Me sing inna B flat." I later came to understand that she meant that her highest note was B flat above middle C.

That was explained to me during a show at the Commonwealth Festival in September of 1965. I was in England with the NDTC, and when the company was returning to London from Cardiff, Wales, Miss Lou, the Frats Quintet and I left the train to do a concert. When Miss Lou's turn to perform came, I gave her the usual introduction. When there was no sound from her, I played it again. Said Miss Lou, "Ah wha wrong wid da little gal. She nuh know say me sing inna sea (C), me nuh sing inna river." I created an introduction modulating through several keys with complex chords, ending up in the original key, and she sang with aplomb.

I was involved in several Little Theatre Movement pantomimes as musical director, and the rehearsals were wonderful examples of Miss Lou's amazing creativity. In many of these plays, she showed her skill in writing songs in the vernacular, using traditional folk melodies, or composing her own melodies, which used the rhythm of the language to guide the flow of each melodic line.

Driving up to Miss Lou's house was not the easiest of trips. Leaving Papine, the Gordon Town Road is winding and narrow, with cars parked haphazardly, requiring patience and skill to negotiate the multitude of corners to Gordon Town Square. Then came the steep incline up to the Coverley residence, and the careful parking required on arrival.

From the front lawn, one could view the surrounding mountains and the Hope River winding down to the valley below. Surrounded by bougainvillea, hibiscus, crotons, aralias, Chinese lantern, Chinese privet and triple poinsettias, this was a lush garden. The house was a huge stone edifice with a large living room and bedrooms to each side. A flagstone patio stretched across the full width of the house. Stepping down from the living room was the formal dining room with pantry and kitchen behind. There were other bedrooms and a swimming pool to the eastern end of the backyard.

Soon after my arrival, Miss Lou would move into her bedroom, which opened on to the patio. She did her writing and planned her programmes seated at a typewriter with a large wooden chair. She often held court stretched out on her king-sized four-poster bed. We talked about everything under the sun. Family, politics, entertainment, theatre, festival competitions, a little gossip here and there and stories which were not to be repeated. As time went by, she would call for chicken and Syrian bread with a large jug of lemonade. But there were also many visits to seek material for suites to be sung by the NDTC Singers for the upcoming season of dance.

There were occasions when the visit was for more than just sharing songs from her collection. Miss Lou was a mentor, and a gracious one at that. When I was appointed head of the Folk Music Research Department at the School of Music at the Edna Manley College for the Visual and Performing Arts, I went out on initial field trips to areas close to Kingston and St Andrew in St Catherine and St Thomas and, through my years as an adjudicator at competitions in traditional folk forms and consultations with the dance coordinator, some work was done.

Miss Lou shared with me the research methods that she had used during her years of working at Jamaica Welfare, now the Social Development Commission. She always made these trips opportunities for sharing. She would teach a song that she knew, and then when the ice was broken, the group with which she was working would warm to her, share songs, accompanying movement and rhythms. She also advised me to observe what may be needed by the members of the group, or the host at whose yard we met, as researchers were often offered fruit and ground provisions and so on. I learned and made sure to travel with groceries, a few beers, and white rum, depending on the tradition that was being observed.

My closest and most enjoyable period in performing and creating with the Honourable Louise Bennett-Coverley was JBC TV's *Ring Ding* which started as Jamaica's answer to a foreign children's show in which the kids were Do Bees. *Ring Ding* was telecast live between breaks of the scheduled programme. Miss Lou taught the children folk songs and ring games, clapping games and action songs, and told them Anancy stories. I was her sidekick at the piano and, as it grew popular, it was extended to a one-hour presentation. The format of the programme changed, allowing for children to perform, reciting poems, giving jokes, coming up with riddles, singing, with school groups performing dances and choral speaking. The children would write to JBC asking to participate, and postcards with a drawing of Miss Lou would be sent to them with the date for attendance; short auditions of those wanting to perform would be held and the order of performance programmed.

One morning some time afterwards as I was entering my bank, the security guard greeted me by name and proudly showed me his postcard from many years earlier, a precious memento that he had kept in a little plastic case. I then realized just how loved and celebrated Miss Lou was.

The programme would open with:

> Pass di ball an di ball gawn roun, Mawga Nanny show me how di ball gawn roun,
> Pass di ball an di ball gawn roun, Jigga Nanny show me how di ball gawn roun,
> Play boy, play boy, play boy play, Mawga Nanny show me how di ball gawn roun.
> Play girl, play girl, play girl play, Jigga Nanny show me how di ball gawn roun.
> Short and fat but a play we da play, Mawga Nanny show me how di ball gawn roun.
> Tall and slim but a play we da play, Jigga Nanny show me how di ball gawn roun.

As the performing opportunities grew, Miss Lou came up with a variation on a traditional song that opened concerts, allowing adult audience members to perform, paying a penny to be allowed, and paying also to stop the item if it was not up to par.

After a period of amazing popularity, watched for a decade by adults and children, and with a history of being watched in village squares at a shop or bar that had a television set, or by people sitting with neighbours who were fortunate enough to own a set, the series came to an abrupt end with absolutely no warning. One Saturday, I drove into the parking lot in front of the television building, noting that there were only a few children sitting on the wall by the patio. Miss Lou soon drove in, and suggested that we go inside, as usual. The studio was in darkness, the dressing rooms similarly. There were no cameramen, no director, no floor manager, and no production assistant in sight. We waited outside to welcome children and the odd parent to apologize that the show had been cancelled.

To date, there has been no apology from management, no explanation, no thank yous nor appreciation for the years spent creating, hosting, and presenting a programme that had exposed a generation of young ones to Jamaican culture in an entertainment package, presenting material from Miss Lou's collection, using her magical love for children and her sense of impeccable timing.

Not to be forgotten are Miss Lou's programmes on radio, one produced for entertainment, the other for social commentary. On Sunday nights, families gathered at home to listen to the radio programme *The Lou and Ranny Show*, a half hour comedy produced live on the stage of the Carib cinema, before the scheduled movie. The cinema was filled, usually to capacity. JBC had to set up sound and props, with the large outside broadcast truck parked and director and sound technician in place.

The script was written by actor and comedian Randolph "Ranny" Williams, with him and Miss Lou as the main characters and Maude Fuller and Tony Henry as the supporting cast. There were two separate scenes, one with a newspaper setting with characters Glenna Brydon as Miss Pollolopsky, and the other in Susumba Walk, with the two stars playing husband and wife. Ranny was always getting up to some bad behaviour to which Louise objected, and she would chase him shouting, "Whey me piece a flat board?"

My brother, Dwight Whylie, who was the announcer for the show, and who provided sounds of running feet and other sound effects, would never have to hold up a sign which had the word APPLAUSE written on it. People listened as she commented on actions, decisions, social commentary. Dwight would always have to make the gesture of a quick movement of a hand across the neck to indicate that the laughter should be cut for the purpose of continuity of the show.

Miss Lou's Views was her other offering on radio before the news at midday. There were no sacred cows. There was gentle humour underlying serious social commentary on decisions and actions at different levels of society. She had a following of loyal fans who listened regularly to this five-minute programme. It meant that she had to be aware of daily happenings and write on subjects that were relevant, cogent and thought-provoking.

There are so many ways in which the Honourable Louise Bennett-Coverley can be described: writer, actress, comedian, educator, historian, language artiste, poet, philosopher, nation builder. If one were fortunate enough to be listed as a friend, she can be described as mother, a lover of children, a mentor, a Jamaican with a deep sense of spiritual strength, a hostess "with the mostest", an advisor and someone who revelled in the success of others.

A Journey of Love

BARBARA GLOUDON

Louise Bennett is a study of love. She was filled with love for her family, her friends, her people and her nation. Her journey of love began with her mother who encouraged her talent. "Miss Fiddie", as she was known, raised her daughter in difficult times, a time when poor black Jamaicans did not think that the culture they possessed was worthy. Louise's love for her culture and the language of the people defined her career as a writer, performer and social worker (in the years when she worked with the Jamaica Welfare Programme).

Of course, there were those who did not think much of her writing in dialect, and when her work was first published in the *Gleaner*, there was backlash at the thought of the common language being reproduced for all the world to see. She was not deterred. She knew the beauty of our language, the way we "mix-up and blend-up" English and Twi to express ourselves with humour and succinctness. We speak and move and live with rhythm, and Lawd de riddim sweet.

She gave us no end of proverbs, which were, in fact, parables. They were almost biblical in their connotation: "When trouble tek man, pickney shut fit him." The British say, "Any port in a storm", but how clear is "When trouble tek man, a child's shirt will fit him" (even that will cover him)?

She loved her Jamaican people. Her ability to capture the essence of the proud, strong "Jamma" woman was reflected onstage in many a pantomime, bringing dignity to those who knew that "rain a fall but the dutty tough" and the medicine to what ails us is to "tek kin teet kibba heart bun". When Louise first became involved in pantomime in the 1940s, the cast was mainly expatriates or white Jamaicans. There were a few black Jamaicans here and there. She set out to change that, to make sure that Jamaicans could see ourselves onstage and feel proud of our Anansi stories and our folk songs, which she always wove into the work.

Louise's other love was her family. She shared many years with her beloved husband, Eric. He was a man who saw in this young girl tremendous talent, and she often told the story of the great love affair which started with Coverley. They were a pantomime in themselves. He played the straight man to her comedic character and you never got between them.

There was a lovely story of when they just got married; they were living in New York and they didn't have much money. Every day Louise would send Eric to the meat shop to buy a pound of mince, and she became very creative in cooking minced meat. It finally came to a head one day when he arrived at the butcher and before he could say anything the butcher said, "Mince, sir?" and Eric never went back to buy mince. She used this joke for a long time.

She loved her extended family, the many children she took in and looked after at her home in Gordon Town. As a result, there were always children around. Nobody knew where they came from or where they went after they had lived there. Eric, who was a man of great dignity, put up with a lot from Louise and her foolishness. He came storming out of his room one day and said, "Louise, this has reached the lowest it has ever reached. A boy just met me in my bedroom and said, 'Hello Papa.' I have never seen the boy before in my life and I have never seen his mother." Louise thought it was hysterical.

Louise did not love blindly. In her works, she spoke of the things that troubled her, about how we sometimes treat each other. The injustices that were present in society. She couched it all with her full-throated laugh or her rhyming words, but she never shied away from the things she thought to be wrong.

Louise was part of a political movement at the point in history when Jamaica was building itself into a new nation. One of her strongest political statements was the one she was making against the British. It was accepted then that all things British were good, hence a generation grew up being made to feel ashamed of their tongue because that was thought of as bad; it was not British. Now, you can find foreigners singing her songs and quoting her words. She had the last laugh when she wrote "Colonization in Reverse", when the mighty Britain needed our strength to rebuild. Sadly, things have changed again, but Louise would probably say, "Today fe you, tomorrow fe me."

Louise spoke of "water more dan flour" and "jackass sey de world nuh level". These are all similes she developed out of her domestic knowledge, and she gave them to us like pebbles to carry in our pocket. As we go through uncharted difficulties today let us draw on her words of wisdom and comfort. Louise loved and she received love in return. Let us continue to love each other. "Aii-yai-yii."

Boonoonoonoos

LINDA GAMBRILL

Miss Lou and Eric were guests at our wedding, up in the hills near Newcastle in 1970. I wore a copy of my grandmother's wedding dress; Barry Chevannes sang "Ruth and Naomi"; Buddy Pouyatt and I swirled in the quadrille; *Star* columnist "Stella" (Barbara Gloudon) stated that caviar rubbed shoulders with saltfish and ackee; my three sisters looked so beautiful, and Miss Lou and Eddy Thomas (the best man) taught the Gordon Town mento band "Here Comes the Bride".

Soon after, Tony (my husband) and I came to live in a teeny one-bedroom, ivy-covered cottage up on Enfield Road, Gordon Town, which we rented from Miss Lou. Through the open kitchen window, after a heavy rain, you could see the mist creeping over the mountain. Early on a Sunday morning you could hear women singing, all dressed in white, coming down Enfield Road to a baptism at the river bank or carrying cakes to a wedding

On a Saturday night, Mr Savage, with his donkey, staggered up the hill, cursing every bad word imaginable and stopping at the corner by our cottage for a rest. A few days later, he would send me Resurrection lilies. To us romantics, it was a magical time and a special place, so after consulting with our landlady, Miss Lou, we called the cottage "Boonoonoonoos".

We were privileged to enter into a unique circle of friends who lived in Gordon Town and who were all connected to Miss Lou and Eric. Miss Ivy (Eric's sister), a gracious lady, lived in a house below us. Then there was dear old Mother Coverley, who loved to bake us cakes, especially carrot cake. But she usually forgot the sugar! The indomitable Lois Kelly-Barrow (known simply as Barrow) was Miss Lou's dearest friend and stage colleague. It was a treat for me to be in a play, *Paradise Street*, which Tony wrote and in which Miss Ivy and Lois alternated as the leading lady.

We also met Ancile and Barbara Gloudon, Lorna Goodison, Mr and Mrs Jacobs, Mrs Simon (the postmistress), Mrs Little (the shopkeeper) and Mrs Parks (the owner of El Paso). Miss Lou and Eric knew everyone in the area; she was the queen of Gordon Town.

Going to visit Miss Lou was not an easy matter. The hub of the house seemed to be her bedroom, from which she conducted the events of the day. "Come in, mi chile," she would call out as I entered the house. There she was in her housedress seated in a large comfy chair in front of her old four-poster bed, looking out onto the hills. There was a window seat in front of her for visitors; there was a cluster of "curouchies" (a mishmash of this and that) and papers all around, mostly written in her flowery script and some faithfully typed by her assistant, Valerie, from the village.

We would settle down and both have a cigarette. She smoked Matterhorn, although she always seemed a bit bronchial, and was always wrapping up her throat or chest, fearful of catching a cold. In the middle of our conversation, you noticed she was looking around for something. A cry of "Pickney!" would go out and, from the cavernous house, one of Miss Lou's children would arrive and be asked to find some piece of clothing needed for a meeting later, or a page hidden among the various things, perhaps a vital end of a poem. Then a little later perhaps the phone would ring, someone wanting an interview (much laughter and chatter), or a university student needing guidance. She would always oblige. I tell her, "Miss Lou, I have to go." A reply, "Hold on little, mi love."

And then, inevitably, Eric (Coverley, as she called him) would arrive, pipe in mouth, to ask her something, and sometimes he would go down memory lane and chat about how he discovered her and encouraged her career and how he had to win her mother's approval. And if you were lucky she would join in and remind him of shared experiences; it could become like a play between them.

She recalled, "Remember the time when you managed those visiting evangelists and they owed you" – much laughter from Eric – "and we heard they were leaving the island today so we rushed down to Myrtle Bank Hotel where they were staying?" Miss Lou bawled out, "Coverley!

See dem deh!" and they would both collapse in wonderful laughter! Miss Gladys would wander into the bedroom to find out about dinner, or Gracie was called to check on Miss Rob (Miss Lou's mother) who lived in the room beside hers and who she adored. Perhaps Desmond, her driver, might want to know what time to take her to the theatre. One day, after at least two hours of being there, I asked her how many people lived in the house. She gave out one of her sighs and then her laugh – she just loved having people around her, so the door was always open.

When our first daughter was born, we had no name for her, so the task of naming her went around our friends and family. A book was bought, a list of names produced, and soon I had to go to the University Hospital to finalize the registration. Miss Lou arrived at Boonoonoonoos and, in her inimitable way, announced, "No fret mi chile, call di pickney Beeny-bud!" We both dissolved in laughter. We called her Ashley. But the name stuck and a couple of years later I started a small cottage industry in the village making, among other things, a little cloth doll named Beenybud, and writing a series of children's books about a little girl, Beenybud, who lives in rural Jamaica, all thanks to Miss Lou.

One day the news came down to me from Miss Olive that Miss Lou was not well. I went up the hill to see her. There she was, lying on her bed with many sweaters and scarves wrapped around her throat and chest and a rather scary tie-head with all sorts of bush sticking out from under it. She looked bad, and in a very feeble voice, she said, "Dengue, mi love." It took the laughter from her for weeks. Miss Lou was a believer in old time bush remedies.

I also remember when I was prop mistress in Brooklyn for Air Jamaica's travelling show *Come Home to Jamaica* and Faith D'Aguilar, a member of the cast, lost her voice. There was much panic among the cast as she was to perform that night to a full audience. Miss Lou and Lois took charge! They fixed her up with some concoction, which she was persuaded to drink and wrapped up her throat with various remedies. She sang like a bird that night! What amazed me was how nervous Miss Lou was, waiting in the wings. And then the cue. She did a delicate glide across the stage to centre, held up her arms and gave a warm laugh. She was home.

One of my fondest memories is going down the hill to Mona in Miss Lou's blue Volvo. At Papine, due to traffic congestion, she had to slow down, and all of a sudden I heard, "Lawd, see Miss Lou deh!" and people came up to see her in a most respectful way and they just wanted to reach out to her, to touch her, and she would sigh or smile or say something kind and I saw the love.

The 1980s came along and a lot of things changed. After she left, I would call her from time to time. Miss Lou had moved to Canada. The magic circle was broken; the world I had been privileged to touch was gone.

Early in 2006, Buddy and Cissy Pouyatt, Lois, Tony and I were having lunch at our house and we felt to call her. She sounded a little old and sad. Eric had died and Miss Lou without her Coverley wasn't whole. We tried to be cheerful. "Come home."

"Ah, mi chile," she sighed. And as usual she sang in her loving far away voice, "Walk good on you way, mi darling, just walk good."

You Can't Bury Creativity

NEIL ARMSTRONG

As the host of a literary radio show, I would often invite Miss Lou to be my guest and, somewhere in our conversation, she would pause and say, "Dem tief mi" – meaning her work was being copied, used and sold all over the world, but she was not receiving any royalties. Many years later I reflect on this and ask her stepson, Fabian Coverley, about her comment and he confirms that to be the case. He notes that there are still people using her work without giving her credit or contacting the executors of her estate.

In 1994, while working at CJRT-FM (now Jazz FM) on the Ryerson University campus in Toronto, I proposed the idea of interviewing Miss Lou for one of CJRT-FM's current affairs programmes and to send it back to Radio Jamaica Limited (RJR) for its Christmas programming.

Having started my journalism career at RJR, I maintained my connection with the company by contributing stories from Toronto. Christmas was approaching and I wanted to revisit Christmas traditions in Jamaica – like Jonkonnu, Christmas morning church service and Christmas market. Miss Lou was receptive to the idea and invited me into her home to record the interview, which I subsequently sent off to Jamaica.

Working at CHRY 105.5 FM (now VIBE 105 FM) at York University, I would cover many events where Miss Lou was being honoured or was a special guest. Oftentimes, I interviewed her about various aspects of Jamaican culture.

My interview with Miss Lou about Anancy informed a story I contributed to the Black History Month special feature published in the student newspaper *Excalibur*, at York University in 2003. Entitled "Spreading Ancestral Wisdom: A Veteran Wordsmith and Jamaica's First Lady of

Folklore", it noted that the master storyteller, at eighty-three years old, had been keeping the oral tradition alive since she was thirteen.

This is what Miss Lou told me about Anancy, the trickster hero in many Jamaican folktales, "I got most of my stories from my grandmother, Meme, who would tell stories at recess time and lunch time. I used to fall asleep every night in Meme's lap just to hear the Anancy story. Every story had a little song somewhere. Many nights I went to bed singing an Anancy song."

She said that when telling stories, "your whole body has to take up the story, yuh know". Speaking of the history of Anancy, the trickster and folk hero, Miss Lou shared that "he was the only hero. My grandmother used to say he was a trickified little spider man but rememba you caan be like Anancy, yuh nuh, because Anancy is a magic person. Yuh caan be like Anancy but you can enjoy the Anancy story. Anancy is the only folk hero that makes himself also the villain because he points out the weakness of the human being and shows you how you can be tricked by your own greed or envy because you don't examine what you're doing properly."

As a folklorist Miss Lou celebrated the African cultural retentions of Jamaica's folklore. She would have known, as Laura Tanna shares in her book *Jamaican Folk Tales and Oral Histories,* that the original Akan-Asante name of Kwaku-Ananse has been shortened to Anansi, or Anancy, but the word still means "spider", as in the original Twi. Anancy has the appearance of a spider and also human characteristics.

In February 2004, I organized an event at York University in collaboration with Dr Omi Soore H. Dryden, who was then an advisor at the Centre for Race and Ethnic Relations at York. We called it Reading with Miss Lou, featuring Miss Lou performing some of her poems and stories, and guest performers Elaine Lyons, Danae Peart and Sankofa.

If you know anything about Miss Lou, you would know that people are drawn to her and she draws people to her, so visiting her home means that you have entered Jamaica. The food, art, music, singing and storytelling are all there. Her husband, Eric "Chalk Talk" Coverley, whom she affectionately called "Rico", was usually doing calligraphy, and Rosie Johnston, whom Miss Lou called "brawtadawta", was always nearby.

Miss Lou's get-togethers were familiar places to see veteran RJR, JBC and later CBC journalist Keeble McFarlane, the late Dwight Whylie, the Heritage Singers and many more public personalities. Of course, there were friends who held her dear such as artistes and scholars Joan Andrea Hutchinson, Marjorie Whylie (musician on *Ring Ding*), Leonie Forbes, Charles Hyatt, Barbara Gloudon, Oliver Samuels, Owen "Blakka" Ellis, Carolyn Cooper, Sandra Whiting, Letna Allen, Phyllis Walker, and so many more.

Over the twelve years I knew Miss Lou, there were people who were constants in her life whenever I saw her in public: Carl Henry, Carolyn Goulbourne, Rosie Johnston, and stepson Fabian Coverley and his family. It was Goulbourne who called me while I was working at the *Gleaner*'s Canada office to inform me of Miss Lou's passing.

When Miss Lou died in 2006, Maud Fuller wrote, in part, this tribute to her: "A linguist by intuition and a poet by inspiration, Louise set out to transform the speech of the people around her into a written language – and this while still a teenager. She managed to devise an orthography that, with its inconsistencies, conveyed mood change and tone shift in the speaker."

At the service of thanksgiving for the life of the Honourable Louise Bennett-Coverley, ambassador and special envoy of Jamaica Maude Fuller eulogized Miss Lou by saying:

> How do you bury creativity, imagination, originality, artistic integrity? How do you bury laughter? Miss Lou cannot be buried for she is indelibly etched in the collective psyche of a nation and a people. It was as if she'd received a divine mandate to unfurrow the wrinkled brow, turn the tear into cheer, bring joy to the saddened heart and above all – "hold the mirror up to nature" that we may see ourselves reflected – warts and all, and laugh at our foibles (and no one could laugh harder at her own foibles than Miss Lou herself).

That really captures the essence of Miss Lou.

A Family Connection

LINCOLN ROBINSON

Wat a ting! Yu see me dying trial . . . yu see how life stay. Some a we beg fi family, while others have it and not even know.

All my life, I had always heard that Miss Lou was our cousin. Some members of the family took it seriously and delved deep in the family tree; others relished the connection, and still others simply went along with the narrative. My brother, Claude, in his usual anecdotal self, says Miss Lou would always mek you know "we a cousin" but would also add words to the effect "im doan mek nobody know cause dem sey me chat too bad". Then again, everybody and Miss Lou a family . . . even Aunty Roachy!

I remember my grandfather Claudius Robinson – Puppa we used to call him. For Miss Lou he was Maas Claudie. I remember too my grandmother Miss Ketty. The ruins of the old family house at Hamilton Mountain are still there and the family burial plot below the house where everybody – well, a good portion of the family – is laid to rest. I always say that is where I want to go when my time comes, not at Dovecot or somewhere else.

From the work on the family tree, dating back to the 1800s, we have now established that the Hamilton Mountain family property was owed by "Bulla" Byfield, father of Mary Byfield, who is Miss Lou's grandmother. We have also established that Miss Lou's grandfather was James Robinson, father of Kerene Robinson, Miss Lou's mother. James and Arthur Robinson were first cousins, and Arthur and my direct family line from another Robinson – George Robinson – were brothers.

If the strength of the relationship appears tenuous, it could perhaps be because Kerene lost her father when she was five years old. Added to that, there is as yet no information of other siblings of Kerene, and the family lines of Arthur and George Robinson appear somewhat more definitive. However, the connection is clearly established. Miss Lou's mother was present at my uncle Lincoln and Jean's wedding reception held at Miss Lou's Gordon Town home.

Aunt Gloria, my father's sister and the last surviving sibling, traced the Robinson family/Miss Lou connection. Incidentally, my father Maas Horace, or Skipper, as he was called, would also be one hundred years old, having been born in 1920. And even as the mix of memories linger, I do recall at least one occasion when Miss Lou stopped at my family house at Bogogie and how she was literally swarmed by the excited neighbourhood children who gathered around to greet her. Aunt Gloria says Miss Lou would visit on a regular basis, especially at holiday time.

From those long ago days of my youth back in the 1950s, my grandmother, Miss Ketty, used to prepare lunch for Miss Lou when she came to visit the family, from Jacks River to Bogogie (where we lived) to Geddes Mountain to Hamilton Mountain. My aunt Gloria, now well into her eighties and the last child of my grandfather Pupa, says there was even "Robinson Yard", where it is said three Robinson brothers started the district back in the late 1800s.

Fast forward to the mid-1970s and my more recent recollection as a young trainee programme producer at the now defunct Jamaica Broadcasting Corporation (JBC), where one of my duties back then was to welcome Miss Lou when she came to record and present the very popular *Miss Lou's Views* programme, aired on the station on weekdays after the midday news and sports segment.

Miss Lou would pull up in her old Volvo in the heat of the noonday sun, with sweat jus' a run dung her face. She would always have a rag with her to dry her face before coming into the cool of the JBC studio.

I had no idea then that this "likkle bwoy" who was meeting and welcoming Miss Lou at JBC was family to her, even though I must admit to holding the thought, to myself of course, how Miss Lou reminded me so much of my mother – Mother B. I don't think Miss Lou knew I was

Claude's younger brother, and I certainly did not mention it. I think it is fair comment that although I was greeted by her: "How yu do, me cuz", I just embraced it as vintage Miss Lou greeting.

Miss Lou and the Robinson family bear an important thread of national history with the likes of others like Teacher Robinson (who started Jack's River Primary School); Professor Leslie Robinson, former pro-vice-chancellor of the University of the West Indies; my brother, Claude (former press secretary to Prime Minister Michael Manley); my uncle Lincoln (barrister); my daughter, Renee, who presently serves as Jamaica's film commissioner, and so many others who have contributed to a rich history and proud family legacy. In fact, there may well be another piece of history written, with Claude and myself as brothers from a small rural district going on to serve as press secretaries to Jamaican prime ministers; he served Michael Manley and I, Portia Simpson Miller.

In later years, I had the opportunity for my family – wife, Barbara; son, Marcel; and daughter, Renee – to visit Miss Lou at her Scarborough home in Toronto to cement the bridge in this piece of the Robinson family/Miss Lou connection.

Like all Jamaica, we salute you, cuz. We proud a yu so till and good duppy always follow you!

Learning from Her Dynamics

PAULINE STONE MYRIE

I first met Miss Lou in 1966, when Greta Fowler asked me to play in *Queenie's Daughter,* the twenty-fourth National Pantomime. I was nineteen years old. Mrs Fowler wanted me to be Miss Lou's understudy. I was horrified. I couldn't sing. She told me not to worry, to just be present and to listen to the director.

When she handed me the script, I was filled with trepidation. I studied it on my own for a while before I met Miss Lou, who came to rehearsal several weeks later. As a child, I had seen her on performing on television, and had dreamed of meeting her in person. When Mrs Fowler told Miss Lou that I was to be her understudy, she gave me one of the biggest hugs possible. She said, "Pauline, a want you to stick close to mi." I was in awe of this beautiful lady.

When we started to rehearse at the Ward Theatre in December 1968, I got to see the love and admiration that people had for her. I remember there was one member of the backstage crew called Reako. He loved Miss Lou so much that he would bring her an orange every night. One night she said to me, "A don't really want the orange every night, yuh know, but Reako think it is his duty and I not going tell him is not him duty to bring it."

I questioned my role as her understudy. Could I ever get this kind of reception? Miss Lou would encourage me to learn my lines, to be focused "because one night you going to get a chance to do them." I listened carefully, but never thought it would come to pass.

One evening in 1970, while I was at my Saturday job, my manager came to me and said, "Mr Henry Fowler and Ms Doris Duperly are here to see you." They told me that Miss Lou had sprained her ankle and was unable to do the show. We were doing *Rockstone Anancy* that year. I had to do it and there would be no time for rehearsals.

We headed straight to the theatre. I looked at the set and almost cried. Mrs Kelly-Barrow brought me a message from Miss Lou. "Just go out deh go do the thing; you are capable," she wrote. At the end of the show I was drained. It was a heck of an undertaking, but I had done it! Miss Lou was out for a week so I had to do the show again. However, she came to one of the shows. At the end of it she gave me a big hug and said, "I come to watch yuh and yuh do good girl. You do good."

When I first started as her understudy, Miss Lou encouraged me to pay careful attention to the dynamics of her exchanges with others on the stage. That advice helped me when I had to play with Ranny Williams in 1972. I knew I was talented, but I was new to acting and needed to understand timing. So she taught me how to wait and how to present my lines in an effective way. She was an extremely skilful actress.

Some young people came into pantomime with a stupid belief that they were going to upstage Miss Lou. They would put on ridiculous costumes and walk on stage while she was there, so the attention would be on them. She would push them off the stage and say, "Gwaan, yuh look like yuh have marly gripe and fluxy complaint!"[1] They learned their lesson. She taught me to hold my place on the stage. She also pulled me into her inner circle and kept me close until I created a space of my own.

Initially, Miss Lou faced a lot of resistance from the establishment, but she knew that average Jamaican people who came to pantomime loved it. Like anthropologist Olive Lewin, Miss Lou was an expert in Jamaica's folk history and music. She blended everything into the pantomime experience. Miss Lou understood the psyche of the Jamaican people; she knew what they wanted to hear, and what would inspire them. Aunty Roachy knew everything about everything, and many people showed an appreciation for that.

---

1. "Molly gripe and fluxed complaint: Stomach ailment caused by eating a harmful mixture of foods or fruits" (*Jamaican Folk Medicine: A Source of Healing*, by Arvilla Payne-Jackson and Mervyn C. Alleyne [Kingston: University of the West Indies Press, 2004], 203).

I had a friend who was head of the Dental Association. He came to me and Miss Lou to help them with their Dental Association Week events. Miss Lou invited him to her house and he told her what he wanted the public to know. Miss Lou talked about dentistry on her radio show for one week. The dentists were so pleased. They hadn't realized that we could actually use this method of communication to talk to people about complex issues. If someone wanted to say something important to the masses, they had to say it through Miss Lou.

When she decided to leave pantomime in 1971, I assumed her role, but it was a tall order. I played *Hail Columbus* in 1972 and *Dickance for Fippance* in 1974. She was doing *Ring Ding*, which was taking up a lot of her time, but generally, she seemed to have lost interest in performing at pantomime.

If the World Was Like Miss Lou

BONGO HERMAN

Interview with Opal Palmer Adisa

Opal Palmer Adisa: Miss Lou would have been one hundred years old in September 2019. I know you were close to her.

Bongo Herman: Miss Lou was one of the most wonderful persons to ever walk on this earth. Almighty God made only one Miss Lou. She was very special to me. Back in the days, after we attended Clancy Eccles's Christmas morning concerts at Carib theatre, Miss Lou would sit backstage with us and give we a whole heap a jokes, and me, Bim and Bam, Charles Hyatt, Sista Fae Ellington, would a just deh deh a laugh. We used to have three Christmas morning concerts – one at Regal theatre, one a Carib, and the other at State. Sometimes, when Clancy Eccles ran out of emcees, I was chosen to introduce Miss Lou to the audience.

Miss Lou and I were together from JBC days. The two of us, and some other brethren, including Wycliffe Bennett, Mystic Revelation of Rastafari, and Mortimer Planno, put 250 drummers into the National Stadium at CARIFESTA in 1976. There were twenty thousand dancers. The stadium was packed from one end to the other. The dancers come from the four corners of the stadium; every beat of the drum dem come with their hands stretch out ina dem costumes. Jamaica never see nothing like that yet.

Miss Lou was really respectful to the I. One of the reasons she was so respectful was because I played the chimmy, the mug, and other percussion instruments that she really liked to listen to. She loved certain things, like when me go for little frog sound. People might say it's a bullfrog, but you have to know how to make the sound musical. I haven't met another person like her.

OPA: What are some important things that you would say Miss Lou has done for Jamaica and Jamaican culture?

BH: She taught Jamaicans to love the language, to just talk plain and no bother with the twanging. Dem ting deh mek you feel good ina yuself. Even at Carib theatre, when we used to step out pan the stage, you find some people would start twang, and Miss Lou would say, "No bother with the twanging ting, just talk raw chaw Jamaican." Me did love dem kind a vibes deh wid har. Is a different type of drama dem time deh.

OPA: Did you participate in *Ring Ding*?

BH: Yeah – *Ring Ding* was a wonderful thing for the children. During break time, Miss Lou would sit down wid we and tell jokes. We were just joyful. If the world was like Miss Lou it would be a better place right now, trust me.

I feel proud that I am here still. I mek sixty runs now and I am still batting. I am still singing good on stage, still performing wonderfully, and the people them love me for it. I am an entertainer. I don't go on stage to curse or to tell people to go to church. When I go out there I go to entertain. I learned a lot about entertaining from Miss Lou, Charles Hyatt and Sista Fae.

OPA: That's right. Have you ever taught at the Edna Manley School of Music?

BH: I go and play down there, but dem never go in history like how you going in it. For instance, most of dem never know that I was so close to Miss Lou. The Bible says, "careful how you entertain strangers for you might entertain angels and don't know". So I am glad for this opportunity that I could express myself to you, I feel proud of that, you know.

Lessons from Miss Lou

OLIVER SAMUELS

An Interview with Opal Palmer Adisa

Opal Palmer Adisa: What is your first memory of Miss Lou?

Oliver Samuels: My first memory of her is from the radio serial *Life in Hopeful Village*. I had always admired her: her use of language, how she spoke, this feeling that she was so proud of speaking the Jamaican language; and I admired her comedic skills too. At that time, though, I was not capable of explaining my feelings in this way. I felt as though I wanted to be where she was and I wanted to talk like her.

OPA: When and what was your first physical meeting like?

OS: I met her in person when I joined pantomime in 1970. We were rehearsing either *Queenie's Daughter* or *Music Boy*, I can't remember now. I met her at the rehearsal; it wasn't an official meeting or anything like that. We were like students at the school that was formed by the Little Theatre Movement, so I was among the students participating in pantomime. Naturally, as the rehearsals progressed, I tried to push up miself and talk to her. She was very accommodating.

She had so much knowledge of the Jamaican experience, so she would be guiding even the director, "No, no, no, a no so dem say it", and then she would just explain the historical background of that phrase. One evening down at the Ward Theatre, she called me and seh, "Tell mi something little bwoy, a weh yuh come from?" and I said, "From Heritage in St Mary." She said, "Oh, people in St Mary were kind to me during my research there. Lord a neva have to suffer, a neva hungry. When mi ha fi go ova river, dem put mi pon donkey and carry mi. Dem just tek care a mi." She had a special love for St Mary.

OPA: And this worked to your advantage?

OS: How you mean! I went through the gate! After that, every evening when Miss Lou come I would go outside to meet her and carry her little basket. She always walked with her food. A lot of people would surround her – "Miss Lou, Miss Lou, Miss Lou" – and I would get very upset and seh, "Why uno no leave her alone?" A mossi jealous mi jealous because mi waa carry her basket fi har and thing. Poor me neva think seh is admiration and love dem a pour out. Mi just think seh dem nuff. Mi neva think seh mi hegs-up, mi think seh mi meds-up.

OPA: Because you wanted to get to know her better?

OS: Yes. One day a seh to her, "Miss Lou, all dem people ya – how dem dis a bodda-bodda you so? Wah mek yuh no run dem?" She seh, "Mi pickney, yuh ha fi learn fi tek kin teeth so kibba heart bun." It was the people who made her and she knew she had to share her love with them. That was a real lesson for me.

In all of my work with her, I never see that lady seh, "Lord, wah dem a bother mi fa?" She always gave them a beautiful smile, no matter how she was feeling.

OPA: Can you cite an example of how Miss Lou influenced you as a comic, as an actor, as someone who celebrates Jamaican culture?

OS: One incident that made me realize that it is important to be aware of one's space, the creative situation one is in, was when we were doing a promotion called "Come Home to Jamaica" with the Tourist Board, for people in New York and England. We were doing a scene where Miss Lou and Lois Kelly recited a "tracing poem" they had written, and Faith D'Aguilar's role was to go between them and seh, "Lord, lord, uno stop it man! Two big ole oman like uno a behave dem way deh!" and so the two a dem now were to bump her an' seh, "Who yuh a call ole?"

There was this big fish basket on the floor, and when dem bump her she fell inna it and my role was to run an'she, "Mama, mama, dem ketch pupa." When I see Faith inna the basket, I couldn't go on, I was dying with laughter! Peter Ashbourne in the orchestra pit saw mi and start to laugh and mek it worst. So when Lois realized the dilemma she seh to Miss Lou, "Tell me something, yuh did sen out yuh bwoy, no?" Hear Miss Lou, "Yes, yes, fi go buy goat meat." I was dying. I don't know how I find the courage to run on and seh, "Mama, mama", then hear har, "Dem ketch yuh pupa eeh, ketch him a tief goat meat." That was not in the script.

OPA: In what capacities did you interact with Miss Lou outside of the theatre movement? Tell us about her impact on the wider Jamaican culture.

OS: Miss Lou had a life filled with creative adventure and the stories of some amazing people. I was fortunate enough to have been invited several times to Miss Lou's home. She would tell us stories, including one about a man called Mr Mitchell who went on the banana boat to England and eventually became a servant to the Queen.

I can't tell the story the way she did, but what happened was that Mr Mitchell became the spokesperson for the people on the boat. The people were tired of eating potatoes and he went to the captain and seh, "My name is something, something Mitchell and I am here to tell you the people are starving. They are tired of potatoes. They want something else to eat." They gave him what he asked for and he saw to it that it was prepared for them.

Miss Lou told us that once she went to an official function in the United Kingdom and was asked to sit in a posh area. She said, "Lord is how mi reach here so?" and at that point she hear, "Miss Bennett, Miss Bennett." When she look it was Mr Mitchell. Him seh, "My name is Mitchell and I am here to serve you." I think that is how she got the information from this man regarding how he got to England on this banana boat and what he did when he went there. He was smart and outspoken. That's how he was able to move up to the point where he was serving Miss Lou in this prestigious place. It was Mr Mitchell who arranged for her to be in the posh area. Anyway, if Miss Lou had told this story it would have been much more amazing.

At a session at the Royal Academy of Dramatic Arts, she told the audience, "Mi come fi hone mi craft, not to learn and accept." That is what made this woman so real. She did not want to lose that Jamaicanness. I so strongly believe in that. Wi caah be too proud, wi caah be too educated, we caah be too learned not to memba wi language. She took the language to the highest level. She gained recognition which mi don't even think she cared bout anyway, but people respected her and I think the respect came out of the fact that here was this woman who come from this little country, who spoke on any topic in the language of her people. I loved her for that. I've always wanted to be like her.

Now there are so many universities throughout North America that are studying her work. One of her most valuable contributions is that she's raised awareness of the importance of women, especially women in the workforce. Women were sidelined, you can seh them tek over now. She contributed to that movement.

OPA: How many pantomimes did you do with Miss Lou? Share another interesting stage moment with us.

OS: I did five with her and they were all amazing. One time when the late Raymond Hill was to come on stage, nobody could find him. Miss Lou created stories around the whole thing, she ask if nobody no see har son, and when he came on stage it was such a relief for the rest of us. She grabbed him and seh, "Weh yuh did deh?" The audience had no idea what had happened. She covered it up so well. Afterwards, she was a bit angry though because Raymond had fallen asleep.

Another time we were on a bus in England, and the bus driver, Malcolm, looked lost for the whole time. We were going to the Alexandra theatre in Birmingham and some a wi seh wi want to go get food. Malcolm was a lovely man, but him just never have any sense of direction and dem time deh wi no have GPS. Miss Lou said, "Mi caah badda fi go git up" and she stayed on the bus.

When show time come, not a bus, not a Miss Lou. Malcolm lost inna Birmingham. A police have fi escort Malcolm back to the theatre and we had a great laugh over it. When we finished our tour and was leaving we gave him a little package. The poor man cry yuh si. Him seh him neva seen such sweet people in his life.

OPA: What would you say to her if she were alive today?

OS: Miss Lou and I had become extremely close. I was one of the persons that she would call and ask to do favours. I started to call her Mama Lou Lou. I would say thanks to her for empowering Jamaicans to speak the language without fear. She put pride into speaking it, defended it. She struggled in order to get that recognition because you couldn't talk Patwa pan radio or inna commercials. That has changed because of her.

Today, children are doing her work at Festival. Some Jamaicans in the diaspora use her books to help their children to understand their culture, so I thank her tremendously and Jamaica owes to her memory a great debt.

OPA: How did she mentor other actors and comics during pantomime and did you ever work with her on *Ring Ding*?

OS: She was such a giving person, like a schoolteacher. She was always willing to give advice and gained a lot of knowledge from her work at Social Welfare, which is now the Social Development Commission. Sometimes you go to the theatre and Miss Lou would have a few people around her just telling them how she thinks this or that should be.

Jamaican Through and Through

FRANKLYN HORACE CAMPBELL

Interview with Opal Palmer Adisa

Opal Palmer Adisa: When and where did you first meet Miss Lou? Tell us a bit about your relationship with her.

Franklyn Horace Campbell: I met Miss Lou for the first time after driving home Tony Duvall, who lived with his family right behind Miss Lou's house. In the '60s, I was the cast coordinator for a young group called Sing Out Jamaica. I had joined the group as the bass player. Tony Duvall played the guitar, and in the evenings I would take him home because the band finished playing late. One day he told me that he lived behind Miss Lou's house. I got excited because, while we were growing up in the 1950s, Miss Lou was our first superstar. I really wanted to meet her. We started to go up to her house and we all spent a lot of time together. She was very interested in us as young musicians. We would go on her veranda and sing.

OPA: What was your first impression of her? What was the first project you did together?

FHC: She was like our mother, our grandmother, our aunty; she was everything to the young people; everybody loved Miss Lou. These days, everybody has easy access to information, but in those days information was limited, so when we met Miss Lou we were absolutely in awe. She was just as we pictured her – fantastic, kind, sweet, you name it. We loved her before we knew her. She fulfilled all of our expectations, and more.

For one pantomime skit, Miss Lou wanted someone to act as a "peanut boy", and she asked me to do it. I was shocked. Miss Lou worked out one little song for me to sing. I went to pantomime and, of course, nobody could "talk" to me because Miss Lou had brought me in. I got to the theatre twenty minutes before I was supposed to go on stage. I didn't rehearse or anything.

OPA: What are some of the things she taught you?

FHC: The general lesson which she taught everyone was to be compassionate and to love the culture. She was Jamaican through and through. In those days, we didn't think about language much because we spoke Patwa, though Patwa was not allowed on RJR or JBC. At the time, Miss Lou was the only person who spoke Patwa on the radio. At school we were taught proper English. She taught us to enjoy our language. Pantomime was done in Patwa, and it was all about Jamaica – our culture, our dance, our clothes. Pantomime was the biggest annual cultural show and it ran for weeks.

Younger people will never understand how important pantomime was. We didn't have theatres like we do now. Every single school pickney wanted to attend, whether they lived in the country or not. If they lived in the country they might have been lucky to go to a school that was going to pantomime. Miss Lou and Maas Ran couldn't do anything wrong. They taught the entire nation what it was to be totally Jamaican, and even now Jamaicans from all backgrounds are discussing and celebrating their work.

OPA: Can you remember a specific advice she might have given you?

FHC: Not a specific advice. After we formed Fab 5 she took us on our first trip to America; that's how close we were. We went to Hartford and did a series of shows. The first time we played as a pop band was at the Gordon Town Methodist Church, where she worshiped. We also played at Fabian's [Miss Lou's stepson] wedding on the lawn of her house. Fabian has been my friend from dem days. It's hard to think of a specific advice because we were there with her and her family for many years. I am one of the lucky ones, I suppose.

OPA: How many pantomimes have you participated in with Miss Lou? Tell us about other notable Jamaicans who helped to make pantomime a success.

FHC: There were some big stars such as Oliver Samuels and Leonie Forbes. Everyone wanted to be a part of pantomime, and of course the whole production was led by Miss Lou and Maas Ran. I did one by myself, and then Fab 5 did *Queenie's Daughter*. We were the band, and Rex [Nettleford] was the choreographer. That was fantastic.

OPA: In 2003, you were a part of a committee that tried to get Miss Lou to return to Jamaica from her adopted home, Canada. Talk about this.

FHC: By then, she had been living in Canada for a long while. We were very distressed because nobody knew that she had made plans to leave Jamaica. Miss Lou was proud, and so whatever difficulties – financially or otherwise – she and Maas Eric were facing were kept secret. A few years after she left, Louis Marriot and I, and a few others, decided that we had to bring her back home and have a celebration because she was getting on in age.

We actually wanted her to relocate to Jamaica. Our plan was going very well, but she felt obligated at that point to stay in Toronto because the Canadian people had embraced her. I understood exactly how she felt, but we wanted our national living treasure to be back home. We put on a big concert for her at Emancipation Park. We felt good about doing that, and I'm grateful that the recordings of the event survived.

OPA: So many other things have not survived.

FHC: Yes, including *Ring Ding*. One of the stories behind the loss of the *Ring Ding* recordings is that a manager from abroad who came to JBC threw away the tapes. I guess we didn't understand our history. A couple of the *Ring Ding* tapes survived, thank goodness. Future generations will have a small glimpse of what she did. Do we preserve our history enough as a nation? I don't think so. We don't have a lot of information about many of our cultural heroes, and so our young people don't know anything about them. I was most distressed when, about six years ago on the *Ity and Fancy Cat Show,* the hosts showed several photographs of Miss Lou, and two-thirds of the people did not know who she was.

Thank heavens there are kids who are doing her poems today. That's helping to keep her name alive. Some don't go beyond the poems to find out who she was, but at least her work is still being read. This is more than what we can say for someone like Delroy Wilson, who was a fantastic rock steady singer. Few people under forty know who Delroy was.

OPA: Talk to us about the album that Fab 5 did with Miss Lou.

FHC: She wanted to do a studio album with a live band and, of course, she came to us. Most of the recordings were done at the Federal Studios, and that was really fun. We did about eight or six songs on the album. Nobody can take this away from Fab 5 – we did that with Miss Lou.

OPA: Do you agree that she should be made a national hero?

FHC: Yes, but I think she needs to be recognized in a different way, perhaps as a cultural hero. She didn't sacrifice her life, but she did so much for the nation. Some people want Bob Marley to get it. If we are going to give it to a cultural icon, then obviously it has to be Miss Lou.

Miss Lou fe Real

PAUL KEENS-DOUGLAS

See she stan' 'pon de stage
Wit' she han' 'pon she hip,
De Jamaica ole talk
Fallin' sweet from she lip,
See she smile, hear she laugh,
Watch she dance, hear she sing,
De whole place does swing
When Miss Lou do she ting.

See she costume it reachin'
Right down to de groun',
An' watch when she spin
How de skirt does fly roun'.
See she smile, hear she laugh,
Watch she dance, hear she sing,
De whole place does swing,
When Miss Lou do she ting.

See de crowd how dey shout
When she open she mout',
An' all de folk-story an' poetry
pop out.
See she smile, hear she laugh,
Watch she dance, hear she sing,
De whole place does swing,
When Miss Lou do she ting.

Hear she say "boogooyaga"
An' shout "talawa!"
When she talk 'bout Uriah
All man laugh ha, ha, ha.
See she smile, hear she laugh,
Watch she dance, hear she sing,
De whole place does swing,
When Miss Lou do she ting.

An' when time come to go
An' she wavin' goodbye,
Yu does hear big man say,
"Look ah laugh till ah cry!"
See she smile, hear she laugh,
Watch she dance, hear she sing,
De whole place does swing,
When Miss Lou do she ting;
De whole place does swing,
When Miss Lou do she ting.

I always tell the story how, after listening to Louise Bennett perform on the Mona campus of the University of the West Indies in 1972, where I was pursuing a postgraduate degree, I decided to try my hand at writing in the vernacular, trying to put the sound on the page, making it real. Prior to that, all my efforts at writing were in standard English.

So right there on campus, in Irvine Hall, I sat down and wrote a piece called "De Band Passin". I can only say that it must have been an inspired piece because, in writing it, I somehow discovered the power of the vernacular, the power of myself, my voice, and never went back to my traditional English style. I was hooked on the freedom that writing in the vernacular gave me. The rest, as they say, is history.

Over the next few years, my career as a writer/performer blossomed and I became Mr Tim Tim. Up to that point, I had never met or seen Miss Lou again since that encounter at Mona. Then in 1979, Black Theatre Canada brought the two of us together in Montreal, to do a show called *Miss Lou Meets Mr Tim Tim*. It was a huge success and the beginning of a warm friendship with Miss Lou that grew over the years, albeit from a distance.

To me Miss Lou was a pure personality. On- or offstage she was still Miss Lou. As a matter of fact, I sometimes found her to be even funnier and more intuitive offstage than onstage. Over the years, we did several performances together, each one creating its own set of memories. We would do some quick rehearsals before a show started, because you really can't script people like Miss Lou. We had to decide on generally what we were going to talk about, and which pieces would strike a balance.

After that, it was up to God's grace and our ability to ad lib. She would say, "Tim Tim you goin' to say dis, an' I goin' to say dat , den we going to say everyting, yu know what I mean!", and I would say, "Yes, Miss Lou." Then we would go out there and make it work. Every mistake was a style. The thing is that it was always fun and enjoyable. There was love on that stage between us and the work and the joyful audience.

One memory that has remained with me over the years was the time we spent together in Barbados in 1981. We had been invited to perform at the opening of the new DLP headquarters. They put us up in a cottage on the beach, so we had plenty time to relax and talk and exchange ideas and just enjoy the ambience of Barbados. Miss Lou would tell me at breakfast that she was not supposed to eat certain things, but that she would eat them anyway, because she had brought along certain "medical remedies" to offset them.

She would say, "Tim Tim, these medicines here is for me to take before I eat, and those over there is for me to take after I eat . . . so let's eat." But the greatest memory of that episode was that Errol Barrow's hobby was cooking. He fancied himself a chef and he would send over some special dishes that he had prepared himself. So we had the Prime Minister of Barbados cooking for us.

Some things you remember some things you forget, but one thing I will always remember was the time I brought Miss Lou and her husband, Eric, to Trinidad to do a show at the Little Carib theatre in 1982. My car at the time was a small Toyota. Knowing Miss Lou's size, I decided to hire a big station wagon, which I knew could handle Miss Lou, Eric and her little helper.

Night of the show, wagon arrive. Guess what? You had to step up to get into the wagon. Miss Lou couldn't make the step-up. So guess where everybody end up? In my poor little Toyota. I felt sorry for it. All de spring gone through. Two months later, I had to trade it in and get myself a brand new, bigger car . . . thanks to Miss Lou.

Miss Lou and I remained friends over the years and, on my annual trip to Toronto, where she then lived, I would always make it to her apartment for a little chat and some tea. The last time I was there, we took photos and I performed the poem "Miss Lou fe Real" which I had written for her and which she had never heard.

I am delighted to be a part of this one hundred years' tribute to Miss Lou and may the memories of her inspire others to think, as I did, "I can do that too!" You never know who is listening.

"Ac' chile, ac'!"

She Helped Shape My Life

FAE ELLINGTON

"Ac' chile, ac'!" (Act child, act!) Those three words from Miss Lou propelled me into character. I did act . . . and I sang, as any lead must do in a pantomime. But in that performance, I sang as if my life depended on it.

This evening the curtain went up, as usual, and we were off to a rollicking start. The chorus members were out on stage in a scintillating opening number. The legends would give their usual command performances and the young lovers, playing the juvenile leads, were preparing to wow the audience with their love story. A few minutes into the production, the female juvenile lead, Faith D'Aguilar, would enter from stage left.

Only, this evening, as I looked across the stage, from my position at stage right, I didn't see the usual figure in the wings. And truth be told, I cannot recall if stage manager Audley Coulton was signalling to me because, in that split second when reality hit, I sidled up to Miss Lou, who was seated down stage right. I whispered, "Faith isn't here", to which she replied, "Ac' chile, ac'."

As I stood on the outside of the cell – seeing my lover behind bars – and singing these words, "I'm alone, I'm alone, I'm alone with myself, tonight", I knew that I wasn't alone. I knew that Miss Lou had my back. And so did the other members of the cast and crew. That evening would signal the start of a very special relationship with Miss Lou.

This was my very first National Pantomime, *Music Boy* (1971), written by Trevor Rhone. I was still a student at the Jamaica School of Drama which, at the time, was under the auspices of the Little Theatre Movement, but a few of us had negotiated and lobbied our way into the production.

I was made understudy for the juvenile lead. I was elated. However, it didn't take me long to learn that being an "understudy" is vastly different from being an "alternate". You see, the lead would have had to drop dead, or be so ill that she couldn't perform, for an understudy to don the costumes and play the role. So, I was content with being in the chorus. At eighteen years old, I was sharing the same theatre stage and tripping across the same floorboards as legends such as Ranny Williams and Miss Lou – Louise Bennett-Coverley. What else could a girl want?

MISS LOU AT THE GARDEN THEATRE

It was also in the early 1970s that I would sit in the audience at Paul Methuen's Garden Theatre, 72 Hope Road, and see Miss Lou in a production of Shakespeare's *Merry Wives of Windsor.* I was mesmerized. The production was being staged in a garden, on a generous property that was reflective of the privileged class of colonial Jamaica. Seeing these stalwarts of theatre enter and exit from behind the trunks of large trees or deliver a speech through branches and leaves had me wide-eyed and filled with expectancy. And the sheer opulence of Miss Lou's costumes! She was so light on her feet with all those clothes on!

Miss Lou, people like Easton Lee, Wycliffe Bennett, Olive Lewin, Bobby Ghisays and Louis Marriott, created for me the blueprint that would direct my life in the performing arts and media.

THE JBC EXPERIENCE

A few years later, I would share a radio production room at the Jamaica Broadcasting Corporation (JBC) with Miss Lou. While she put the finishing touches to her *Miss Lou's Views* – a five-minute commentary on social, contemporary or cultural issues, or waited for her studio booking time, she would treat us to patties or icy mints, share from her vast reservoir of knowledge, encourage us, or just simply relieve the tedium of a day with her infectious personality. Or she would explain why she had two spectacles dangling from her neck. You guessed. One to see in the distance, the other for reading. She didn't fancy bifocals then. I'm not sure if she ever made the transition.

It was in that very production room at the JBC that she autographed my copy of her publication *Jamaica Labrish*. In it she wrote, "To dear Fay [*sic*] Ellington with sincere compliments and best wishes dat she wi kip awn leggo har labrish pon de *Morning Ride*. Louise Bennett 18/12/80".

I had been the presenter for the early morning programme on JBC Radio One's *Morning Ride* (1978–81). Those weekly interactions with Miss Lou were invaluable and certainly memorable.

Some of the gems and significant historical happenings she shared from our production room conversations found their way into my on-air utterances and helped to heighten my interest in the Jamaican way of life. And her philosophy became my philosophy: "Tek kin teet suh kibba heart bun. Yuh haffi laugh or yuh wi go under."

I was really privileged to rub shoulders with such greatness, a larger-than-life persona who did not dwarf me in her presence. She was always an encourager. I suppose back then, in the 1970s, I may have taken a lot for granted. She was so easy to be around. I do not think I got the full import then of who this person was or what she represented. We regarded her as we would a caring grandmother or aunt who just wanted the best for us. But the decades would prove her to be a trailblazer! An icon. A most powerful *political* figure.

MISS LOU AND THE JAMAICAN LANGUAGE

Miss Lou it was who chopped through the woodlands of linguistic prejudice and cleared a path for the acceptance and use of the Jamaican language. For me, Jamaican talk is a language – not just Patwa, dialect or Creole. Louise Bennett-Coverley legitimized the Jamaican language. And decades after she began her pioneering work, the Bible Society of the West Indies would publish *Di Jamiekan Nyuu Testiment (The Jamaican New Testament)* in 2012.

Di Jumiekan Languij Yuunit at the University of the West Indies was established in 2002. Some universities overseas both teach and accept the Jamaican language as a legitimate second language. At the same time Jamaicans continue the debate, arguing, "Is there such a thing as a Jamaican language? Should it be a language of instruction? Jamaican is broken English."

A VOICE FOR JAMAICANS

Many Jamaicans never had a voice when we were a colony, nor even after achieving political independence in 1962. We couldn't and wouldn't share our views and opinions, as we were made to feel less than, simply because some of us didn't speak the Queen's English. So, helpful, insightful, carefully thought through ideas were left in the field, in the markets, at the rum bar, or at the river as women washed clothes. But Miss Lou was forging ahead. She became the voice for the voiceless. And in her deft, cunning use of the Jamaican language, she tackled the issues.

If we look back to the 1930s and 1940s, we will notice a movement to *smadditization*. We were on our way to self-government and, ultimately, independence in 1962. We were coming into our own culturally and politically. Becoming. During this period, political parties and trade unions were formed, galvanizing the people. There was the actualization of universal adult suffrage in 1944. This was not lost on Miss Lou. She wrote several poems highlighting the pertinent issues – "De Latis News", "Census", "Votin' Lis", "Rightful Way". In this last poem she played her part in helping people understand how to vote:

> Yuh doan haffe cross out nutten
> Nor haffe draw no line,
> Jus mark a X side o' de name
> A who deh pon yuh mine

Louise Bennett, a young Jamaican woman who was following closely the sociopolitical developments in her island home, captured and recorded for posterity the developments and unique circumstances that would go on to define the Jamaican ever-evolving psyche using the Jamaican language. Bold. Courageous. Visionary. Her poem "Yuh Nephew Sue" was written after the 1944 hurricane; "Back to Africa" was written in 1947;

"Him Deh Yah" in 1948. In this poem she captured Paul Robeson's visit to Jamaica and his fight against racism.

THE COVERLEYS

It wasn't uncommon for Miss Lou and her husband, Eric Coverley (Uncle Eric), to have young people up to their home. Of course, we all were delighted to take the ride to Gordon Town. I remember the warm hospitality, the food and the nuff-nuff laughter. The Coverleys' hospitality was abundant.

BACK HOME

In 2003 the Government of Jamaica brought Miss Lou home as the highlight of the Emancipation and independence celebrations. I was honoured to have been included on the planning committee. Meeting her on the tarmac of the Norman Manley International Airport as she disembarked from the plane was one of those moments which can't be adequately or accurately described. For my part, I experienced a roller-coaster ride of emotions. And when, on seeing me, she said, "You too?", with her special brand of affection, mi glad bag buss.

There were several events staged in her honour in 2003. I had the pleasure of interviewing her for the JIS feature, *Masters of the Arts*. When I asked what had meant the most to her of all the events planned, in typical gracious, elegant Miss Lou style, she remarked, "Everything." And then she said the people out on the streets to meet her and the children performing for her meant a great deal to her. She never expected such an outpouring. I believe it was only then that Miss Lou understood what she meant to Jamaicans from all walks of life. Her work had not been in vain. There were throngs of people in the streets, waving flags, cheering and dancing. As she was driven past, she could see and hear them, and they saw her because her window was all the way down. The people's cultural ambassador, the Jamaican icon, was back on terra firma. Our Miss Lou was home.

The concert staged in her honour in Emancipation Park will always be etched in my memory, for so many reasons. The crowds could not be contained in the park. People just wanted to touch her. I co-hosted the performances with another Jamaican legend, Easton Lee. Miss Lou had lifted the Jamaican spirit. We were soaring.

AN UNUSUAL REQUEST

Miss Lou died on 26 July 2006. Earlier that year, she made a rather curious request of Leonie Forbes, who had been working on projects in Canada. Leonie was scheduled to visit Jamaica for a short break. Miss Lou asked her to do all in her power to find her mother's grave, take pictures of it and bring them back.

When Leonie called advising me of the assignment, I did not hesitate in agreeing to accompany her. I picked her up and we were on our way to the churchyard in Gordon Town. Several of the graves at the small St Martin de Porres church yard are precariously perched on a hillside. As women born and bred in rural Jamaica, we were not daunted. We found sticks to anchor our steps as we searched the hillside for the grave. We combed that hillside, clearing weeds and debris from gravestones until, at last, we found it. I had the pictures printed that very day. Yes, printed.

A few days later, Leonie returned to Toronto with a most prized possession. To say that Miss Lou was delighted would be an understatement. She desired to have something of her mother's memory before it was too late. Miss Lou would die months later. I played my part at her farewell.

I was responsible for doing the commentary for the televising of the thanksgiving service at the Coke Methodist Church, East Parade, downtown Kingston. It rained heavily that day. Upstairs, where I was seated, the ceiling leaked. I did some of the commentary using the Jamaican language. I had mentioned earlier that Miss Lou would share her icy mints with us in the production room at the JBC. She loved icy mints. A few were put in her coffin. So too was a face cloth. She was never without those two items.

The Coke Methodist Church was her family church. Also, this was where, at seventeen, she first performed for impresario Eric Coverley, at a Christmas morning concert.

I also covered the leg of the broadcast at National Heroes Park, where she would be interred. When we arrived, the earth was inundated. Water covered my ankles. As I did in my first encounter with her on the stage of the Ward Theatre when she advised me, "Ac' chile, ac'", I simply delivered. Done in her honour.

Exit stage left

Walk good Miss Lou, an' may gud duppy waak wid yuh.

Memories of *Ring Ding*

ERIC DOUGLAS

About nine o'clock every Saturday morning, about fifty children gathered at the entrance to the television studios of the Jamaica Broadcasting Corporation. They came from different parts of the city and they came without invitation. They would mill around, chat and laugh, unsupervised and guided only by an instinctive recognition of the need for good conduct. Innocent, happy faces all hoped to get through the door. They came to appear on *Ring Ding*, the premier children's show of the period. More than that, they came to be with Miss Lou.

While the kids waited outdoors, props men in the studio built the set with adequate seating for the kids and Miss Lou. The technicians for lighting, camera and audio all set about completing their tasks for an on-time live broadcast. Seasoned professionals, they all knew their roles working on a show that lasted on television for twelve years.

Satisfied that everything was in place, the front door was opened. All of a sudden, a flood of kids rushed down the passageway and into studio B where the show was done. Under the guidance of the floor manager, the children took their seats, happy to be in this strange place of big bright lights on grids and pantographs above them and large orthicon cameras being manned around them. Most of all, they were just happy to be in the same place with Miss Lou, an idol to both them and their parents. Marjorie Whylie took her seat at the piano while Miss Lou whipped up the kids' enthusiasm. A short run-through of the opening, including the theme song, and all was ready to go.

The director of the show is at the control, audio man is ready with his microphones, one of which hangs on the telescopic arm of a Mole-Richardson boom, tracking the performers' every move. The floor manager has everybody on standby as we waited. Seconds to go. Master Control gives the countdown . . . 3, 2, 1, cue "B". Marjorie hits the piano keys. The kids, led by Miss Lou, begin the theme song: "There is a concert here for you and me. There's a concert here today . . . "

For the next hour, the nation is treated to what might have seemed a spontaneous televised display of Jamaican folklore in music, dance, stories and poetry. It was the only show of its kind on television. It was, in a way, a link between annual festivals; meant for kids, but enjoyed by all.

Ring Ding was both a TV show produced for the enjoyment of children and a learning experience. The host, Miss Lou, was an exceptional comedian, a poet par excellence, an original thinker of ideas beautifully expressed with clarity in Patwa, and a reservoir of Jamaican folklore. In an entertaining fashion, she taught kids, and indeed all viewers, much about the grass- roots culture of the Jamaican people and, in so doing, raised their level of appreciation of the worth of their native language. She taught by entertaining kids with folk songs laced with the expressions of ordinary folks as they experience life, with lyrics like "Di man from Panama wid im brass chain a lick im belly bam bam" and "Dis long time gal mi neva see you, come mek mi ole yuh han".

Throughout the years, guest performers were invited from schools and elsewhere to appear on *Ring Ding*. I remember that young people from St Andrew Technical High School and from Denham Town Comprehensive High came there to dance; stories were told by people like Christine Craig and others. There were individual performers, like a very young and flamboyant Orrett Rhoden, who later became an internationally acclaimed classical pianist.

But the dominant feature of *Ring Ding* was to pass on, through entertainment, the creative expressions and cultural legacy of ordinary Jamaican folks, whether through riddles, poems or music, and especially folk songs. And there was no one better equipped to lead in that regard than the woman who had become the personification of Jamaica's folklore, the one and only Miss Lou.

Being Miss Lou

FAITH D'AGUILAR

I first learned about Miss Lou in the early 1960s. I used to listen to her on JBC Radio doing skits with Ranny Williams. It was very exciting and very entertaining and, while my parents listened, I would listen too, without them knowing, of course. My father was very strict about us speaking proper English, so he would not encourage our listening to these skits which I found very entertaining.

I was in third form at Clarendon College when I joined the Girls Brigade and my teacher asked me to perform a Miss Lou poem, "Cass Cass". While preparing and learning the dialect, I paused to get my thoughts together. My father, who was in another room, marched out and angrily demanded, "Turn back on the radio; why did you turn it off when Miss Lou was on?"

I replied, "Sir, the radio was not on."

My father insisted that I had turned off the radio. I said, "Miss Lou wasn't talking about anything, sir, and she was not on, Papa." I added, "Miss Lou wasn't on the radio. It was me." My father was very upset and did not believe me. He reflected for a moment, then said, "Okay ma'am, you go ahead and do what you said you were doing and let me hear you now!"

I was amazed and also somewhat fearful since he was so strict about us speaking proper English. But I knew I had to do what he asked, so I recited Miss Lou's poem that I had been practising. I will never forget the look of surprise and admiration on his face. He shook his head and declared, "You know, you sound just like Miss Lou. You fool me you know, you fool me good. You must keep doing Miss Lou."

I was delighted. My Papa declared that I had done a good job. I could talk just like Miss Lou.

I came to Kingston in 1968, and Ruth Hoshing and I became friends. She invited me to an audition at the Little Theatre and, once there, she encouraged me to perform a few items, including one of Miss Lou's dialect poems. I did and I got the leading role. That was really funny because I had not planned on doing anything, really. I just accompanied her, but I landed the junior lead in the pantomime. Miss Lou was the big lead.

I met Miss Lou at the Ward Theatre when I was introduced as the junior lead. What a great moment that was for me! I was overwhelmed and overjoyed to be in the company of someone so famous. When I did the poem for her, she told me she enjoyed it and encouraged me. I was shy, but she was very helpful and encouraging, never criticizing, just suggesting other ways to do the lines. She would say things like, "Do it this way. Work with the programme, and it will all work out. You have to understand there is an audience."

I didn't do Miss Lou's dialect in the "Miss Lou voice" at that time. I think I might have been too overwhelmed by her. I remembered that I did the "Miss Lou voice" for the first time a few years later, in her company. She told me, "Go ahead, let me hear you." When I did the piece she said, "But Lord have mercy child, you sound just like me, even better." After that I started doing "Miss Lou" as a matter of course.

I was asked at the time to do something on the radio and I replied, "Yes I can talk like Miss Lou. I think I will just do that", and I did. Miss Lou later told me that I fooled her husband because he thought she had left the island to do a performance, and there she was on the radio. She said he asked her about it. Ever jubilant and laughing, Miss Lou said to me, "You know seh you nearly mess up mi marriage, girl!" That was really funny, but then I thought I must really sound like her if even her husband heard me and thought it was his wife.

From then I started doing poems in Miss Lou's voice and it was a real hit; people loved it. I loved it too because it made me feel like Miss Lou was in me, and that was a joy.

We did the show *Come Back Home Jamaica* in the 1970s. The cast included Oliver Samuels, Peter Ashbourne and his band, Monica Lawrence, Cathy Levy, and Lois Kelly-Miller. We performed at a few places in the United States. By then Miss Lou knew how much I sounded like her and she was quite impressed. She called over Lois Kelly-Miller and said, "Lois I want you to hear this little one. I want you to hear her." So I did it and Lois Kelly-Miller was excited. She looked at me in amazement, "What! You sound just like Miss Lou."

Performing like Miss Lou became a part of me then; I was performing on a regular basis all over the place. It was always good to be in Miss Lou's company. I remember one night on stage I stepped on her foot and I felt so bad about it. But she said, "Lord missis, no badda, no badda, no badda. No don't touch it, do not touch it chile. Lord, woiiiiiyooiiii." She went on and on. I said, "I am sorry, Miss Lou", and she said, "No, no, no." It was hilarious how she went on and me trying to appease her and make her feel better and she saying, "No, no, no." It was one excitement. That's one of the moments I really saw how funny she really was, and she brought a lot of laughter to me and the members of the pantomime.

I remember the time when Miss Lou was abroad and I was asked to impersonate her on an ad, which I did. When she returned to Jamaica, she said, "Huh, mi hear sey dat dem gi yu mi part fi do, but mi no deh ya, mi chile. But doan worry because what a wi do, I will mek dem pay yu same way because after all yu do the thing but mi no dead yet." So, true to her word, she made sure that I got paid.

After that I was always being called to do a commercial to do the "Miss Lou voice". She was happy, and when I asked her what she thought of me doing her voice, she said, "Lord me chile, I like how you do it, that big mi up and mek mi feel good."

I performed with Miss Lou on *Ring Ding*, and I performed with her in three pantomimes, *Music Boy, Love Is the Thing* and *Queenie's Daughter* – Miss Lou's special. That's when we went to the United States, then later that year we went to Canada. When the Creative Production and Training Centre did *Miss Lou's Ring Ding*, I was asked to perform with her.

I moved to live in Gordon Town so I was even closer to Miss Lou and I would often go to visit her. I remember one time she had pork for dinner, and she invited me to dine with her. I said, "Miss Lou, I don't eat pork, you know." And she said, without skipping a beat, "Um um . . . all the better, mi chile, that deh something deh nice so till! Mi just get more."

Many years after she died, Mutabaruka asked me to do a "Miss Lou from the grave". "Miss Lou from the grave?" I asked, startled. He said, "Yeah mon, pretend you are Miss Lou in the grave." And I did just that. That performance was a hit, and can be found on YouTube. Many people called up Muta and asked him how he got Miss Lou's duppy to speak. That was funny.

Miss Lou celebrated the language of the masses; it has been accepted and very soon I think we will have more books on Patwa. As soon as Covid-19 disappears, I will reappear on stage being the voice of Miss Lou. Miss Lou is here to stay and so am I.

Miss Lou, Miss Lou

MUTABARUKA

Miss Lou Miss Lou
Wi love yuh fi true
Wi love how yuh chat
Som' nuh love dat Miss Lou
Miss Lou Miss Lou

Yuh heavy fi rue
Mi seh wi love weh yuh seh wen
Yuh seh wey yuh seh
Miss Lou
A years now wi si
Wey yuh do fi poetry
Here in a Jamaica
Usin our patwa
Mi knoo nanny a hero fi true
But me tink yuh a hero too
Mi watch de children a dance an sing
An' yuh teach dem how fi play
Ring ding

Miss Lou
Miss Lou Miss Lou
Wi love yuh fi true
Wi love how yuh chat
Some nuh love dat Miss Lou

Miss Lou Miss Lou yuh heavy fi true
Mi love wey yuh seh wen
Yuh seh wey yuh seh
Miss Lou
Miss Lou yuh mek dem know
Dat is from de base tings Jamaica grow
Dem use fi seh wi must speak an' twang
But yuh mek wi proud seh wi a Afrikan
Now wi si dem a teach in schools
Dat Jamaica Patwa is not fi fool
Wen yuh chat it soun' suh sweet
An' all a Jamaica jus a skin dem teeth
Miss Lou
Miss Lou Miss Lou wi love yuh fi true
Wi love' how yuh chat
A Patwa dat
Miss Lou Miss Lou yuh heavy fi true
Mi seh wi love wey yuh seh wen
Yuh seh wey yuh seh

Miss Lou
Mi know Nanny a hero fi true
But me tink yuh a hero too
Wi watch de children a dance an sing
An yuh teach dem how fi play ring ding

Miss Lou Miss Lou wi love yuh fi true
Wi love how yuh chat some no
love dat
Miss Lou
Miss Lou Miss Lou yuh heavy fi true

Things My Mother Taught Me

LOLITA KNIBB PHILLIPS

Interview with Opal Palmer Adisa

Opal Palmer Adisa: Tell us about your relationship with Miss Lou.

Lolita Knibb Phillips: We were extremely close. When I first met her, she and Uncle Eric were very interested in my last name. They knew about my grandfather, Enos Knibb, who was the first black Jamaican umpire. From the first day, they took me under their wings. Uncle Eric was a good friend of my grandfather, and Louise Bennett was a good friend of my uncle's wife – educator Mary Morris-Knibb. Actually, I didn't know these people well because I grew up in England. Miss Lou and Uncle Eric said they wanted to teach me about my ancestry. We became close to the point where Fabian started to refer to me as his sister.

OPA: What are some of the things Miss Lou taught you about Jamaica?

LKP: She taught me how to speak the dialect and about the history of slavery, including about how enslaved Africans made Easter bun. Apparently, the British would give them bun to eat without cheese. So they developed a way to make the bun with the cheese inside. Miss Lou told me how to do it.

OPA: Her father was a baker, so I guess that's where she learned this.

LKP: No, she learned that particular recipe from her mother, who learned it from her mother.

Anyway, one of the things that surprised me was that she mentioned my aunt Mary Morris-Knibb in her book *Jamaica Labrish*. I couldn't believe it. We became very close and she gave me the first dress that she wore on stage. My daughter in Canada has it. I told my daughter that I want to donate it to a museum here.

OPA: While living in Canada, did Miss Lou talk about her desire to return to Jamaica?

LKP: Yes. In fact, when I visited Jamaica, she would ask me to go to her former house in Gordon Town just to look at it and to look at the land. When I returned to her in Canada, we would sit and talk about what I saw, talk about the river near her house and she would reminisce on the activities that took place while she lived there. She talked about the Gordon Town Square, the people in the community, about her children.

OPA: What did she think about the square and the people, about the river?

LKP: She talked about the people who had impacted her life, like the ones who had worked in her home, the food they cooked, their stories. She had this way of linking the surroundings – especially the river – with stories about food. She shared stories about her time at Buckingham Palace. She told me that once she was invited there and that all of the people were speaking in their nation languages because it was an international gathering.

She was there with a Canadian actress who had Jamaican links, and both of them had no idea what was going on, so they started to speak in Patwa. Then people gathered around them because they wanted to know what language they were speaking. She said this was her "Anancy way" of dealing with situations like that. She said they felt equal, because initially people thought the only language they could speak was English. They were no longer seen as "language-less" West Indians. They used the opportunity to educate the people there, particularly the Africans, about Caribbean nation languages.

OPA: How did Miss Lou feel about being Jamaican and African?

LKP: Having been brought up in England and having gone to Catholic school there, I really was not into Jamaican history, but after meeting Miss Lou, I learned so much about the culture and it changed my whole life. She spoke proudly of it. We had a discussion once about her taking the bus from Spanish Town to go to school in Kingston and she said that she looked forward to it, to listening to the market people, observing their behaviours. She attended a high school where she had to speak the Queen's English. These bus trips excited her and she wanted to learn more, so she asked her mother to teach her the language.

Her mother was a dressmaker, so she would sit with her while she sewed and ask her about the "other side" of Jamaica. No one at her high school could give her the kind of information that she was getting from her mother. She also learned a lot about the culture and food from Uncle Eric's mother and his sister. She liked a lot of the old-time cooking with coconut oil and I'd use that whenever I was making her something. She was quite sad when she lost her sense of smell. I remember on one of her last trips to Jamaica, people brought her baskets of fruits and food, stuff she hadn't had in years, including stinking toe, gizzada and grater cake.

OPA: What conversations did you have with her about how she was feeling about Jamaica, shortly before she died?

LKP: Well, as I said, she felt very homesick after she left. After Eric died, that feeling became even stronger. She knew every nook and cranny of Jamaica. She would tell me her memories of different places. She loved the Jamaican people and her time working at JBC. It is such a shame that they lost all those *Ring Ding* recordings.

When I told her that I wanted to leave Canada to make a contribution to Jamaica, she wrote a letter to CUSO International to help me fulfil my dream. I worked for the YWCA and then I worked as a volunteer at the Office of the Prime Minister. While I was working at the Office of the Prime Minister, I informed Prime Minister P.J. Patterson that Miss Lou would love to return, and I made all of the necessary connections. He brought her back and asked me to be her chaperone while she was here.

When we travelled across the country, Jamaican kids would touch her hands and say they would not wash their hands after touching their queen. She really appreciated the opportunity she got to engage with young Jamaicans. Miss Lou wanted to have an impact on children who did not know her. When I returned from England at age eighteen, a lot of children used to watch her on TV on Saturday mornings. By the time she came back, those kids were grown and she felt it was important to engage with the new generation.

OPA: I am glad that she was buried in the land she loves.

LKP: While she was in Canada, they talked about what would happen if she died. Miss Lou never liked talking about it, even though she had a discussion with P.J. Patterson and some decisions were made about her body coming back to Jamaica. I know that she told him that under no circumstances would her body be coming back here without Uncle Eric's. She said wherever she lies, Eric has to lie there also. As a matter of fact, I went up to Canada and came back with her body.

Reflections and Memories

PAMELA APPELT

Memories of the Honourable Louise Bennett-Coverley flood me with smiles and laughter. This phenomenal woman of so many talents and accomplishments was indeed precious to me. She exuded a majestic sense of the presence of a higher power, self-confidence and a beautiful commitment to the country of her birth and to her people. Laughter, pride, joy, hopefulness, peacefulness and a steady willingness to help were second nature to her. Miss Lou, as she was affectionately called by her friends, colleagues and admirers in her native Jamaica and around the globe, was not only instrumental in preserving and promoting Jamaican culture in her beloved country, she did so with equal vigour in her adopted home of Toronto, Canada.

My first encounter with Miss Lou was in the mid-1980s, through her friend Lolita Phillips. My husband and I were invited to join Dwight Whylie at his home for dinner, and there was Miss Lou, whom I had heard so much about. Her charm and her personality were captivating. She regaled the gathering with her memories of Jamaica, her time in London, England and her varied experiences. I left Dwight's home that evening extremely thankful that I had had the opportunity to meet this incredible lady.

Over the next few months, we saw each other often at events in the community and would greet each other with warm embraces. At the time, Miss Lou and her husband, Eric, had recently relocated to Canada for health reasons. She shared with me her connection with Canada, going back to the 1970s when she performed to capacity crowds in the Toronto Public Library, Parkdale Branch.

In the same year that we met, Dudley "DRB" Grant, a well-respected

Jamaican educator, did a needs assessment with respect to early-childhood education that was submitted to the Jamaican consul general in Toronto, Canada. Out of that emerged the organizational structure for the Project for Advancement of Childhood Education (PACE). Dr Mavis Burke, a well-known Jamaican educator in the Ontario Ministry of Education, was selected to be the president. Dr Burke asked Miss Lou to be the first patron. This gave further legitimacy to this charitable organization, as well as a sense of pride and possibility. I was then asked to be the next patron.

When I shared this with my husband, his first question was "How do you plan to support this organization?" In short, my husband offered to host a dinner in our home and invite guests who he thought would be interested in the organization and would make a financial contribution. That fundraising effort was a huge success. Thanks to the efforts of Miss Lou, who entertained the guests, twelve schools in Jamaica were adopted that night. Today, over three hundred basic schools in Jamaica have been adopted through the Project for Advancement of Childhood Education.

In the months following, I saw Miss Lou fairly often. With infectious pride, she would share the contributions of Jamaicans in Canada. She also shared with me her memory of her composition in 1988, *You're Going Home Now*, which won a nomination from the Academy of Canadian Cinema and Television. Her reflections on these milestones brought her great joy. She was especially pleased when she was the featured artiste at Westmount High School in Montreal. The invitation was extended by Thelma Johnson, the founder of the Caribbean Pioneer Women of Canada, which had sponsored the show. They were happy to have her as their special guest. That night, the large auditorium was packed to capacity for their first fundraising event in aid of the Reverend Charles H. Este Scholarship Fund.

In 1990, I was honoured to be the judge who administered the oath of Canadian citizenship to Miss Lou, along with many other Jamaicans. Needless to say, everyone was quite delighted to be photographed with this remarkable lady.

Canada became Miss Lou's home for the last two decades of her life and she served the nation with great pride, leaving a remarkable footprint on its sociocultural landscape. There was not a request made of Miss Lou that she didn't honour if she could. She never said no to an invitation. She was very supportive of the Jamaican consulate in Toronto and the Jamaican Canadian Association. She went beyond the Jamaican diaspora and generously shared her knowledge, talent and wit with Canada's melting pot of people groups – Europeans, Asians, Africans and her very own Canadian Caribbean compatriots. Miss Lou's authenticity modelled to immigrant communities how to enrich the Canadian fabric and yet be comfortable in their own skin.

Many years ago, on one of my visits to England, I was walking the streets of Brixton with my brother, who lives in London, and he pointed out to me an area where many famous and world-renowned artists, such as Langston Hughes, regularly met. Much to my surprise, there was Louise Bennett Close, a street that had been named in honour of this famous lady. My brother, a photographer, was naturally compelled to take a picture, which she received with great joy.

Miss Lou would say very often, "Wherever I live, I am in Jamaica." She meant it and she created the atmosphere for you to experience it. She was a cultural ambassador par excellence. In 2003, she was invited by the Jamaican government to return home to be honoured during the independence celebration. She was invigorated by the reception she received. The many tributes for her work and influence were overwhelming. Then prime minister Percival James Patterson presented her with a citation from the Government of Jamaica. In part it read: "Miss Lou helped us to break the barriers of cultural ignorance. She inspired confidence in ourselves. . . . Dr the Hon. Louise Bennett-Coverley has enriched and empowered us all." Miss Lou shared with me how the love and appreciation of the Jamaican people at that event elevated her and how she returned to Canada more invigorated. "Lawd, it sweet me, it sweet me", my dear friend remarked. That was her last visit to Jamaica.

Looking back, I think that Miss Lou shared these memories with me because she intended for me to play a role in maintaining her legacy. When she died in 2006, the minister of culture in the Government of Ontario made a commitment, in the presence of several hundred mourners, that Miss Lou would be remembered by the province. Soon after that pronouncement, I was invited to meet with the minister and his senior staff members. He asked what I would consider a fitting tribute to Miss Lou. I did not hesitate to share my thoughts with the minister and his staff. In anticipation of this task, I had done my research. I hastened to inform the minister that Miss Lou had received the honorary degree of doctor of letters from York University for her groundbreaking contribution to literature and the performing arts, which legitimized dialect writing, and that she was also honoured by the University of Toronto. So it was fitting that such a cultural icon be remembered in a public space where all Canadians could benefit.

Exactly six months after this meeting, the Government of Ontario named a room at Toronto's Harbourfront Centre in her memory. Interestingly, the Harbourfront Centre was the first place where Miss Lou performed when she moved to Canada in the 1980s. The Miss Lou Room at Harbourfront Centre houses a permanent exhibition, honouring her and her achievements. There you'll find photographs and recordings of her storytelling and performances. Hundreds of students and teachers visit annually. Many talks and presentations are given in that room and many cultural events are held there. Not long ago, another well-known Jamaican Canadian, Denham Jolly, had his first book launch in the Miss Lou Room.

In 2012, I had the pleasure, as the co-executor of Miss Lou's estate, along with her son, Fabian Coverley, to gift McMaster University the Canadian archives of Miss Lou. The archives are used on a regular basis and have been digitized. These can be found online in the digital archive and are open to everyone. On Jamaica's fiftieth birthday I co-chaired the Canadian committee which commemorated our independence. We published a coffee table book, *Jamaicans in Canada: When Ackee Meets Codfish.* It featured 250 individuals who have made extraordinary contributions to their adopted land. Notable among them is Miss Lou.

In 2016 at the second annual Palaver International Literary Festival in Wasaga Beach, Ontario, the works and accomplishments of four outstanding individuals, including Miss Lou, were acknowledged. Miss Lou was cited for her historic achievement in getting the Jamaican people to throw off the yoke of colonialism and to accept their own language and culture as legitimate.

Miss Lou's legacy lives on among the second and third generations of Jamaican Canadians who are fluent in the mother tongue and who, through her work, find belonging, inspiration and connections to the roots of their culture. The Louise Bennett Exchange Fellowship in Caribbean Literary Studies at the University of Toronto, offered in partnership with the University of the West Indies, also became another significant milestone that has helped to pass the baton on to younger generations to build on the foundations Miss Lou laid and keep the light of her legacy glowing.

Someone once said, "We live in deeds, not years; in thoughts, not breaths; in feelings, not figures on a dial." Miss Lou crossed the mysterious river to the other side thirteen years ago and I am honoured to remember her on the anniversary of her one hundredth birthday. Thank you for carrying on her legacy of caring for others, keeping our culture alive, carrying the candle and lighting the world. Her memories will grow more precious and will forever glow in our hearts.

My sincere thanks to the Government of Jamaica, the Ministry of Culture, Gender, Entertainment and Sport, Dr Palmer Adisa and the entire team for the work that you continue to do in keeping the memory of Miss Lou alive.

"Mi just like people"

LOUISE BENNETT-COVERLEY

Interview with Opal Palmer Adisa

Opal Palmer Adisa: You have said that your writing is not about championing a particular cause, but to simply show that Patwa is a viable language. Yet many of your poems seem decidedly pro-feminist. Please talk about this.

Louise Bennett-Coverley: Yes, it's true that my work glorifies the Jamaican woman, who is often put aside and is rarely taken seriously. I feel like a lot of Jamaican women are doing good work and are not receiving any credit.

OPA: Were you conscious of the early efforts of the women's movement?

LBC: Yes, I was conscious of the work of the Women's Federation. I felt though that a lot of women who went into the federation wanted to see what it could do for them and their families. They needed a great deal of leadership themselves.

OPA: Was it initiated by a middle-class woman?

LBC: No, it was initiated by the governor's wife, Lady Molly Huggins, who felt that the Jamaican woman should have a movement because when she came to the country she found that there were a lot of male organizations. So she started the Women's Federation and she got a lot of different women interested, like Mary Morris-Knibb and Amy Bailey.[1]

---

1. Mary Lenora Morris-Knibb was one of the pioneering and vocal women of pre-independent Jamaica who challenged the gender and race status quo and advocated self-sufficiency and self-reliance. She was in the forefront of social and political activism in the 1930s and 1940s and was the first woman to contest electoral politics in Jamaica (*Gleaner*, 21 March 2021, https://jamaica-gleaner.com/article/esponsored

At the beginning, people like Mrs Knibb had great influence on my work. She was the first female councillor, I think.

Amy Bailey and Morris-Knibb also created the Women's Liberal Club and they were quite political and militant. There was Madame Aitken too, who was very strong. She was an American black woman married to a Jamaican man and she was very active in the Garvey movement in America. They were very supportive of my work and I used to perform at a lot of their social gatherings.

OPA: So, was the movement open to all Jamaican women, to market women, for instance?

LBC: It was open to all women, but the women who needed it most, whose voices we needed to hear, it was quite hard for them. They would come out to meetings, but these women had great stresses and pressures on them – family this, family that, work, so those voices were not really coming through in the way we wanted it to. Lady Huggins used to have big meetings at King's House and invite women from different country districts. For many of them it was the first time they got a chance to go to King's House. One or two would get up and say something.

OPA: What did they talk about?

LBC: The social conditions, the things ordinary women needed.Their needs were so great that they overwhelmed everyone. What we were doing was so inadequate. I was supposed to be coordinating and administrating and what not. It was extensive but not intensive enough. You went to a place and you were gone. You would have liked to stay a little longer to do more work.

/20210321/mary-morris-knibb-pioneer-women-politics). Amy Bailey was an educator, social worker and women's rights advocate. She was a co-founder of the Jamaican aid organization Save the Children and was the driving force behind the efforts to introduce birth control to the island. She gave voluntary service to numerous underprivileged girls in the field of education and social service training. She founded the Housecraft Training Centre in 1946 with a mission to train girls to bring out the best in themselves, to teach them respect for the self and the job. Here she mothered six thousand girls along with her adopted daughter (https://nlj.gov.jm/project/amy-bailey-1895-1990/).

Some people, like Lilly Mae Burke from Lucky Hill, were able to follow up. There were a great deal of grassroots people who tried but, as I said, their positions were so pressed already that it was very hard to sort of get it moving there. It got a little frustrating for me.

OPA: For some reason this makes me think of your poem "Colonization in Reverse". What situation inspired that poem?

LBC: I was living in London when I wrote it. From the first time I went there, when this big *Windrush* boat came.

OPA: This was while you were at the Royal Academy or after?

LBC: Well, I was finishing up at the Royal Academy and doing a whole lot of work with BBC. The manager wanted a programme for the Caribbean and so we created one called *Caribbean Carnival*, which was done partially in nation languages. People would come in; this was radio but we had an audience. Initially, it was common for me to walk along the street and be the only black person; then all of a sudden mi start to meet all these black people.

OPA: They were coming from the West Indies or from Africa?

LBC: Which Africa? The West Indies! The Africans had been there, in the universities, mostly. But the West Indians, the ordinary West Indian man and woman, were there now. I was meeting them in the streets and yuh hearing Jamaican language talking like nothing no happen. As a researcher, I was interested in how things were happening. I begged a friend one night to take me to a place called the University College. It was on Tottenham Court Road, which was a dance place. Everybody did mix up deh. A lot of West Indians were there, mostly Jamaicans, and I went there to hear the tales of Jamaicans.

The students were afraid to say anything if somebody insulted them. Dem just mek it pass, but these that come there wasn't making nothing pass. This friend was going through the underground ticket place and the steward thought something was wrong with his ticket and said something under his breath about "Nigga". This fellow just looked at him and was about to pass him (this is what him telling me now), "Louise, all of a sudden I hear buff, and when I look I see the ticket man lying down on the ground!"And a little Jamaican man seh, "A fix him up fi yuh!" Oh gosh!

One day mi and a friend went into a restaurant and we sat there and we realized that the people weren't serving us. I wouldn't say it was prevalent, but it happened. We noticed this waiter passing up and down; it was a Chinese restaurant, so I didn't expect this. Him pass and serve other people who came in after us.

Then two bwoy come in and I spoke to dem. Dem siddung and when him pass, one a dem seh, "Pssst" and him don't notice; him pass again and the bwoy seh, "Hiiiii", and the next time him a pass the Jamaican just grab him inna him collar so and shake him and seh, "Is yuh a talking to. Yuh neva hear me?"

Him shake that poor man and seh, "You know how long wi siddung yah and yuh pass we up and down. Serve we!" I never see people get serve so fast. So all these things inspired "Colonization in Reverse".

OPA: I believe that poem has transcended time, which is what good poetry does. I am wondering if you were to add another stanza to it, what are some of the things you'd include now? Have we succeeded in making England take stock of us as people, as human beings?

LBC: They have carved out little spots of Britain that are for West Indians. Well, West Indians have carved out little spots and made it their own. Truth be told, Britain has hit back by sabotaging the culture, by not giving us sufficient room to express ourselves. But West Indians are there and they are working.

OPA: You are now in retirement. Have you been writing new work?

LBC: Little things, you know. Within the last year [1987] I have had such a traumatic time because of my husband's illness, and so I have not really done anything crazy. A lot of things have come to me and I make notes. Just this morning when I was coming, I saw some of them which I intend to sit and write soon.

OPA: Do you want to continue performing?

LBC: It is very difficult for me not to perform because my work lends itself so much to performance. Actually, just last week I got an invitation to play a very important role in this storytelling festival in Britain.

They are making up their itinerary and they want me to tell them by the middle of this month whether I can be there and I want very much to be a part. I am supposed to go to Toronto for a show around that time. I have a whole lot of plans. Missis, the heart willing, but mi no know if the flesh strong – well, yes, mi strong yes!

OPA: Is the personal Miss Lou as jolly as the public Miss Lou? Where do the personal and the public merge?

LBC: A one sumady, man! I could never have weathered all the storms of my life if I didn't have joy and tek kin teeth kiba heart bun. I believe that we have the strength to overcome difficulties, and a lot of it lies in our ability to laugh at certain things. To just bust out a laugh and blow off steam. Sometimes we blow off steam by just cussing, but we have the ability, like in the dinki mini, to banish grief that is underlying all the sorrow. You seh, deliberately, I'm going to banish this grief for now and the only way to do it is to be as active as possible. To dance, to sing, to move. This is wonderful therapy that is much better than sitting and grieving. This business of just standing and biting you tongue, I don't believe in it. I believe in saying, "Woiiiie" – letting it off. So I do that.

Sometimes my husband seh to mi, "Yuh chat too much. Yuh tell people yuh business. Yuh telling everybody." I tell him that I have to do it; I have to tell people; I have to talk with people. It is very important that you share all that, that you share everything.

OPA: Who are some of your close friends, people you go to for support?

LBC: I have a friend that just called me the other day. She used to sew with my mother. In my mother's sewing room, I learnt a lot and met great friends, but this girl used to go to school with me. She migrated and we didn't get to see each other for long periods. When wi get a chance fi talk wi talk. But before she left, anytime there was anything to do with me she would come. Sometimes when I'm on stage I would look down and see Una there in the audience and I just laugh. We siddung and chat and let off steam, you know.

Throughout Eric's illness, we had two men friends; whoa bwoy, I don't know how we would have got through without them. They were so good to us. And sometimes it's even just the people yuh meet in the street who bawl out "Miss Lou!" The funniest thing is sometimes I'm driving through country districts at night and people bawl out "Miss Lou!" and you seh to yuhself, "How them know that you are there?"

I have been in a car that is not mine, just relaxing, and I hear, "Miss Lou, but no Miss Lou that?" It does something to you, warms your heart because it is an expression of endearment.

Friendship is a wonderful thing. I remember just last year, when Eric was really sick, and the day I was waiting for news at the theatre after he did surgery. I kept on asking, "No news yet?" and a doctor said, "No, Mrs Coverley. I'm so sorry. As soon as we hear we will let you know", and so on and so on. Then I just saw a group of Jamaicans coming, some of them in their theatre things. Dem seh, "Miss Lou, he is alright. The surgery was successful; don't worry." And then they left, because they were working, but they made that time to come and let me know, to set my mind at ease. Three of them came first and then they were just coming in droves, different groups of Jamaicans coming in to say, "Miss Lou, he is alright." It was wonderful; you feel the support, you know.

Sometimes, I'm in the middle of mi work and a whole heap a pickney just arrive and I seh, "Lord have mercy, I have plenty things to do, but tell them to come in and sit and talk."

Sometimes dem hiking and somebody tell them seh Miss Lou live up there so, so dem come look for me. I would say, "I can't stay too long" and we sit and talk for a little while. I like that, mi just like people.

This is an excerpt of one of two interviews I conducted with Miss Lou in 1987 and 1988, respectively, when I entered the doctoral programme at the University of California, Berkeley, and initially, I was considering writing Louise Bennett's biography. You can say that this anthology is my tribute and homage to Miss Lou, whose bravery and unapologetic use of the Jamaican language gave me permission to infuse my own creative writings with our language.

SECTION 2

REAFFIRMING OUR CULTURE

Marcus Garvey said, "If you haven't confidence in self, you are twice defeated in the race of life. With confidence, you have won even before you have started." Miss Lou believed in herself and she believed in the lived culture of Jamaican people, where they claim the right to speak in a language with which they are comfortable. And thus it was that Louise Simone Bennett said to herself, "These people are good people, so they cannot talk bad. These are nice people; they are kind people, so the way they talk cannot be bad." And just like that, Louise Simone Bennett found her purpose in life. As Lorna Goodison reminds us, Miss Lou's lessons in self-identification became a basis for cultural identity formation. She truly believed that a nation's culture resides in the hearts and soul of its people, and she set out to validate the culture of the Jamaican people. The way they talk cannot be bad, she said. This was a powerful message that she broadcast to the length and breadth of Jamaica and beyond. Many heard the message and Patwa gained respectability. This section features works by people who were strongly influenced by Miss Lou.

Noh Lickle Twang

LOUISE BENNETT

Me glad fe see you come back bwoy,
But lawd, yuh let me dung,
Me shame a yuh so till all o'
Me proudness drop a grung.

Yuh mean yuh goh dah 'Merica
An spen six whole mont' deh,
An come back not a piece betta
Dan how yuh did goh wey?

Bwoy yuh noh shame? Is soh you come?
Afta yuh tan soh lang!
Not even lickle language bwoy?
Not even little twang?

An yuh sista wat work ongle
One week wid 'Merican
She talk so nice now dat we have
De jooce fe undastan?

Bwoy yuh couldn' improve yuhself!
An yuh get soh much pay?
Yuh spen six mont' a foreign, an
Come back ugly same way?

Not even a drapes trouziz? or
A pass de rydim coat?
Bwoy not even a gole teet or
A gole chain roun yuh t'roat.

Suppose me las' me pass go introjooce
Yuh to a stranga
As me lamented son wat lately
Come from 'Merica!

Dem hooda laugh afta me, bwoy
Me could'n tell dem soh!
Dem hooda sey me lie, yuh was
A-spen time back a Mocho.

Noh back-ansa me bwoy, yuh talk
Too bad; shet up yuh mout,
Ah doan know how yuh an yuh puppa
Gwine to meck it out.

Ef yuh want please him meck him tink
Yuh bring back someting new.
Yuh always call him "Pa", dis evenin'
Wen him come sey "Poo".

Speaking Jamaican, Talkin Farin'*

AMINA BLACKWOOD MEEKS

Missa Shepherd where is thy sheep . . .[1]

You know my fren Likkle Miss Jing Bang use to wonder if it did eva occur to certain people dat de UNESCO convention on national treasures dat sey dey are not to be removed from de shores dat spawn dem did mean to include Louise Simone Bennett-Coverley.

Bring them back into fold . . . for they have gone astray.

Look here! When dem invite me fe come talk at de Sixth Louise Bennett Festival up into Broward me Jamaican upbringing kick in. Every properly brought up Jamaican – meaning sey dem age drop offa almanac – know sey you cannot go to where people invite you wid yu two long hand. Modern day people might tink dat mean sey yu mus cut dem shart. No, dat is reserved for if dem offend yu as per de biblical injunction. What my madda meant was to shorten dem by putting something into dem han an curling yu fingers around same. So I tried to find a few tings to put into mine.

De likkle girl in de shop, meaning she was under thirty, did not know anyting about Bustamante[2] so she knew even less about him backbone.[3] She show me some soff-looking sweetie and said it was flavoured with

*Edited version of a lecture delivered at the sixth Louise Bennett-Coverley Reading Festival, Broward College, Pembrooke Pines, Florida, 2013.

1. From a Jamaican Revivalist song.

2. Sir Alexander Bustamante, first prime minister of independent Jamaica.

3. Bustamante Backbone was a hard toffee enjoyed by primary school children up until the 1980s. Sometimes simply referred to as Busta. A more modern version is soft.

rum an coffee. Which one me prefer. Well thanks, but no thanks. I was unaware that anyone cudda have two backbones. Moreover that they could be flavoured.

Worse tings was to await me when I asked for Jackass Corn.[4] She said she only had coconut biscuits. Taste dis. Jackass Corn is suppose to treaten yu jawbone. Not melt in your mouth. Dat soun like an ad for a chocolate from farin.

Take comfort from the fact dat all this took place in the airport shop. De tings were meant for people going behind farin barriers so dem tek out some of de good Jamaican hardback resilience. All de language soffen. Puddin what cook wid "hell atop, hell a bottom and hallelujah in de middle"[5] have in something dat is not found in microwave. Taste it and tell me is a lie.

Now excuse me please, I need a likkle privacy to write a letter.

Where is thy sheep . . .

Dear Miss Lou:

Pinch me a pinch you and tell yu something what me know sey you already know. Yu know sey all now, seven years after yu shut yu eye, thirty-three years afta dem shut down *Ring Ding,* thirty years afta Jamaica nearly shut down yu house uppa Gordon Town, people nuh stop open dem mout pan yu?

Yes Miss Lou, me hear yu, so I stand corrected. Me really waan fe sey people nuh stop live pan yu name. Live pan yu name betta dan you did eva live when yu was pan teevee an radio. Nuff a dem neva waan hear yu name much more de language what come outa yu mout, an barely pay yu while dem elevate people who fa mouth affee twist up before dem cudda speaky-spokey. If it wasn't people like Easton Lee and John Maxwell, Daddy Manley and Bari Johnson, dawg nyam yu Jackass Corn. But

4. A hard, flat biscuit also enjoyed by children up until the 1980s. A softer version now exists.

5. A Jamaican riddle referencing the style of making cornmeal or sweet potato puddings.

a life! We nah go talk bout dat part today. But we have fe cut an clear,[6] so you know sey we know how de ting go.

Shepherd where is thy sheep . . .

So, dem invite me fe talk an ask me for a topic. Hear me now how me write back an sey:

> Try this: Speaking Jamaican: Talking Farin.
> I want to look at how the content of what we speak is alien to our heritage, mitigates against the values on which we were raised and thus disrespects/does battle against the imperative of liberating the language.

Cooyah! All a dat? In how much time?

Miss Lou, yu know sey de people dem call my bluff an accep de high-falutin suppen, so dere we all were. One night yu see, Miss Lou, into July 2006, dem did keep a concert fe yu uppa de National Arena in Jamaica. You was not dere, in a manner of speaking, but Oliver Samuels was dere. Him did launch a protest in your name.

Dem did have someting dem call "A Send-Off Concert". Dat sound like somebody was going away on de SS *Windrush*. Memba old time Send-Off Party when people going on long-distance travel? Look like dem did fraid fe call it Nine Night. And every performer did well rehearse ascarding to a carefully designed script.

Miss Lou, Oliver teck de stage, literally and went completely off script. Before him sey what dem rehearse him fe sey, hear him: "Well Miss Lou, a now me know sey duppy nuh have no powers. For if you had any powers yu wudda bax dung some people inside yah tonight. For I hear dem is planning to bury you into Hinglish."

Miss Lou, me go off script too. For we were to sit down an smile in a imitation of some definition of decency. Miss Lou, me stan up an clap, me mean applaud Oliver. For de ting was choking nuffa we and we shut we Jamaican mout and go quiet like we a fariner an did not wish to intervene into another nation's sovereignty.

6. Spiritual cleansing among practitioners of African-based religious practices.

Dem crass de border and take dem might
Crass de border and teef we right . . .[7]

Bury yu inna Hinglish, yu know Miss Lou!! Nat wan word of Jamaican was spoken or sung into de official ceremony in de church. Is like God would not understand what dem was talking about except it was into Hinglish. Dat would mean to say dat today, God does not understand the latest VW ad and cannot participate in the raging debate about wedda VW a mock we or honour we.

Bury yu inna Hinglish, after all what yu do fe nation language? I like that term. Edward Kamau Brathwaite sey a so we fe call it. Is nat Patwa or screech owl. A screech owl or a Creole? Nutten like dat. Is nation language. Dem was not going to bury you in de language of de nation dat dem sey yu liberate and in which you live forever in the hearts and minds of de people. Dem was going to bury in a farin tongue. Is hide dem was planning to hide yu from we?

Dem crass de border and take dem might
Crass de border and teef we right . . .

Crack dem crack?

Miss Lou, you remember dat once upon a time dat word was reserved fe yu madda plate. De one dat she use during de week when nuh stranger nat dere. Stranger use to get to use de crockery.

Today when yu say a ting like dat you have to know is in which language yu speak. For when an American says, "he's on crack" he does not mean the same thing as when an Englishman says, "he's gone crackers". But yet we undastand de two of dem. An if yu tink yu bad inna Jamaica tek whey somebody two crackers, especially if is de laas two dem have an dem have no idea where de next two comin from. Yu head, yu hand, yu foot, de whole a yu wudda crack up jus so. That's called speaking crack in any language.

We are a multilingual people. Fariners marvel at how easily we ketch on. When we going to travel yu know we jus look at de map of de place

7. From Peter Tosh, *Fight Apartheid, Equal Rights* (1977).

we going and we speaking dat. Puerto Rico. Germany. France. Show we Hungary and we know we all born wid a full knowledge of dat. Hungry a go kill we. De only ting we want to ask you, is what you going to do about it.

Hear de problem as I see it. In order to accept that you have nation language, you have to believe and know that you are a nation.

Big-word people sey all manner of tings bout what is a nation. Small-word people have no problem wid dat. For if dem hear Rev. Easton Lee chop some Mandarin, I do not mean de fruit or dat him mekking suey, I mean if dem hear him speak and dem do not see him, hear de fus question dem ask, "Den is which nation dat?" De minute dem see him now, problem solved. Hear dem, "Oh, a likkle Chinnee Man."

But big-word people have to deconstruct de ting. In adda words, mash it up. Dem sey dem excavate but sometimes dem leave it outside of realms of reconstruction.

Hear dem: "A *nation* may refer to a community of people who share a common language. (Hole on, see a problem here, dere is nothing common about de Jamaican language. De uncommonness of it leaves many people flabbergasted. I really want to say grudgeful, wish it was fe dem. It inna movie soundtrack. Dem cover it pan hip-hop.)

Moreover, dem sey *nation* "can also refer to people who share a common territory and government". Stop again. The whole world is common territory to Jamaicans and we know that had it not been through our influence and instrumentality, Mister Barack could not win any elections. Miss Lou, you did see de Big Jamaican flag a wave inna de man inauguration?

"The word *nation* can more specifically refer to people of North American Indians such as Cherokee Nation . . . " Den Miss Lou, doan dat is de root of de confusion about if Jamaica is a nation?

What is a nation? (Qu'est-cequ'une nation?)

Into 1882 yu see one Frenchie parlez-vous name Ernst Renan sey a nation is "a daily referendum". Prekkeh. Imagine everyday dungtown Kingston have two group a people separated into different colours square off like 1950 how-much with chants reminiscent of federation a go "Federation No, Independence Yes!"

And I believe that if we try our best it could be a great success
So let us live in unity for progress and prosperity.[8]

Mr Frenchie parlez-vous put de icing on de cake when him sey nations are based as much on what the people jointly forget, as what they remember.

Me remember my fada tell me nuff tings bout de intestinal fortitude of Sir Alexander Bustamante but me nuh memba de sweetie what name Bustamante Backbone have in any rum or coffee. Dose were forbidden items to children my age when I was dat age. De ingredients aforementioned put in fe fool or please de fariners as dictated by de exigencies of de market. An sometimes de market put pressure pan we fe chat foolinish bout weself to satisfy what dem want to believe till we come to believe sey dat is de rightful way it go.

Miss Lou, you did know de man who did miss de plane fe go a farin an reach back a him yard gone pint out live lobster inna bucket a wait fe tun him dinner and ask him wife, "What is dat crustacean creature?" Den suppose him did board de flight?

Betta question is dis; I can ask you for you did live at farin an abraad an overseas places: What dem have up dere? Lobster or crustacean creatures?

Me hear sey de man neva know sey de labsta did still alive and see him when him pint like him was a informer a view identification parade. Me hear sey de labsta jus jump up an grab him finga. Same time him memba a wha, an him memba wha fe do. Hear him, "Wifey queeze de yeye!"

Heh. When chubble tek man, him pickney boot fit him. I do not know what kind of chubble haffe tek we an which pickney boot we is going to fit into. Cannot be de one who do not know Jackass Corn. You cannot send dat one to feed your jackass. De poor animal wudda mawga dung pan coconut biscuit. As a matter of fact if dat little girl did ever read dat farin sey coconut is nat a good ting, she wudda meck de poor jackass starve till farin again declare dat coconut is a miracle ting. For it look like our size go up an come down ascardin to what farin commodities we consume.

Den stop laugh and ansa me nuh, Miss Lou? Is labsta or crustacean creatures? I firmly believe dat if yu feget what de ting name yu going to

8. Lord Creator, "Independence Song" (1962).

feget its nature and en up in serious pukketary. For is de failure to know de difference dat did cause some of us to write up pan wall back in de '80s before dat December election dat "Michael Manley is a fruit cake". Dat is farin talk fe when we mean to say smaddy head tilt. Den dem get into a shock an awe when some people interpret dat fe mean sey him is a sweet man an vote him fe dem Chrismuss.

Bad mout people sey President JFK did nearly commit a faux pax like dat. For ascarding to how me get it when him did went to Germany gaan talk bout "Ich bin ein Berliner", him was really saying him was pancake, a common pastry.

People sey him shudda really sey, "Ich bin Berliner" to mean "I am a person from Berlin". By adding the indefinite article *ein*, his statement implied he was a non-human Berliner, thus "I am a jelly doughnut". So me get it, so me sell it.

De people of Berlin laugh bout de whole ting. Dem know whether dem is people or jelly doughnut. We now, we haffe a wait fe discover if we is eida one or de adda, six a wan half a dozen a de adda, one or de adda.

Mussie choo becausen we know everyting bout everybaddy except weself. Instead of searching we history fe find weself, we expect to find weself pan Google. Look an see whey dem put as de significance of Feb 1. You will not find that Amina travelled from Jamaica to Broward County for a most auspicious occasion. Yu find uncountable tings of which every Jamaican know de details and discuss anyone and everyting like dem was dere, in person, in de front row. An dat is to be commended. "I salute you kimbo."[9]

Oh yes, you will find numberless tings but nowhere will you find de proclamation of Reggae Month dat sey, "Jamaica's exports of Heritage, Culture and Music are phenomenal, setting our Tourism Product apart from competition, giving Jamaica the greatest potential for a sustainable competitive advantage."

For if dem put dat dem wudda have to put for example, de Hon. LBC is heritage, culture and music in one phenomenal package. Miss Lou, you are still part of the conversation. It is about how can we find anything

9. Line from a children's game.

beautiful and dignified in the language, if we cannot find it in ourselves? If black, gold and green never look good pan we nobody wudden know sey dem winters could be colourful.

What colour is the rainbow
Check it never it show
No matter what they do no matter what they say
All a Jah Jah children a go Harambee[10]

10. Rita Marley, "Harambe" (1982).

Miss Lou We Celebrating

JULIET HOLNESS

Prime Minister, dignitaries, all a who me voice can reach
Judge, police and soldier and di parson weh dah preach
Teacher nurse and farmer, woman man and pickney too
I does glad to take this microphone and wish you howdy do!!!
Dis auspicious celebration near and dear to fimmie heart
And me proud fi seh me glad bag buss dat me can play my part
Is Miss Lou we celebrating and me haffi shout it loud
For this product of East Rural dat mek dis MP proud
Proud fi chat we native language,
Proud fi use we native tongue
Mek we nah fi hide we face nor mek we proudness drop a grung
Proud fi lift we head and beat we chest and with a joyful heart
Make high fashion from bandana and don't call it table cloth
Big big scholars and bright people mek collections from her life
And di whole Toronto Canada sing her praise
Dem all put her name pon building celebrating Maas Eric wife
And McMaster library chronicle her work in many ways
All her letter dem and story, all di Bible she did read
Big and broad a foreign library, Louise Bennett gone a lead!!
Yes she lef ya go a Englan'
Yes she went to school at York
Yes she use we language boasy
Like a Royal knife and fork
And so now we celebrate her as we Royal cultural queen
Royal poet, Royal teacher, Royal pon di stage and screen
Now we come fi celebrate Miss Lou, me welcome one an all,

Even those with nothing good to say are welcome to this ball.
For we raising up a statue, in honour of Louise
One big boasy statue that can stand all rain and sun and breeze.
And as her house keep watch over the Louise Bennett school
So shall her statue watch this town and none shall form di fool
For pride in this is pride in her and pride in our land
A pride to teach our children to believe and take a stand . . .
for the things that we believe in, whether language, whether art
Mek we all preserve we culture mek we all just play we part.
Joining hands and heart together in boonoonoonoos song
That we people and we visitors can all just sing along.
For the love that will share must last foreva and be true
(Sing) strong and eva lasting ONLY FI YOU.
Jack Mandora!! Me no choose none!!

Keep We Culcha Alive

PATRICIA REID-WAUGH

Miss Joycie, yuh see wat a happ'n?
Yuh see wat a gwan me chile?
How people a mess up wi heritage
An a mek we culcha spoil?

It grieve me spirit suh much, mah
It bring water to me yeye
Fe see we traditions a disappear
An watch how we culcha a die.

Likkle pickney kean play hopscotch!
Yuh ever hear of such a ting?
Yuh see de blankness pondem face
Wen me talk bout Miss Lou *Ring Ding*?

An jacks; is like me did speak in tongues,
Miss Joycie, me feel suh shame
When de pickney ask innocent as ever
Ef jacks is a video game.

Miss Lou up dey a shake har head,
Marse Ran a tun eena im grave
When dem see how people a cook
Duckoonoo and pone inna microwave.

Yes, all de food a suffer culcha decay,
When last yuh see a stinking toe?
When last yuh eat a handful a asham
Or dig yuh teeth eena Bustamante Backbone?

Ole time dance, ole time music,
Everyting wata down in a bad way,
An is only few likkle people lef
Who a try dem best fe save de day.

Miss Joycie, we haffe emancipate we culcha!
We cyaan sidung an mek it die.
Dis rich heritage dat was pass to us,
We haffe mek sure it stay alive.

Suh, mek we organize some bruckins
Sat'day night eena Emancipation Park.
Mek we draw long bench an tell Anancy story
An bring back some good ole time laugh.

Mek we gather de pickney dem an teach dem
Bout de richness of we pas'
Soh dem can teach de next generation
An mek we culcha las'.

1-2-3 Aunty Lou Lou

MICHAEL HOLGATE

Yuh never invent language
Yuh never invent me
Yuh never invent Patwa
But yuh certainly set it free

Miss Lou
This is my un-sung
Tribute to you
Squeezing rhymes in
Di lines
Like the way you used to do

Wading through spellings
To write what is new
Yet old as the folk
Who struggle anew
To love how dem talk
And write it down too

Poor mi
Me cyah even read
Wi own talk
In school dem nuh
Teach wi fi crawl
Much less walk
Di whole a we
Know how fi run

Wid di ting
But walking wi
Langwige
A different sinting

Me well cudda write this
In prose wid more style
Wid metaphor, metre
And grace
Lawd mi chile
Nuh matter how much
Degree UWI dem gi mi
Your gifts to this nation
And world still a school wi

Bless you Miss Lou
Mi Aunty Lou Lou
Di Miss sound so formal
And as our folk do
We aunty-up people
We love and respect
A you dat fi sure
I must interject
And force in a word
To rhyme up di ting
A nuh me name Miss Lou
Me a nuh Ring Ding

Not aiming to do
Your life in review
But pausing to say
A hearty thank you
Not just cause
Yuh write what yuh grow up
And hear
The voices that schooled you

Scolded you dear
Cause yuh chat how WE chat
And nuh speaky spokey spoo
Your courage is legend
And now
So
Are
YOU.

Smile Queen

ASHLI-ANN DOUGLAS

Where we goin
Weh we goin?
A bet Sammy a turn inna him grave
And Paul bex caan done
Youths – disgrace
What is this pon mi likkle island in di sun?

We have a few makin it tru the U
Years pass
Dem still a wrestle against the flu
Coughin up interest
Pocket sore
Bank account weak
devaluation
underemployment
What a situation!

The rest a dem

Missis
You can find dem on the corner rubbing dem hand
Making calls
Carryin Jamaica name abroad
No likkle twang dem twang, Miss Lou
Dem speakyspokey the dollars all the way from foreign lan
Day in day out: "Heller"
But they doan have a plan
No one plans lest hope abounds

We come too far no fi nice and green
So a wha a di solution
What a go gwaan
Whai pree?
Aunty Roachy seh we must stimulate sporadic change
So a favourable future we may see

Where we goin?

A full time all a we agree
Wi plane caa reach no weh
If we doa build it some wings –
Strong, steady wings
Island in the Sun
So it can dip and rise back
So it can fly

So fly Jamaica
Smile Jamaica –

She has a rich history
A beautiful woman with the sweetest gifts
Beautiful sunrise and an evenin kiss
I find a nice sunset on the evenin seas
But she tell me seh she wear out and tired
Har bone dem sound like grater inna mento band
Missis, she feel the abuse and misuse of years past
She convince more heartache a come and she no think she go last

And I want to say
Don't you worry yourself, Mama
Your people are here for your aid, Mama
Can I say
Don't you worry yourself, Mama
Your people are here for your aid, Mama
They will rebuild your wings
Pristine

They will sing
Thank you Mama for the fifty-seven years you carry me through
All the pain an' sufferin'
No one knows the pressure you bear; it's only you
Mama, I will never let you down
I'll never go away, I'll always be around
You know why you do it such love that you found
I'm always gonna let you wear that crown

Smile Queen
Smile Jamaica

Eloquently Expressed in Patwa

JEAN SMALL

I had the distinct honour of sitting with our great Miss Lou for an interview on her return to Jamaica from Canada after the passing of her husband. She was still, even under the circumstances, open and jovial with her gutsy, hearty laugh. Many knew Miss Lou as someone who gave honour, distinction and recognition to Jamaican Patwa, the people's language.

Whereas most people were of the opinion that only jokes and comedic stage performances are expressed in Patwa, Miss Lou demonstrated through her poetry that serious philosophical, psychological, cultural and general human issues, their strengths and their weaknesses, could be eloquently expressed in Patwa and she devised a way of documenting her commentaries in her own orthography, which made this oral form legible on the page. In the process, she invented words and expressions that have become a part of the Jamaican language.

In the 1980s, when I joined the staff of the French department of the University of the West Indies, I was able to bring a Guadeloupian, Lise Marie-Sainte, to Jamaica as the first exchange student from the French Caribbean.

In my anxiety to introduce her to the culture of Jamaica I could think of no better way than to introduce her to Miss Lou who, always proud and passionate of introducing her culture to the world, willingly agreed to meet with her and even invited her to be a guest on her *Ring Ding* television programme for a sharing of cultural experiences and information. In this way, Miss Lou introduced the French Caribbean to her audience and Jamaica to her guest.

When I questioned her about her passion to popularize Jamaican Patwa, she informed me that it was already popular, being the language of the masses of Jamaican people and that in fact we, as a people, are bilingual, with Patwa being the maternal language of the vast population of Jamaica.

In my own radio programme, *A Festival of Words*, I had the opportunity to interview many poets and the dub poets all recognize Miss Lou as the mother of that form of poetry, as she gave pride of place to Patwa which, as it developed, gave form to the rhythm and basic language structure of dub poetry. Miss Lou maintained that Jamaican Patwa is not broken English and she found a way to extend the Patwa, the rhythm and cadence of the Jamaican voice, in folk songs, her most famous being: "Dis long time gal mi neva see yuh . . . "

My son created a Caribbean jazz piece titled "Kas Kas" as a tribute to his father. The title of the song represents his father's initials. Recently, I was told that Miss Lou invented the expression "cass cass". I did not know this and I adamantly insisted that my son had created that expression from his father's initials. However, when I told him that people were saying that it was Miss Lou who had created those words, he explained that when he created "Kas Kas" it was, in fact, a play on the original "cass cass" created by Miss Lou.

Miss Lou has had a great influence on poetic expression, folk music and even Caribbean jazz. She lives on in our memories, dressed in her Jamaican national costume, as a Jamaican icon.

Mi Miss You Bad

fabian m. thomas

Dear Miss Lou,

How yuh do? Mi deh yah a gi tanks fi life an every blessin wedda big or small. Bwoy, Miss Lou, mi miss yuh bad. But mi grateful fi di membrances, an fi wan in particulah. Now, old age is a serious ting because I cyah remember when it was I did get the gift an blessin of workin wid yuh and being di stage manager fi di performance yuh did do a Lickle Theata afta yuh did migrate a Canada! Yuh memba?

Yuh did come back after a period a time after yuh did lef . . . no Miss Lou, dis nuh tan good, me cyah memba a when! A which bush tea dem seh good fi memory? Rosemary, don't it? Mi affi go eidda ask smaddy or do some research fi certain a di date, but Miss Lou what a blessing it was fi me as a young man in dem time deh fi work an draw lang bench wid yuh!

Mi memba how yuh did si people. Mi nuh mean si like jus true yuh eye dem a work, yuh did si all wi, yuh look ina wi face direck. When time yuh talk to mi it did come een like nobady else was inna di worl. Up to tideh-day mi still tell people dat inna di lickle time mi spen wid yuh, yuh nat ongle teach mi what it mean to be a boonoonoonoos performer and a linguist and a lover of Jamaican Patwa but yuh teach me about being a good smaddy – a decent human being. Di grace, love an respect weh yuh show mi, mi will neva figet.

And Lawd, Miss Lou, yuh laugh was full a joy! It was like chocolate tea with cinnamon. An yuh laugh from your belly bottom an it rise an fill di room! Mi woulda love fi hear yuh buss a big belly laugh right now.

Mi memba when yuh talk to me yuh used to hole mi han an squeeze it. Yuh memba di night wi did deh a Buddy Pouyatt house fi a dinner party inna yuh honour an mi siddung side a yuh an yuh tell me di story bout how yuh come up wid "menticus"? Bout di doctaman . . . him was German or Greek? Mi cyan memba. Yuh did hurt up yuh foot an him say, "Madam, you have damaged your meniscus." But yuh seh it neva soun so righted or roll offa yuh tongue comfatable so yuh change it to "menticus" and talk bout it inna yuh story dem and pon stage!

Yuh memba di performance a Lickle Theata? Yuh did tiyad, but seh, "Fabian, mi haffi push through do mi part a dat mi deh yah fah. Tiyad or nuh tiyad!" Lata inna di night wan whole heap a wi bungle up inna di wings a peep pon stage pon yuh wid Miss Lois. What a piece a niceness? Unoo ack out wan scene from *Queenie's Daughter*. Meck mi tell yuh something – mi cyah neva pay fi di gif of dat experience, yuh know Miss Lou! Unoo timing, di way unoo seh unoo line dem, di way unoo use di language dem. Di Patwa and di Hinglish! It did sweet!

Mi memba when yuh remin har seh di two a unoo come from Bollo Lane, an Miss Lois seh, "I don't sew, I only 'em" an a talk bout her "clionts". Mi did a watch unoo an wish mi was around inna yuh pantomime heyday fi si yuh a do yuh ting wid Maas Ran an dem odda wan.

Even widdout di rosemary, mi memba when yuh did a talk bout some a di new play and performance yuh go watch an yuh seh some did nice, but some a dem was "so-so booguyaggary!" Mi nearly dead wid laugh.

Miss Lou, wi cyah tank yuh enough, Jamaica cyah tank you di way yuh deserve. We cyah pay di debts for di work, di love, di dedication, di pouring of yuhself inna yuh writing, performing, research and broadcasting pon Jamaican issues, wi culture, wi history an wi language. Bless yuh.

Bwoy, Miss Lou, me nah tell you no lie, it grieve mi seh wi still a disrespeck people who talk Patwa; some a dem a jump pon the bandwagon now wid dis 100 Miss Lou excitement. Between me and yuh: when the celebration done, dem wi go back to nah pay Patwa no mine and a seh a dunce people talk di Jamaican language. Meck dem gwey!

Mi wish yuh neva had to move away to farrin. Mi wish we were able or did tink it was important enough fi keep you here, look afta yuh and treat yuh with love and respect and see yuh as royalty right here inna you owna country. Memba when yuh carry mi wid yuh go up a di house inna Gordon Town? Yuh went to get some tings and yuh gi mi a quick tour. Mi did fall in love wid di house. It did full a love an light, like yuh.

Miss Lou, is pure love inna mi heart fi yuh, bans a respeck. Mi will neva figet you, Miss Lou, and di shart time mi get fi work wid yuh – mi grateful so till!

Walk good Miss Lou, walk good.

Nuff love,
Fabian

We Could Be Whoever She Was

VELMA POLLARD

Miss Lou did not know me, but I certainly knew Miss Lou. I was and still am a great fan. I first saw her close up on a platform at a Monday morning's assembly at Excelsior High School somewhere in the early 1950s. She was a past student of that school. She attended when it had been housed on North Street in the city, before it moved up to Mountain View Avenue to new buildings and vast spaces heavily wooded with lignum vitae.

The principal, Mr Wesley Powell, had this habit of inviting former Excelsorians who had done well to speak to the current crop of students. The intention was to have us appreciate what we could become.

I had already been enjoying her poetry published in the *Gleaner* and her performing voice on radio. I do not remember what she said but I remember how she laughed and how effortlessly she engaged us. The excitement in the assembly hall was palpable. It was the ordinariness of such a great performer that surprised us. She easily narrowed the distance between ourselves and herself; between us and a performer already a household name in Jamaica. At one point it became interactive as she invited us with "Chichi bud-oh" and the response "Some a dem a halla, some a bawl".

It was many years before I got that close to Miss Lou again. I was an educator by then, sharing some of her poems in classrooms with student teachers. We were in the car park of a supermarket where she was to meet some friends on their way up to her house in Gordon Town. It seemed as if nothing had changed. She was as engaging as ever. And she laughed. It was the same effusive and embracing warmth that she brought to Excelsior that long-ago Monday morning.

Miss Lou's infectious charm affected all ages. I was at the house of one of my friends early one Saturday morning. Her daughter, about five years old then, was sitting between the knees of her grandmother, who was plaiting her hair. The child was in tears. Her grandmother was too slow. She might be late for this one chance to be on *Ring Ding*. Miss Lou had done it again. Every child wanted to be on her television show. That was Louise Bennett, exciting adults and children alike for so many decades of Jamaican time.

In spite of her achievements and her popularity, she was so humble that we definitely felt we could be whoever she was.

Patwa Pride

MELISSA McKENZIE

Mi seh a doh know where to begin,
But all mi know joy full up mi heart right to di brim.
Di pride inna mi lef mi so heavy
A can barely stan' up or kip miself steady.

Dere was a time people use to seh yuh dunce lakka bat
Or yuh cawna dark ef Patwa was di language weh yuh chat.
So sake a dat nuff people use to preten'
An a so comes dem people deh cudda seh dem have fren.

All wen dem doh know di fuss wud in English,
Some people start to speak like dem is British.
Yuh fi hear how dem just a twang,
Till dem swear seh choo dem speaky spoky
Dem intelligence tan up strong.

Di people dem was so shame a di Patwa
Dat pan di radio it hardly use to play
Yuh wudda swear seh Patwa do dem summen
An' dem a carry feelings fi it same way.

But yuh did have wah lady
Weh dem call Louise Bennett-Coverley
Patwa was near an' dear to har heart
An' she mek dis clear clear from di very start.
Wen Miss Lou talk di Patwa everybody seh how it sweet,
It mek man, woman, boy and girl kin off dem teet

Miss Lou was a serious ooman pan a mission
An' she neva short change or dilute har passion.
She twis' an' tun' di language so till
People start talk lakka seh a prophecy a fulfil.

Likkl by likkl all who use to skin up dem face
Or style Patwa lakka it a big disgrace
Start sing an' dance to a difran tune
An' open up dem heart fi gi Patwa likkl room.

A neva know a wudda live fi see it
wen di prestigious university mek a Patwa language unit.
Unno see how Patwa get big position
till it become a part a tertiary level education.

Because mi grandawta plan fi tun big teacha
She carry mi pan a likkl tour a UWI an' a dis mi buck up eena.
A tenk Massa God fi mek mi Miss Lou.
A she mek wi start realize all a weh Patwa can do.

Mi seh di gladness inna mi heart kyah hide
It jus' a jump an' prance an' kin puppa lick inside.
Mi cannot wait fi see what next is in store
Cah mi know seh Patwa have greater tings a come fi sure.

A *Ring Ding* Love Affair

KEVIN A. ORMSBY

Interview with Lisa Tomlinson

Lisa Tomlinson: How old were you when you appeared on the *Ring Ding* television show?

Kevin A. Ormsby: I did the show between ages three to seven years old.

LT: What are your most memorable moments?

KAO: The most memorable moments were sitting at Miss Lou's feet and having her and Maas Ran go through all the songs, all the music, the songs that we would sing, and how she would interact with us. She was such a motherly figure who nurtured us. She would make sure all who were on set were okay. The experience of being on the show was one of the best things that I can remember. Even though so young, I can still remember those experiences.

LT: I noticed that I asked you to give a memorable moment, but it is obvious that you are unable to pinpoint any one moment. For you, it was just about being on the show.

KAO: Yes, for me it was also about the preparation involved in the show, where you get the opportunity to say a one- or three-line poem or just to sing a song. Those were some nice moments. It was not just programming that the producers catered to or what they believed the show should be. However, kids from the community who came into that space on Saturday would have the moment of their life.

LT: How did you get the opportunity to be on *Ring Ding*? It seemed like a once-in-lifetime opportunity not open to everyone.

KAO: I had two things going for me. One was location. I lived on Molynes Road and Jamaica Broadcasting Corporation – JBC, as it was called at the time – was just up the street in Half Way Tree, literally a five-minute walk. When the announcements started coming out that the show wanted children to be regulars on the show or who could make it out to the programme, my parents knew I was this little brazen, bright, loud-mouth boy. So, they decided to take me into the studio. And this was the opportunity I got.

LT: So, it was not about knowing Miss Lou or having a prior relationship with her?

KAO: No, not at all. I did not know of her until I was on the programme and then later, I started to get more involved in the arts.

LT: So, you were not even in the performing arts yet?

KAO: No. That was my first set of artistic experiences and interaction, I would say, with folk culture in Jamaica.

LT: With that said, with the interaction with folk culture, do you think there will ever be a replacement of the *Ring Ding* show, given that folk culture in Jamaica is seen as outdated, old and oftentimes primarily associated with the Jamaica Cultural Development Commission (JCDC)? It is just not contemporary or in line with today's popular culture or a part of mainstream culture.

KAO: I think a show like *Ring Ding* needs to come back. There are many of us of a particular age group who grew up in the *Ring Ding* period and it gave us a sense of cultural appreciation. That appreciation is missing now, beyond JCDC. We are favouring North American children's programmes and our children are being raised with a value system that is foreign to traditionl Jamaican culture. This is something that CVM and TVJ need to begin thinking about. I am not suggesting that they recreate a *Ring Ding* television programme. But they need to think about a children's show that is relevant to Jamaica.

LT: You are suggesting a cultural show for children that can incorporate aspects of the Jamaican culture like *Ring Ding*. Can you elaborate on what form or shape this programme could take?

KAO: What we are missing in Jamaica and what *Ring Ding* was portraying were the values of our cultural practices. For example, the value in understanding the role our language plays, or the role that the stories play, the Anancy and Big Boy. There are stories that we are losing because maybe parents are no longer sitting down and sharing these stories with their children. So, this programme not only has the potential to influence the children growing up now, but it could also have a great influence on intergenerational conversations, conversations between parents, grandparents, and children. It can definitely unearth certain values around Anancy stories, for instance. All these things have a place in our society. And if we do not continue those stories either in an oral tradition or written tradition or, in this case, visual tradition on television, we are going to lose them.

LT: You mentioned Anancy and using these stories to teach morals or lessons to children. I am sure you are aware of the controversy around Anancy. I have read recently where scammers are being linked to the ginnalship of the Anancy tradition, and not in a nice way – rather, looking at Anancy as being dishonest and cunning. I recall a member of Parliament pointing to Anancy among other factors as contributing to the scamming culture. How do we reconcile with Anancy's ginnalship, given that the stories are so heavily tied to Miss Lou's work, including the television show *Ring Ding*?

KAO: As a cultural practitioner, there is no way I will accept that this character that exists in the African pantheon of knowledge and culture is the actual trickster. I think the tricksterism is the way Jamaican society has been influenced by colonialism that allows for scamming to happen. What we need to reconcile with is not the ginnalship, but how colonialism has impacted Jamaica. It has divided the society into the haves and the have nots, where minimum wage is below the basic standard of living. And to have elected ministers not understand the psychological trauma that Jamaicans have gone through is problematic. You cannot give me the example of Anancy as the reason for scamming. That is the degradation and defamation of our African cultural tradition. Anancy is a griot, a character that holds truths that in our stories communicated morals of good and evil, decision making and consequences. How can Anancy be reduced to influencing scamming in our cultural pantheon?

LT: Another point I want to bring to the fore is the social aspect. We oftentimes look at Miss Lou as an entertainer. When you were on the show, did you see her work going beyond entertainment?

KAO: I did not see Miss Lou's work as entertainment. *Ring Ding* was a cultural programme. People religiously sat and watched. They laughed and made associations. And that is more than entertainment. There are many ways in which Jamaicans are participating in the culture. The woman at the market who you are bartering with represents the culture Miss Lou and Maas Ran represented in the visual form on television.

LT: What are your feelings about Miss Lou's lost or damaged *Ring Ding* archives?

KAO: By quoting Miss Lou herself: "Every time mi memba Liza wata come a mi eye." The reason it does is that in losing some of the recordings, we have lost history. The Caribbean needs to do a better job of archiving culture. I do not want to hear that we do not have the resources or the money. Today, we have the digital capacity to do so. And we have people and organizations that we can partner with. I would love to have even seen at least one video of *Ring Ding*. I have memories of my parents telling me of how I got on the show. These are valid stories, but I have no visual reference of those moments where I can smile and say, "Wow!" But more importantly, what we might have from those visual references that are lost is that other people working in cultural practices in Jamaica and across the world cannot trace back to that cultural stream that *Ring Ding* would have supported.

I operate a technically but also racially diverse company and so that requires artistic leadership that is culturally sensitive to the dancers. Patwa informs my instruction in class and it's incorporated in the technical codification I am creating with my company. We even have a concept of "TANUPPANYUHMAHLA" which we use when dancers are falling off their balance.

For us, the expression of Jamaican Patwa and the affirmation of language to physio-cultural awareness of people was something I am sure

Miss Lou had to consider. The phrase is such a statement of presence, awareness, confidence and expression of all things that started as a seed, watered and fed in Jamaica by my participation in the arts, grown and matured in the United States and Canada. I share this in a spirit of reciprocity through my ongoing engagement and research in the Jamaican/Caribbean culture.

For Miss Lou

LILIETH H. NELSON

Mi cyan bawl and thrash about
But mi can open mi mout and shout
Fi mek everybody hear
How mi respec' and hold yuh dear
Miss Lou, the mother of dialect verse
Who put Jamaica language
Pon de map
In poetry, prose, song, story and even rap

Miss Lou we proud a yuh cyan done
Fi some yuh is a icon
Fi some a wonder woman
Fi some a mother, a matriarch, and fi some
A sample that God put here
Then throw weh the mould when Him done
For there is truly not another
Living or honoured legend under the sun

Mi cyan forget the times
Spent at yuh feet
Learning and laughing
Flinging back head when joke sweet
You was a walking encyclopaedia
Of Slim and Sam songs
Of stories and anecdotes
Of wi rights and wi wrongs

Yuh was nevah mean or coomoodgin
Wid yuh knowledge and insight
But would share wid generous spirit
Leading all to the light
For yuh did know dat information
Lock up under yuh arm
Was of no use to anybody
So you share wid all who wan' learn

Long before the highway buil'
From information was pon dirt road
Yuh did a disseminate and spread wi culture
To all who did wan' log on and crack di code
Fi understan' how likkle Jamaica
Was so rich in heritage
An' how dis few few people
Mek such a big name pon de worl' stage

So walk good Miss Lou
An' good duppy go wid yuh
We will nevah forget what yuh stan' foh
We will continue the work yuh start
And wi know yuh woulda proud fe see
Dat we always have yuh in we heart
And from yuh principles nevah depart

Tan Tuddy wid Har Pen

SHELLEY SYKES-COLEY

Mi was listening di radio, when mi hear di news.
Dem waan Miss Lou tun National Hero, despite conflicting views.
Some people seh she deserve it, but some seh "Not at all"
Dose seh dat Miss Lou nuh fit, fi ansa di "Hero" call.
True she neva fight gainst colonialism, like di likes of Nanny or
Sam Sharpe,
Dem use dat criticism fi seh fi har credentials fi "Hero" nuh valid.
"If we mek Miss Lou a National Hero, den whappen to Bob?
Fling Bolt inna di mix, an smaddy bound fi get rob!
We have too much hero areddy fi a country dat so small . . .",
Is one bounsa dem bowl afta Miss Lou wid dat deh ball!
A suh we backwuds, we cyaan move wid di times?
Our definition of "National Hero" cyaan redefine?
Miss Lou tan tuddy wid har pen, she neva need nuh sword.
She jus keep dashin it pon dem, all dem try fi ignore.
A she mek we proud fi chat Jamaican, an tek wi culcha far an wide,
Suh dat evry Jamaican, can big up dem chest wid pride.
Look like Miss Lou too ordinary, like di people she did promote.
Elevatin di unassuming Jamaican, wid evry word she wrote.
Mi fine it suh strange, dat even now Miss Lou still a get a fight,
Afta she advocate fi social change wid all di ting dem dat she write.
Me is of di view, dat is lack of vision mek dem blind
Cah wi cyaan put a value pon di rich legacy she lef behind.
Suh unno vote Miss Lou fi National Heroine! Everybaddy seh "Aye!"
Mek a new chapta of her-story begin! Big up, Miss Lou! Ayayeye!

Birthday Beach Bonfire

BEVERLEY ELAINE WRIGHT

Bright-eyed, dark-skin sugar plum
Tun you tail, cum dance and spin
Rum punch lips, mi chocolate cake
Bus a smile, kin you teeth and grin

Mackerel rundown, sweetie pie
Brush de spiders from you hair
Grill de lobster in champagne
Wine up you waistline if you dare

Wear de pearls mi barefoot gyal
Mek de sand cum thru you toes
But as Aunty Roachy woulda sey
No mek de sandfly bite you tho

Ride de wind mi fry dumpling
Tek de moonlite, star and sun
No matter what, dis is you day
Midnight come, mek fire bun

If It Weren't for Miss Lou . . .

NORMA DARBY

If it weren't for Miss Lou, we would not have learned to embrace our culture. We have traditionally taken our culture for granted and, like a child who leaves home for the first time, these things are rarely fully appreciated until they are no longer available. We all need our "groundation" – the things that are part of our heritage, making us who we are as a people. Miss Lou, "the mother of our culture", gave us that with her stories, proverbs, folk songs and traditions that were passed down from our unlettered but wise West African griots – Sankofa and the backward-looking bird – "remembering your past, to protect your future".

She was a cultural activist who made invaluable contributions to our development. After three hundred years of conditioning, which led to contempt for local culture, she dared to validate and give us permission to love our own Jamaican culture.

Dr the Honourable Louise Bennett-Coverley, OJ, OM, MBE, captured the hearts of the Caribbean and black folks everywhere as she addressed the social injustices of the times with humour. She elegantly insisted that what was fundamentally Jamaican was worthy and that nothing, not even colonization, can keep people of colour down.

Miss Lou was a cultural activist, playing a major role in shaping my early concepts of being Jamaican and validating who I am today. As a product of the British school system and all its influences – speech, penmanship, music, decorum and even the games we played – it was an open act of rebellion to espouse Miss Lou and her Jamaicanisms.

Mary Morris-Knibb, well-known educator and disciplinarian, captured her objection of Miss Lou with, "I don't know what's wrong with that Louise Bennett; trying to reverse all our years of hard work in guiding these children in the proper, accepted ways of British culture." My response: "Cuya puppa!" Mi teacher never knew the prophetic influence Miss Lou was to have on our Jamaican people. She had underestimated the self-love, respect, acceptance and cultural emancipation that Miss Lou would give us.

If it weren't for Miss Lou, I would not have fallen in love with our culture. I couldn't wait for the annual pantomime to see and hear Miss Lou and stage partners Ranny "Maas Ran" Williams, Charles "Maas Charlie" Hyatt and "Miss Lois" Kelly-Barrow in person and living colour. Yes, I watched Miss Lou in every pantomime, with her various partners, and, like most Jamaicans in the audience, I always eagerly anticipated the evening's entertainment, where our Jamaican version of childhood fairy tales gained a new twist, with Brer Anancy supplanting the traditional fairy godmother.

Over the years, after migrating to the United States, a piece of homesickness teck me and I purchased and collected her early books and recordings. (I even had an autographed first edition of her most popular book, *Jamaica Labrish.*) I was ecstatic when she and her husband migrated to South Florida.

My relationship with Miss Lou began serendipitously in 1980, when the Jamaican Association of South Florida collaborated to produce a fundraiser starring Miss Lou and Lois Kelly-Barrow.

At another event, staged at the Vizcaya Museum and Gardens in Miami, where Miss Lou was being honoured, the Jamaican Folk Revue (a group that I founded in 1975) was asked to be the afternoon's performers. We were elated when Miss Lou hugged us and said to me, "Mi chile, kip up de good work". We had arrived! If it weren't for Miss Lou, I would not have founded the Jamaican Folk Revue.

During the epic twinning of the cities of Port Antonio, Jamaica, and Coconut Grove, near Miami, Florida, Miss Lou reigned supreme, sitting on her "throne" in Coconut Grove and receiving the obeisance of the privileged attendees.

In the years following the founding of the Jamaican Folk Revue, my entire outlook on our Jamaican culture metamorphosed from interest to passion. It became a mission not only to share my discovery with our new neighbours but also to educate those Jamaican nationals who took our culture for granted. For example, when the Jamaican Folk Revue performed a dance or a song, we also explained its origins and the meanings.

Our first real exposure as performing cultural ambassadors was on the stage of Miami's International Folk Festival, where we not only discovered that our folk music was a sensational hit, but this earned us the first place in the festival and two appearances on our local television. The Jamaican Folk Revue became a staple of the Miami-Dade Library's Folk Festival – "The Art of Storytelling". Our audiences loved it, thanking us for a great learning experience that included an introduction to Miss Lou. I think we met the goal to bring Jamaican culture to American audiences. They were awed and absorbed by what we had to offer.

If it weren't for Miss Lou, I would not have been the unofficial Jamaican cultural ambassador to China. When I visited China in 1984 and worked as an English teacher at the Shenzhen University, I employed Jamaican history and folk songs as part of the potpourri of information that I used to colour my lectures. It was a mutually beneficial cultural exchange and unearthed a wealth of information, including the practice of Jamaican Chinese immigrants to send their children back to China to gain a cultural foundation.

If you go to certain provinces in China and say that you are Jamaican, don't be at all surprised in hearing "Chi-Chi Bud", "Manuel Road", "Day-Oh" or the stories of Brer Anancy. Sharing my Jamaican culture helped deflect my initial homesickness, and the cultural exchange as a teaching tool was rewarding.

I remember meeting a Jamaican Chinese student, one of those sent back to the motherland to learn his family's culture. In an effort to improve the Chinese students' command of the English language, I asked each one to say something. To my great amazement, one young man stood and introduced himself by saying, "I come from the same place you come from." On seeing the surprise and disbelief ("Why are you in an English Conversation class?") on my face, he added, "Kiss me neck-back! Yu nuh believe me? See mi han' middle deh!" I was convinced.

When Miss Lou left us in July 2006, I knew what we had to do. She was a cultural icon who made invaluable contributions to our development as a people. We lost a champion in Miss Lou, and I felt a personal void and the pressing need for us to promote, celebrate and further her legacy. Together with other like-minded community friends, we launched the first of the annual Louise Bennett-Coverley Community Tributes on her birthday in September 2006. From the generous contributions of the overflow audiences, two Louise Bennett-Coverley Memorial Scholarships to the Edna Manley College of the Visual and Performing Arts, totalling US$5,000, were awarded as a tribute to her and an investment in the students who would continue the legacy of this amazing woman. Miss Lou influenced and shaped the lives of so many Jamaicans, at home and abroad, with her invaluable contribution to their cultural development.

If it weren't for Miss Lou, I would not have been able to host the annual Bennett-Coverley Reading Festival for twelve years in Miami, Florida. This partnership, with the support of many kindred spirits like Marcia Magnus, Cheryl Wynter, Hyacinth Scarlett and Colin Smith, and the blessings of the Coverley estate in Toronto, segued into what has become one of the important cultural events in Miami.

In the subsequent years, we have been honoured with guest presenters from every genre: Barbara Gloudon, Marjorie Whylie, L'Antoinette Stines, Lilieth Nelson, Owen "Blakka" Ellis, Fae Ellington, Malachi Smith, Amina Blackwood Meeks, the Reverend Easton Lee, Carolyn Cooper, Jamaica's former poet laureate Lorna Goodison, and young writer and poet Dr Susan Davis. The annual event serves as a forum for emerging writers and students of the performing arts through its scholarship programme at the Edna Manley College in Jamaica and the Broward College in South Florida. To date, we have awarded over twenty-four scholarships in Miss Lou's name to students of both institutions.

Because of Louise Bennett and her musical counterpart Dr Olive Lewin, we have been able to present and showcase authentic Jamaican culture not only to the public but also into our schools, which invite us to do presentations during Black History Month in February, and Caribbean American Heritage Month in June.

If it weren't for Miss Lou, we would not have been able to write a musical, *The Hon. Miss Lou*, and host a writers' clinic to honour her. Over the ensuing twelve years, we have written, produced and performed a pantomime, honouring Louise Bennett-Coverley in vintage Jamaica tradition. *Ol' Time Sinting* starred two of Miss Lou's protégées, Leonie Forbes and Volier Johnson, and they did Miss Lou proud.

The writer's clinic, with our resident writers Malachi Smith, Christine Craig and Geoffrey Philp, led the way for aspiring South Florida writers to become familiar with Jamaican culture.

The baton was passed to Colin Smith, new president of the Heritage Council, for our year-long celebration of the one hundredth anniversary of Miss Lou's birth, which kicked off in February 2019 with the annual reading festival titled "Daughters of Miss Lou", featuring Lorna Goodison, actress Pauline Stone-Myrie, and educators/poets Dr Susan Davis and Dr Donna Aza Weir-Soley.

We thank the divine Creator for placing this catawampus woman and her soulmate, Maas Eric "Chalk-Talk" Coverley in our lives and firmly in the lives and annals of *all* Jamaicans – at home and abroad. Miss Lou left her legacy and still moves among us, walking good, with all the other "good duppy dem".

Tenky, Miss Lou.

Find de Riddim

TEJAN GREEN WASZAK

Yuh did hear how dem a praise
Fe we music and style?
Seh words so nice, music so sweet
All when dem cyan mek it out,

Dem a feel de vibes.
So meck sure yuh try teach a ting or two,
Tell dem loud and proud like Miss Lou
Bout de riddim of de language.

Dem already know
Seh de culture so nice.
Now dem waan know
Is where we get it from.

A muss de air, dem seh.
A muss de food!
Like Miss Lou seh,
"We grow it!"

Inna de mento,
Inna de poco,
Inna de revival,
Inna de reggae.

We find de riddim,
Find de beat.
Culture so nice,
Culture so sweet.

Miss Lou Mek History

BEVERLEY LASHLEY

So Prof. Adisa invite me come
to "Miss Lou's Labrish" fe share
bout how Miss Lou mek history
to celebrate her one hundredth year

So me do me internet research and dis is what me find

> Honourable Louise Simone Bennett-Coverley, folklorist, actress, poet, singer, radio personality, lecturer, writer, journalist, cultural ambassador, social commentator and comedian – dubbed as the "Queen of Jamaican Theatre" and "Mother of Jamaican Culture", prominent preserver of Jamaican performance acts – first black person to be admitted to the Royal Academy of Dramatic Arts.

Not a word about HISTORIAN.

So me call on Brer Anancy,
Cause me and you know, him naw go samfie me
Him say, go check down East Street, at de National Library
cause dem have de Miss Lou Archives deh
Him say, dem staff very knowledgeable,
"Chile, just find you self at NLJ!"

So me go through the NLJ archives just to see what me could locate
And the online catalogue give me information
on how to search through NLJ ResearchGate
Me find the resources of the books and many videos too
But the thing dat excite me de most
Was de little black clutch purse and de pickchas of a young Miss Lou!

Then me tek in *Jamaica Labrish*
her most comprehensive work to date
And me find a heap a poem weh she focus pon history
That me and you can relate
De poetic works of Miss Lou reviewed the present society state

Then she mix it up with history and serve it pon a plate
From "Dear Departed Federation" to "Jamaica Elevate"

Miss Lou use her humorous critique
to discuss "the newly Independent State".
Her topics ranged from World War II to politics and migration
Then she dabble in a little bit pon colonial education

Miss Lou influence was international
From UK to Canada – all ova
You know seh she did go de fus Caribana in '67?
Yeah man! big time "featured performa"

All a we can relate to Jackie Guy dance piece
Him call de tribute "Only fi Yuh"
With the dancers gyrating to the beat and hands a "clap, clap, clap"
Remind me when me watch *Ring Ding*
Miss Lou belt out "Clap har, clap har, clap!"

But before me end me presentation
Listen keenly, listen ya
Mona Campus was mentioned in de poem she call "Jamaica Patois"

So find yu self at NLJ dem have all ah dis an more
All a ten-part Miss Lou Series dating back to 1944
Me we see yuh at 12 East Street,
Plenty plenty deh fe see
And if you reach a foreign,
check out McMaster University

Postcards wid de details on Miss Lou Archives give out teday
Know your culture, learn your history, find yuh self @NLJ

She Find Wi Tung fi Wi

CURTIS MYRIE

wi did lose it
shame fi even
look fi it
prefer to be muted
rather than be rooted
backyard pickney
fi speaky spoky
backra-massa
broken-English
dictate dat pon blackboard
fi every story
no other way
to write nor speak
patois was never meant
to reach this peak
look steadily at Miss Lou
scholarship winner to the Royal Academy
taking centre-stage with all that's revolutionary
tale and text our very own dialect
she find wi tung fi wi
tongue we're told
to hide roun house corner
caan put on good clothes
an talk so
communicating intelligently
is fi lose wi identity

so she tek wi to skule
fi set wi own rule
first language is yu own
adopt what you should
to complement how you've grown
pull di padlocks
from yu lips
from Sunday school to our sunset years
no lose yu tung
lose yu fears
she find wi tung fi wi
Miss Lou
tung fi talk fi write true stories
pon di blackboard of our history

Founder of the Heritage Singers in Canada

GRACE CARTER-HENRY LYONS

Miss Lou was a constant supporter and friend to the Heritage Singers (Canada). In fact, the group had enjoyed a warm, colourful and endearing relationship with both the Honourable Louise Bennett-Coverley and her dear husband, Eric.

I fondly recall the occasion when Queen Elizabeth II visited Canada and, in her honour, the Heritage Singers performed with Miss Lou at the Canadian National Exhibition fairgrounds. Miss Lou had already retired and it was amazing to see how she came alive on stage, dancing and energized as if she were forty years younger.

She entertained her friends frequently, and it was always a pleasure to hang out at her home and just "old talk". She never missed an opportunity to speak highly of the Heritage Singers and, in one of our brochures, she referred to our presentation of pantomime by saying, "Christmas time is pantomime and I congratulate the Heritage Singers for their presentation in Canada of pantomime."

Miss Lou's final recording, a CD called *Lawd di Ridim Sweet*, produced by Joan Andrea Hutchinson, was recorded in her living room, with the Heritage Singers as audience and backing vocalists. Plans to do the audio and video recording at a studio were thwarted as Mr Coverley was not well and Miss Lou was uncomfortable about being away from him for an extended period. Such was their love. So we moved out all the furniture from her living room and converted it into a performance space.

That was such an amazing experience as she sang, performed and explained aspects of the culture, the songs and poems to the audience, which also included many children born in Canada to Jamaican parents, and who were sometimes clueless about aspects of the Jamaican culture.

Mr Coverley was fully involved and joined her in the singing of "Under di Coconut Tree". What a day! Forever etched in our memories.

The connection between Miss Lou and the Heritage Singers in performance made the newspapers quite often. Here are a few excerpts:

> It was a night filled with nostalgia for many when the Heritage Singers, one of Toronto's oldest folk groups, celebrated its twenty-fifth anniversary. It was entertainment at its best, and the crowd loved every minute of it. Tribute was paid to Jamaican cultural icon Louise "Miss Lou" Bennett-Coverley, in the form of a video presentation. Miss Lou wrote many of the songs they performed.
>
> (Eddie Grant, "Heritage Singers Celebrate 25th Anniversary", *Share*)

> An audience of over 1,000 crammed Central Tech High School on Bathurst Street last Saturday night to not only hear a celebration of Caribbean folk songs, but also to get a glimpse of the ever-popular Miss Lou. The Heritage Singers delighted the standing-room-only crowd with their production, *Zuzuwah*, which included a guest appearance by Miss Lou, formally known as the Hon. Dr Louise Bennett-Coverley.
>
> (Heather Graham, "Miss Lou and Heritage Singers Attract Sell-Out Crowd", *Contrast*)

> Miss Lou (Jamaica's legendary folklorist, Louise Bennett-Coverley), who has, in the past, collaborated with the group, was honoured by the Heritage Singers at their 20th Anniversary Celebration. In her short acceptance remarks, Miss Lou commended the Heritage Singers and its director, Grace Carter-Henry Lyons, for the contributions towards the promotion of the culture of Jamaica and the Caribbean.
>
> (Sam Donkoh, "Heritage Singers 20th Anniversary Celebration", *Share*)

> The pantomime is an annual musical in Jamaica, which brings out the best in Jamaican folklore and cultural traditions. Jamaica's ambassador of culture, the Hon. Louise Bennett-Coverley, has played numerous roles in pantomime, which has been around for at least fifty-five years.
>
> (Grace Carter-Henry Lyons, "Heritage Singers Celebrating Twenty Years of Musical Success", *Jamaican Weekly Gleaner*)

Tribute Song to Miss Lou
(Written by Grace Carter-Henry Lyons, founder/music director, Heritage Singers [Canada])
(*Tune*: "Dip an Fall Back")

Your Jamaicans they so love you, they cannot let you go,
They know you must be tired as you go to and fro,
So, Lady of our country and Shakespeare of our land,
The culture you have taught us all, has kept us proud and strong.
You performing long ago, your example still a flow,
The performers in our land and far, respect your shining star.
Mutabaruka, the Jamaica Folk Singers, Heritage Singers,
University Singers, Bob Marley, Peter Tosh, Lovindeer, Oliver, and many too numerous to name have exemplified your works.
And now Miss Lou, Chalk-Talk and you feel justly proud, that the torch you lit so long ago, has caused a revolution in our culture, that will NEVER, NEVER DIE.

Neva Bi Figatten

Iconic Miss Lou

JAYNA SHIELDS

De Honourable Louise Bennett-Coverley weh dem call Miss Lou Lou, shi a true Jamaican. Shi born inna Kingston, Jamaica, in di year 1919 pon di seventh September. Shi start fi write poems at a very early age and shi did love fi mek folk songs and dub poem. In di meantime, she did also interested in art, but a think shi find it more excitement in a di poem which shi write inna Patwa. Some a dem mek mi and mi fambily laugh till we tun ova. Some a dem influence mi very much. Shi inspire inna mi a love and appreciation fi di "heart language" of di Jamaican people.

Some time mi feel a way about di language weh we speak. Mi try fi talk in a standard Jamaican English, but Miss Lou influence mi fi be proud a mi language and talk it di best mi can. Mi ave five other topic weh mi waa touch pon about how she influence mi.

Numba one: Shi tell mi fi have a passion fi di diverse nature of the Jamaican culture. Mi love mi rich and diverse culture; it mek up of different things, people and even animals. As a result, our little country on the map is known because of her.

Numba two: Shi influence we fi be proud of wi colour, especially di black people dem. Sometimes di white people look pon we in a disgust way, but mi nuh care cause a dat Miss Lou teach we fi be proud of wi colour. She always seh, "If yuh nuh happy wid yuh self yuh can't be happy wid nobody else."

Numba three: Shi inspire mi and influence mi fi work fi wha mi want in a life cause when mi get olda mi afi guh get mi things mi self. Once wi touch eighteen wi independent.

Numba four: Shi mek mi understand dat it did possible fi explore different interest inna things. Shi said, "Yuh muss always have an open mind to new things; yuh neva know what you can learn." Sometimes when yuh explore new things either from yuh home or when yuh go abroad yuh find out seh yuh good pon something else. Dere is no one talent in a di world and everyone ave wan talent or wan hidden talent suh yuh muss explore the world fi find yuh talent, according to Miss Lou.

Numba five: An di las topic, shi encourage mi through har poem dem fi start fi write poems and sometimes I dedicate it to har. I know dat I am not di only one she inspire in dat way.

Amazing Grace

KEI MILLER

In my teenage years, I consciously disliked anything that was too obviously a marker of Jamaican culture. At the time, I fancied that it made me independent and cool and I didn't see how overly affected and pretentious my disdain for Jamaican culture was. In any case, I decided I didn't like folk music. I didn't even like oxtail or stew peas. However, I have been reminded that the most earnest evangelist is always the one who has had a "Road to Damascus" experience.

So it was with me. When I fell in love with all things Jamaican, I wanted to tell everyone. I wanted to tell them that I love this not because of some accident of birth, and not because everyone else loves it, and not because I had never questioned or interrogated that love. I loved it because I had come to it as if I was an outsider. I had considered its merits and decided that, independent of any nationalism or jingoism, this was a thing worth loving.

To this day I remember the afternoon when I sat listening to Bob Marley's lament: "Yeah, we've been trodding on the winepress much too long / Rebel, rebel!" Tears streaming down my face, and me perplexed that, for so many years, I had denied myself the pleasure and the privilege of being a fan of this music.

But to all of this cultural rejection, there was always one notable exception: Miss Lou. Imagine that – Louise Bennett in her bandana head scarf, in what I know some have accused her as an over-performativity of Jamaican folksiness – wasn't this the easiest target of my affected teenage disdain? It should have been, but that was never the case.

I loved Miss Lou from the beginning, and that love has only grown deeper and more complex. And, to think about it now, I think it is because

I was always able to derive a profound pleasure from her poems and that pleasure wasn't derived from the places people might have expected.

The first thing was this: Miss Lou gave me access to my mother, to what I felt was the most spectacular side of her, which she didn't show on a day-to-day basis. My mother grew up in rural St Ann. By all accounts – even her own – she wasn't academically gifted. She played netball, but she wasn't a stand-out athlete either. Her claim to fame (and it really was a kind of fame) was that she gave the most brilliant recitals of Miss Lou's poems and, for this, she was booked for concerts across the parish. For this, her parents would always sit proudly in the audience shouting above the applause of those sitting nearby, "That's my daughter."

It wasn't often that I actually got to hear my mother read a Miss Lou poem. By the time I entered the world, she was a different person from the little country girl reading on stage and making her parents proud. She had married a city boy and moved to the city. She had a daughter and a son. She took a course in accounting and worked in a government office. It wasn't a job that she enjoyed – just something she had fallen into. In another world, with other kinds of opportunities, my mother would have worked as a creative director in an ad agency, or she would have been an actress or an acting coach – but life had never presented those options to her.

I would never have known that side of her were it not for the two or three family events when someone – a sister maybe – would say to her, "Viv, do a Miss Lou poem for us. Please." She wasn't shy about it and she didn't need to read from a book. She knew the poems by heart. She recited them with her whole body. It was a miraculous thing to see – the effervescent, funny, wise person she became, as if she wasn't performing at all, but just showing us another side of herself – a side that life had somehow hidden away.

To this day, I feel my mother read Miss Lou's poems even better than Miss Lou. You would have had to hear her to understand this, but it is Miss Lou I always thank for writing these poems, these scripts that gifted the unusual grace of revealing my mother to me.

The second thing I loved about Miss Lou was the grace of her intellect. Growing up in Jamaica, we had a model for what the intellectual looked and sounded like. I am thinking here of radio talk show hosts and their derisive laughter whenever someone said a thing that they deemed unintelligent; I am thinking of PhD'ed men and women appearing on our television screens with their frowns and their scowls and facial expressions that often seem on the verge of an eye roll.

This model of intellect was bombastic when it spoke and quietly smug and conceited when it had to listen. Louise Bennett's intellect was a very different model to this. Hers was such a sophistication of thought, a theoretical sharpness that still managed to be warm and generous and was as willing to poke fun at herself as anyone else.

Perhaps my favourite Miss Lou poem is one that, surprisingly to me, is not often mentioned – "Gay Paree", in which the character gives the most hilarious account of the experience of two friends on a trip to France. The trip starts on shaky ground as one character is at first thrown by the new language being spoken around her.

When she and her friend Mary stop to ask for directions, they are unable to understand the responses given to them in French. So upset is the character that she does what several postcolonial subjects do. She looks to language as a crutch to hold on to, to centre herself in a shifting world – but also as a weapon. Big words and hifalutin language are really just a way of putting others down. She misreads the situations or feels so insecure by her own misunderstanding that she tries to put the locals back in their place by saying:

> Den nuff more French man gadder round
> start pop language pon wi
> An me get eena temper seh
> I naah guh stand fi i'
>
> So I legguh English pon dem,
> and a buss big wud so faas
> Some scatta-back, some stagga-back
> Some-stan-up-like-dem loss!

It is the friend, Mary, who has to bring calm and reason to the situation, counselling the persona of the poem:

a nuh show off dem a show off
a suh dem language guh!

The strength of the metaphor always astounds me; how Bennett is able to find in a place as far away as France a new way to talk about Jamaica, about the importance of respecting local people and honouring the language that they speak. And how gracious is the lesson she is trying to teach – that she has found a way not to say, as teachers often do, here is what you must learn. Rather, she says, here is something I had to learn.

The third reason I love Miss Lou might seem the silliest reason of them all, but it is this: in 2013 on sabbatical from the University of Glasgow, and teaching creative writing back in Jamaica, I wondered how I could ease my students into understanding poetic meter – notoriously one of the hardest things to teach. My theory was of course that they mostly understood meter already but the knowledge was instinctive and we were simply adding language to something they already knew.

I started with a relatively simple meter – the ballad – alternating lines of iambic tetrameter and iambic trimeter. I knew that using such language too early would only cause anxiety, so what I did was this: I asked my students to take their favourite Miss Lou poem (the trick works with almost all of her poems) and try to sing it to the tune of "Amazing Grace".

They were sceptical at first. What was this strange thing I was asking them to do? "Just try it," I insisted. Finally, one student who knew "Roas' Turkey" by heart began. You could feel her surprise line by line as she realized each word to this poem she knew so well slotted in so perfectly to the movement of a tune she knew equally well.

Another student could remember a few verses of "Uriah Preach". He did the same and was equally surprised that it worked. As a group they tried to remember "No Lickle Twang", and as each verse came to them they sang it, their eyes wide with astonishment and looking to me as if to ask, What kind of obeah is this?

In one's life as a teacher, we teach hundreds of classes, but sometimes a single class stands out and this still stands out for me – that afternoon so suddenly full of song, that class learning that they could sing their favourite poet, that Miss Lou's poems collected together represented something holy, like a hymnal for an island. After they had belted out "No Lickle Twang", one of my students looked at me and said, "That's amazing!" And I thought to myself, yes.

It is the amazing grace of Miss Lou.

Ode to Miss Lou

KALLIAH WHAYNETTE MINTO

Miss Lou, yuh a wi Jamaican icon. Yuh mek Patwa worl renown. Anywey inna de worl we goh, from we open we mout everybody start sey, "Yeah man! Yuh Jamaican", even when dem no know nuthin else in a Patwa ar English. So till now dem a use big wud bout Patwa dem is advocating fi Patwa tun official language inna wi own likkle country. Miss Lou yuh must feel proud in de heavens when yuh hear dem ya sinting ya.

Lawd, big ahn likkle waan know Patwa. De hexcitement wah dem create fi talk it is sooo great! Not even likkle twang nuh sweet suh. Ongle a reel Jamaican can talk suh. When mi go a foreign lan mi feel important from dem hear me, "Jamaica. No problem man." Yes, a yuh mek dem know we. Yuh mek Patwa be knowst all ova di worl.

Miss Lou, yuh ded an gone but yuh legaci tan up tall, tall. Pan yuh shouldas wi stan for Patwa revolution. Miss Lou, all pon a sudden every bwoy an gal waan talk like we!

Cooyah! Yuh nuh see we a trendsetta? Dem just a fallah we. All a use we language inna dem songs an movies.

Big up yuh self, Miss Lou, walk good! We tenk God fi gi we yuh. Miss Lou, OM. Yuh a mi favourite poet ina di whole wide worl. Yuh poems dem sooo good mi affi read dem ova an ova again.

Miss Lou, a reel reel talk: we likkle but wi tallawah. A yuh fus say it, cause yuh know it lang time. A yuh one use to see it but now wi know fi true cause aldoah yu nuh deh ya now, yuh name large a yard an abroad still.

Miss Lou, yuh was instrumental in wi proudness of wi black skin. From Jamaica, Canada to different parts a di worl weh yu trod widout toning because yu neva did mourn sey yuh black. Yuh stood tall among all de different races, even when yu faced much discrimination.

Miss Lou yuh is a fashion icon enuh.
Yuh auspicious designs of we national claat,
Di bandana, mek wi stand out
Even among di greatest country dem and worl renown fashion designers.
The other day we was so proud to see we own
Miss World Toni-Ann Singh don di cloth wheh yuh bring
A-ya-yaah!
Mi nearly dance and sing: "This lang time gal mi neva see yuh, Come mek we wheel an tun."
We thank God fi di legacy yuh mek so popular.
Mrs Louise Bennett-Coverlyrics
OM,OJ, MBE, Jamaican poet,
folklorist, writer and educator
Yuh name will forever live on!
Pop story gi mi an tenki!

Our Jamaican Queen Comes to St Andrew High School

MARGARET RECKORD BERNAL

Many of the anecdotes about the life of the Honourable Miss Lou, Jamaica's national treasure, Mrs Louise Bennett-Coverley, underscore her instinctive, unfailing graciousness and her genuine interest in her "meeting and reasonings" with all of her people at home and abroad.

Nowhere is this better illustrated than her sixtieth birthday party at St Andrew High School, in 1980.

An impetuous first former (Lavinia Marriott) decided to invite Miss Lou to her own celebratory birthday at the school. The suggestion was immediately pounced upon, welcomed and spread like "bush fire" throughout the school community among students, teachers, parents, and ancillary and administrative staff. The date had to be delayed as the school term had just commenced on Miss Lou's actual birth date, 7 September. In addition Miss. Lou was not in Jamaica at that time. A new date was discussed, and decided upon in February 1980.

The venue was planned.

The menu was planned.

Additions and refinements were insisted upon by the canteen staff.

The AV centre was decorated.

One enthusiastic parent selected, bedecked and dispatched an impressive throne-like chair to the school for the designated day, insisting that Miss Lou is "our Jamaican queen".

The initiative of the first formers inspired the whole school.

On the appointed day, with the entire first form excused from class to attend the grand event (and the rest of the school yearning), Miss Lou arrived for her party. She was ushered into the lavishly decorated AV centre before a combined class of first formers.

There were welcome speeches, birthday tributes, recitations and renditions (of Miss Lou's repertoire).

There were tributes and more renditions of Miss Lou's work. Nadine Sutherland – fresh from her win at the first Tastee Song Competition – sang her tribute.

Overwhelmed, Miss Lou cried; she sang along with the girls, she hugged and kissed and was hugged and kissed effusively in return.

Inspired by hundreds of young schoolers – Miss Lou listened joyfully. She joined in the songs and eventually – in inimitable style – she took over the proceedings, urging on the combined audience choir in her signature rendition of "Chi-Chi Bud".

She signed auotographs.

She insisted on making her way to the kitchen to thank the delighted canteen staff in person.

And she wept tears of happiness – again and again!

It was a never-to-be forgotten visit.

AFTERWORD

Characteristically Miss Lou, always a methodical and organized scribe, returned to Ribba-Bank Oballey, her green and rustic villa in Gordon Town overlooking the Hope River bank. At her overflowing desk, she inserted her personal stationary into her weathered Olivetti and typed a heartfelt, intimate "thank you" to the young schoolgirls who had welcomed her, saying how special and inspirational she had been in their young lives. Amazingly enough for someone known as the "doyenne of words", Miss Lou began, "Have you ever been at a loss for words?"

This note and its weathered, mottled envelope are among today's treasures on display in the Emrie James Museum – Jamaica's first school museum, which opened on the Cecelio Avnue grounds of the St Andrew High School on 8 April 2011:

Ribba-Bank Oballey
Enfield
P.O. Box 11, Gordon Town P.O.
11th February, 1980

Mrs Nadine Marriott,
St Andrew High School,
Cecelio Avenue,
Kingston 10.

Dear Mrs Marriott & my Young Friends,

Have you ever been at a loss for words? . . . wanted to make someone know how much happiness they have given you and yet feel you cannot find the right words to fully express the joy inside you?

Well, it is like that with me in trying to let you know how I feel about the wonderful party you gave me. It is one of the loveliest things that has ever happened to me; something I shall never forget . . . that is why it is not easy to find the right words to tell you all that it means to me.

Would you understand if I told you I feel humbly grateful for your loving-kindness? You have made me feel that everything that I have done since I was a teenager is really worthwhile. My work now means very much more to me because it has earned me your love and appreciation.

As my Aunty Roachy would say "wen yuh find a seed an plant it, yuh nevah know what kinda tree yuh wi get". You have made me feel that the seed which I found and planted and cared for through the years has borne more delicious fruits than I could ever imagine. Through you I have received much, much more than I could ever expect from my plantings and I thank you from the bottom of my heart for your loving-thoughtfulness for me.

May the love you have shown me come back to you multiplied and make you as happy and thankful for giving love, as you have made me feel.

God bless you all.
Sincerely,
"Miss Lou"
Louise Bennett-Coverley

P.S.: May I send my Birthday Card to school one day and ask my young friends to sign it for me?

The modern-day counterpart to this letter was a Facebook thread created in 2019, thirty-nine years after Miss Lou's visit to St Andrew, and thirteen years after her death and internment in National Heroes Park in Kingston, Jamaica. The comments in that thread are an eloquent testament to her impact on the lives of young schoolgirls, who in 1979 were in their formative years, just embarking on a Jamaican life. These "schoolers" have since gone on to establish illustrious careers and useful, community-service oriented lives in many lands – Nigeria, Canada, France, South Africa and further afield.

They recall in their Facebook conversation of 2019 the impression this wonderful national icon had on their lives; that impulsive "honouring" party, that love shared, grounded them in a chapter of their young lives – and inspires them still.

TODAY

Now, many years after Miss. Lou's visit to St Andrew High school, the young women whose lives she interacted with treasure the experience. From her they learned many lessons which they have taken to heart and built on.

Miss Lou is recognized above all as a builder of the hidden history of this island of Jamaica. She embodies the African "griot" – honouring one's traditions, studying them, accessing and interacting with the original "oral" historians and folklorists who lived out the early nation-building experiences of Jamaica. These Miss Louise Bennett-Coverley took, documented and re-presented to her people at a time in their history when the experiences of country folk and urban poor, were little known and little respected. This pioneering work represents the bedrock and the hallmark of her long career.

Miss Lou, however, went a stage further. Building on her inimitable skills as raconteur, storyteller, performer, singer and actress, Miss Lou was able to own the materials that she independently gathered and give them back, as creative, lively "performance" to her countrymen first of all, and then to the world.

Miss Lou lives!

From Miss Lou

2019 Scene

DAVIA ELLIS

"This long time gal me never see yuh",
I wish I could hold your hand.
First lady of Jamaican comedy,
You really loved your homeland.

Yes, I am still growing and learning from you;
You were always on point, Miss Lou.
I´ll tell the people what you would say in 2019 –
For brand Jamaica is a most interesting scene.

You certainly could laugh Miss Lou;
There was no one else like you.
You'd lifted Jamaica up to the sky,
But "Wata come a mi eye".

"Mosquito 1, mosquito 2,
Mosquito jump in a hot calaloo."
Mosquito sick me and give me Chik-V –
Your song sound different, yes Miss Lou.

People inna pretty clothes
But dem no want seem nuff.
Dem can't raise dem hand
Cuz "water scarce and dutty tough".
So when we go overseas we use up the Jamaican talk,

Cuz dem foreigners can't understand enough to bark.
We have to be smart like Bredda 'Nancy,
But reading patois nuh really tickle wi fancy.

Dem bring in patois bible di other day,
But some folks never want it to stay.
Some seh patois scripture sound different – in a negative way,
But Jamaicans love gwaan like a only inna old English dem can pray.

Andrew picked up from Portia's building of roads with the Chiney man,
Because it seems like driving topped the list on everybody's plan.
People still walking and finding fault with everything – such a shame,
And First and Second Peter has never been the same.

Jamaicans still love mix up, and all these things:
"People man nice" is what Mackerel sings.
You would pop up wid Candy's "Can I get a wow?"
But everybody still a hustle fi get a big bus' now.

Miss Lou, you've made your Right Honourable name
And lash out patois throughout your years of fame.
You are a big deal, if you didn't stand up strong,
Even wi language dem woulda steal.

Everytime, I Am a Jamaican

COURTNEY GREAVES

Every time mi think bout Louise, wata come a mi yeye,
Mattee,
yes Courtney,
dem seh mi young, an mi nuh know Miss Lou,
but fi she did deh yah, she wud ah proud fi call me mini Miss Lou,
she wud a vex, fi hear how dem try fi style wi nice nice bandana.
Dem call it dis, dem call it dat.
Dem even call it table claat, but mi Courtney glad wen dem call it dat,
cause table claat a good good sinting.
A betta dem did a wear dis, dan a wear certain clothes
Miss Lou, don't worry, just rest yuh good ole soul and leave mi
Courtney, fi deal with all a them.
ohh, come back Louise, come back gal, wata come a mi yeye,
come back Louise, come back gal, mi kyaan tell yuh goodbye, mi nah tell yuh goodbye.
I am a Jamaican, a proud one too, I wear the colours of my flag with pride, you should too.
the colours in my flag speak of who I am
BLACK is my strength,
GREEN speaks of my hope
GOLD is the sunlight in me.

Talk Yuh Talk Regardless

VIVIAN CRAWFORD

The contribution of Dr the Honourable Louise Bennett-Coverley to the intangible heritage of Jamaica is impatient of debate, and we continue to be mindful of her determination of "talk yuh talk regardless".

It is obvious that she was aware of her life's vocation from childhood when she participated in a concert and her recitation (poem) in the Jamaican language was interrupted by a man who shouted, "Is dat yu madda sent yu a school fe lawn?" The language of the majority of our people then was treated by the minority with derision.

I had the honour and privilege of working with Miss Lou in her role as a facilitator for the Jamaica Cultural Development Commission and at the Institute of Jamaica, where she was elected as one of five fellows. In addition to the support of her husband, Eric, we should remember some of those who recognized her mission, including Sir Philip Sherlock, Professor Mervyn Morris, Professor Rex Nettleford, Miss Marjorie Whylie, Dr Pamela Appelt and the Little Theatre Movement, through the annual pantomime.

Miss Lou told me that her favourite hymn was "All Things Bright and Beautiful", and it was fitting that it was sung at her funeral service at Coke Methodist Church in Kingston. The hymn's refrain echoes to those of us who guard her legacy:

> All things bright and beautiful,
> All creatures great and small.
> All things wise and wonderful,
> The Lord God made them all.

Using the Language of My Heart

FARIKA BERHANE

I was a little black girl who chat bad and lived in a middle-class colour-caste Jamaican neighbourhood when I first became conscious of the presence of a woman named Louise Bennett, who was able to make up poems and stories in the Jamaican language that people appreciated. I was living in a community where talking in the Jamaican language was frowned upon. It was a neighbourhood where I felt like an outsider because of my resistance to its colour/class system of white at the top, brown in the middle and black at the bottom.

It was bad enough that I was the black sheep as the darkest girl who lived on the street, but I added to my lack of integration with the community by insisting on talking in Jamaican language, no matter how much I was scolded by adults to desist from doing so.

My excitement about this woman mounted as the day of her appearance approached. I endured being put in the choir with girls singing Irish and Scottish songs in order to be included among those who heard Miss Lou perform.

The poems I knew as a child were written in standard English about Europeans and British scenery. The few that were in dialect were not in Jamaican language but in the language of the Irish and the Scottish people. Poems by black writers about black people were not available to me. Invited guests at my neighbourhood's community events were usually from the aristocracy who ruled the island in colonial Jamaica.

Although I spoke in the Jamaican language, I showed my love of poetry by writing poems in lofty English and was fond of reciting them to family and friends, who showered praise on me. I remember beginning a school essay on happenings in 1951 with a poem that read:

Nineteen hundred and fifty-one
Thou hast come and gone
But thy precious memories will always linger on.

This ability to write in a language that did not correspond to the way I spoke got me in trouble with my student colleagues and my teachers, both in elementary and high school. I wrote a poem on Joan of Arc when I was in elementary school and was told to write about someone I admired. My homeroom teacher was delighted with my poem but my classmates were not. They told the teacher that I had copied it from a book they had read. My protests against their lying were ignored. Their determination to prevent me from rising above them through my ability to write in the language of the colonial master was indeed painful.

The teacher believed them without asking them to produce the book that contained the poem or to give her its title and author. She scolded me for trying to impress her by copying people's work and pretending that it was mine.

When I went to high school, I met a similar fate. As a teenager and lover of the English writer Charles Dickens, I imitated his writing style in my essays so successfully that my English teacher at the high school I attended called me out for stealing the work of an English writer and pretending that I had written it. She said that I was a thief and let me know that if I did not stop stealing other people's work, I would go to jail when I grew up and would suffer terrible consequences. She firmly believed that children wrote how they spoke and it was impossible for me to "chat bad" and write "good English".

I cried bitter tears for being cursed for my writing that I had worked hard to produce with the hope of getting good grades and praise from my teacher. The fact that my English teacher came from one of the ruling families in Jamaica made her attitude to me especially painful. Some of my classmates laughed at my humiliation by the teacher. Others sympathized with me in secret but did not show their solidarity with me to the teacher's face.

Miss Lou's appearance at my neighbourhood community function was therefore a watershed moment in my life. She put an end to my dilemma by exposing me to writing in the language of my heritage. I was delighted listening to her celebration of the life of ordinary Jamaican people through her poems and songs in the Jamaican language. I no longer felt compelled to write about faraway places and people who I only knew through books.

I began listening to the sound and rhythm of Jamaican speech carefully. Miss Lou freed me to begin the journey towards appreciating the people and scenery around me. I basked in the sun of Jamaican voices talking Jamaican and walked around repeating aloud playful lines from Miss Lou's radio broadcasts, such as, "If a cross you deh cross, beg yu cross mek mi pass. Wat a crosses pon dis yah road crossing."

After I graduated from high school, my cousin who lived in Brooklyn invited me to the United States to spend time with her and to explore going to school in America. My stint in the United States was marked by homesickness. The streets of New York were dirty – not paved with gold, as I had been told as a child. Albums with Jamaican folk songs kept my spirits up during this time. I became attached to our folk culture and became even more attached to Miss Lou as the folklore icon. The inspiration that Miss Lou provided helped me to survive the agony of separation from my beloved country.

On my return to Jamaica, I resolved to begin writing all my fiction and some of my poems completely in the language I heard when I was growing up in Jamaica – the language of my heart. This delighted some people and annoyed others. It blazed a path for my literary career. Several of my stories were published locally as well in *Flamingo* magazine in London and *Short Story International* and *Negro Digest* in the United States. My story "Brother Ben" was a prizewinner in an international black writers contest in London. There was much debate pro and con about it, because it was written completely in the Jamaican language.

Anchored by Miss Lou's pioneering example, I went on to write a play, *These People Never Learn*, and a novella, *The Story of Sandra Shaw*, in the Jamaican language.

Some of the poems as well as the play and a short story won prizes in the annual Jamaica Festival literature competition in the 1970s. Miss Lou's pioneering work for the acceptance of the Jamaican language as a literary form of expression paved the way for the acceptance of my novella and the emergence of the cultural renaissance of the 1970s. The novella was serialized in the Jamaican music magazine *Swing*, a pioneer of the national and international rise of Jamaican music.

Professor Brathwaite published an excerpt of *The Story of Sandra Shaw* in his groundbreaking literary magazine *Savacou*. This is an excerpt of his comment on the cultural revolution of the 1970s:

> There was a cultural revolution in Jamaica and throughout the Caribbean during the 1970s, expressed by Rastafari and the philosophy, lifestyle, music/art they developed and inspired. An essential part of the revolution was literary expression and at the heart of this was Farika Berhane, then developing out of her more middle-class Norma Hamilton, journalist, nativist, scholar, researcher, worker and creative writer.

FAMILY TIES

Eric Coverley and my father grew up in a district close by Gordon Town and had old family ties. They also shared birthdays and often celebrated them together. I was surprised to discover during these family visits that Miss Lou had a sense of humour offstage as well as onstage.

I was doing a stint of writing scripts for the radio serial *Life in Hopeful Village*, introduced by Elaine Perkins, when I heard that Miss Lou had made a call for writers of the Jamaican language to meet with her. I answered her call and she tested me by saying a half-sentence in the Jamaican language and asked me to complete it. When I did so using the very same words she had in mind, her delight was infectious.

I enjoyed those times getting into her time and space and learning from her. She became my mentor. She unleashed my ability to reason. She encouraged me to interrupt her conversation anytime I had a suggestion to make. She did not interpret it as cutting in before her thought was completed. This attitude made it possible for us to relate to each other with ease. Miss Lou wanted to push me out of my hiding place behind print into the forefront of activities. She gave me two pieces of advice that would have put me in the limelight and ensured my stability as a writer, had I heeded them. The first was that I must write for the National Pantomime. She offered to introduce me to that circle.

At the time, I was engrossed in making suggested corrections to *The Story of Sandra Shaw* for the publishers, Simon and Schuster, and had an agent in New York pushing me to pay attention to the book. I did not want the world of pantomime to distract me, so I put off meeting the crew and ended up never exerting myself to take on writing for the pantomime.

Miss Lou's second piece of advice was that I should ask my father to give me an island that he owned and to make him build a writers' haven on it so I could have a retreat to produce great literary works. My father was a building contractor. The island of which she spoke was adjacent to a rural property that he owned in the Enfield community. He was a practical, hard working man who was not fond of the up-in-the-sky ventures of many artists, so I did not follow up on her suggestion.

The last memory I have of Miss Lou in person was seeing her driving while I was walking with my son, who was then a toddler. He had a way of charming people, especially women. Miss Lou was one of the women he charmed. She honked her horn to get my attention and beckoned to me. When I came over to her, she put some money in my hand and said, "Take this for the baby."

She played an important role in enabling me to bring Jamaica to children in the United States when I migrated to that country. I used my ability to write and recite my Jamaican language poems to train children to get used to my accent so that they could not claim they did not understand me and use it as an excuse not to participate. They had to listen keenly and then tell me what my poem was about. Many years later, past students told me how inspiring it was to be introduced to the Jamaican language and how it motivated their reading and writing skills. A past student actually lauded me to a Capitol Hill audience during the annual Congressional Black Caucus sessions in Washington, DC.

After I retired from working as a teaching artist, a parent confessed to me that when she heard that I was teaching Jamaican language poems as a tool to literacy, she had her doubts that such a thing could work. She became enthusiastic, she said, when her daughter's reading score and writing ability showed great improvement. She said there had been excitement and wonder among parents that there was a Jamaican woman successfully using Jamaican poetry to get children to learn to read.

It was during my sojourn at the unique Children Studio Public Charter School for the Arts that I introduced Miss Lou to students directly, and not only through my Jamaican language poems. The school employed artistes to use their art forms to teach academic subjects. I acquired CDs of Miss Lou singing and reciting her work.

The school was truly multicultural. It had students from Latin America, the Caribbean, the United States, Algeria, Morocco, East and West Africa, and Europe. All enjoyed dancing to the rhythm of Miss Lou's performances. I particularly liked to play her song on balancing where children would practise acquiring balance by placing books on their heads and trying to walk around the studio (classroom) without letting the books fall. Students actually tried to imitate Miss Lou.

They really had fun with Miss Lou. They loved her laughter. They loved the joy she brought to them. They could feel cool Jamaican mountain breeze and the spirit of the Jamaican people through her. They loved her as the mother of Jamaican culture. They took her home with them and parents reported they were imitating Jamaican accents and singing Jamaican songs in their homes. Miss Lou, "Yu get large inna Washington, DC, 'mongst DC pickney!"

I admire the works of African American poet Paul Laurence Dunbar. I think that he is the African American counterpart of Miss Lou. They both wrote in the language of their people, utilizing the folk culture and making it acceptable as literature. When I took up residence in an building called Paul Laurence Dunbar Apartments, I made up my mind to use my stay there to inspire me to concentrate on publishing my work. The Dunbar Apartments is the renovated building of what was once the Dunbar Hotel where famous musicians, singers and other artistes stayed in Washington, DC, during segregation.

In such an atmosphere, I began working on a collection of poems for an anthology of my work and asked Miss Lou to do the introduction. When I located her phone number and called her with my request, she readily agreed. It was our last conversation. She died before I completed the book. "Miss Lou, member mi ah member yu pon yu centenary. Miss Lou, ah miss yu. Miss Lou, ah luv yu fi true. Walk good, yu hear."

Beneath the Folk Caricature

TOMMY RICKETTS

It's a privilege to be afforded the opportunity to participate, through the images on the following pages, in the celebrations of one of Jamaica's greatest cultural icons, Louise Bennett-Coverley.

Some of us come to art for amusement and beauty, but it has other aesthetic meanings. For me, art is an alchemy that can genetically help to evolve our humanity to a higher, more wholesome place. Miss Lou's work has always trojaned this subversive evolutionary element. For those of us hungry for a greater and more nourishing self-discovery, her work remains a wellspring, offering glimpses of an ancient past. As we unearth this gift, most of us will be humoured by the vocal cadence and masterful wit of Miss Lou, the griot. But there are deeper opportunities evident in her work, such as the possibility of courageous, priceless self-discovery.

Ring Ding *Nation Griot*

Speaking in Tongues, Engaging the Elements

Monumental

Deploying the Anansi Strategy

Beneath the Folk Caricature

Language and Laughter Laureate

SECTION 3

AUNTY ROACHY SEH

Miss Lou once said, "As my Aunty Roachy would say, wen yuh find a seed an plant it, yuh nevah know what kinda tree yuh wi get".

In har foreword to *100+ Voices,* Lorna Goodison seh, "Louise Simone was granted the gift of poetry and with it came the additional role of freedom fighter; for just as Nanny of the Maroons had to bounce bullets off her body, Louise would have to spend years chucking off the wrath and condemnation of the gatekeepers of society, including many of the people she was defending, who brutally attacked her for championing Jamaican speech."

But Miss Lou plant a seed an it catch an sprout an grow an spread so tidday plenty young Jamaican writer no tink twice bout writing inna fiddem owna language – same way we talk. Cause it soun good an it feel good an we proud a we language.

Dutty Tough

(Excerpt)

LOUISE BENNETT

Sun a-shine but tings noh bright,
Doah pot a-bwile, bickle noh nuff,
River flood but water scarce yaw,
Rain a-fall but dutty tough!

Tings so bad, dat now-a-days wen
Yuh ask smaddy how dem do,
Dem fraid yuh teck i tell dem back
So dem noh answer yuh!

No care omuch we dah-work fa
Hard time still een we shut,
We dah-fight, Hard-Time a-beat we,
Dem might raise we wages, but –

One poun gawn awn pon we pay, an
We noh feel noh merriment,
For ten poun gawn pon we food
An ten pound pon we rent!

Saltfish gawn up! mackerel gawn up!
Pork an beef gawn up same way,
An when rice and butter ready,
Dem just go pon holiday!

Slanguage

CHERRY NATURAL

Remember when wi use to
paint pictures with words
Using wi tongue as the paint brush
Each stroke was a different gesture
Every sentence have its own colour
Nuh full stop, nuh comma
Animated stories use to move wi
Is like yuh watching a movie

Now a days tings change
Long story cut short
Dem youths yah nuh talk or tek talk
As yuh start a conversation
All yuh can hear is
Nuh sey a word!
A weh yuh a sey daaady
Yow dawg yuh done know
Wi have di ting lack . . . maaaad
Baby weh just born a tell yuh
    dem out and bad
Nuh trust nuh one, not even God

Dem nuh have nuh fear
Sicka dan di intensive care
If yuh dis dem, dem mek yuh
        disappear
Give yuh a funeral inna dis yah year

Blood cold, yuh feel a chill
    when dem come near
Nuh heart, just a block a ice
Ha fe eat a food
A yah so nice

From parliament to the market
A so dem talk it
Slanging words no target
Head nuh good again, head sick
Unda pants unda arm, pants pon hip
Swagging right back pon
di slave ship, pon di slave ship

Young girls clueless
Exposing Vctoria's secrets
Leaving nothing to the imagination
Keeping up with the Kardashians
Teen rage gone viral
Spreading like a virus
Twerking, twerking, twerking
    like Miley Cyrus

Six a one half a dozen a di ada
Social media creating antisocial
    behaviour
A whole generation raised
    by gadgets
Bed time stories of neglect
The smallest a youth home alone
Left with a smart phone
Nuh baby sitta
Parents deh a road
Yuh ha fe falla dem pon twitta

Right yah now di pressure slap weh
Nuff survive afa weh others dash weh

Pavaty a happen
The government need fe duh su-uuh
Our little island is swimming
    in a sea of debt
With waves of high prices
Stress gone up . . . way up
The problems deep and nobody
    can cross it, cross it
The Jamaican dalla is sinking
The dalla can't swim
The dalla is drowning
Call the contracta, we need
di contracta to fix di Country's debt
A nuh tutty gran debt
A trillion dolla debt
So call di contracta
Wi need di contracta!!

My Jamaican Tongue

MALACHI SMITH

My Jamaican tongue too sweet
For me to throw it away
When you hear me talk
Ah nuh play me a play
Like my professor friend . . .
Who got circumcised
Dash weh him Jamaican tongue
To get recognized.

My tongue is African, Caribbean
Drum-talk, flute, pan, percussion
Banjo, mento, ska,
Rock steady, Rasta, reggae
Politics, sugar cane
Sweat, slavery, blood and pain
Blend dat with English, Spanish, Chinese, Indian
My tongue is out of many one.

Mi naa dash weh mi tongue
Mi love it to mi heart
Before so mi go back home
Because me and it naa part.
It too sweet like calypso
Your tongue is ballroom dance
Mine is go-go.

I don't have to draw out my vowels
Like Robin shooting his bow.
I make my point,
My tongue just flow
Like notes from Don Drummond's trombone
I don't envy you for yours
So leave me with my own.

You think is everything I say
I want you to understand?
My tongue is a disguise,
Part of my oral tradition.
When our ancestors died
And couldn't afford to leave legacy
Dem wrap up dem tongue eena tie-head
And pass it on to wi.

Stop yuh renk!
Your tongue was derived
And so too is mine
If yours is whisky
Mine is pure wine
Harp, rumba, fire dancer, goat skin
Your tongue is Her Majesty's
Mine a fi wi sinting
So you can cast your innuendos and aspersions
I don't give a damn
Cause when you hear me talk
You must always hear Jamaican.

She Who Laughs the Revolution

ANDRENE BONNER

One hundred years ago
she made a grand jeté,
a classic entrance
onto Love's lap.

The elders blew the Abeng
to wake the town:

a lioness has come
a lioness has come
to laugh the revolution
laugh the revolution.

Same time, one big breeze
blow her first cry
over the Blue Mountains
round Makka Back Lane,
down Half Way Tree,
pass Cross Roads,
over Kingston Harbour
where it pick up speed
before it catch
a Forty North Street,

to laugh the revolution
laugh the revolution.

Matty run leave her clothes
a standpipe,
Aunty Roachy
drag on her slippers,
put on her tie-head,
pick up di Bible,
open di Psalm over di baby head
fi ward off evil spirits and badmindedness,

while peel-head John Crow
look on in wonderment
as di people gather
fi a grand enjoyment

to laugh the revolution
laugh the revolution.

The ancestors brought her gifts:
a heart of cooperation
from the moment
she could raise the barre,
passé and relevé,
leap out di crib,
land on tippie toes,
run round in di yard
with her cousin Fatty,
play dandy shandy,
Manuel Road,
hopscotch,
jacks and ball,
di strategy
to change
di game
began

to laugh the revolution
laugh the revolution.

The ancestors gave her language
of many African tongues
that survived the treacherous crossing,
intersecting European vernacular
imposed by cruel lashings.
Some call it chat bad,
others call it patwa,
but she prefers
to call it soso Jamaican

to laugh the revolution
laugh the revolution.

She used storytelling
to revolutionize
radio serials,
had no qualms
two-party government
to criticize,
for social change a must
from political greed and lust.
For when some people still grumble
that is licky-licky economic power
kill queen pound shilling and pence
to make way for the ever devaluating dollar,

she laugh the revolution
laugh the revolution.

Ancestors gave her euphonic laughter
perfect elixir for the soul
sake a so when she and Aunty Roachy
draw chair fi analyse we foolishness
the ironies of our sorrows
it make we double over laugh loud
just so we can feel whole

to laugh the revolution
laugh the revolution.

And when insurrections
sugar estate revolt
from cities to areas remote
the people demanding
their rights to vote,
better financial compensations
freedom from exploitation,
since bakkra control the wealth
of the hard working class generation,

she laugh the revolution
laugh the revolution.

She revolutionized Jamaican theatre
once reserved for the upper-class elite,
wrote pantomimes of ordinary folks
Ward Theatre pack you couldn't get a seat.
Every time she and Maas Ran
ketch a quarrel is social commentary
establishment rebuke.
Her acting skills and humour educate the masses
how fi kin teet cover heart burn,
take bad things make joke

and laugh the revolution
laugh the revolution.

Ancestors gave her a melodious voice
to recite and sing, revolutionize television,
teach the children *Ring Ding,*
good manners, self-respect and
how to grow them intellect.
She taught that our swift thinking
to strategize a master plan

against our dehumanizing plight
was born in us from Queen Nanny,
Cudjo, Accompong, Quao and Johnny,
who for our freedom put up a stiff fight,

so we can laugh the revolution
laugh the revolution.

And the revolution continues,
a legacy of works from writers and artisans like me,
Lorna Goodison, Mutabaruka, Malachi, Opal Palmer Adisa,
Donna Aza Weir-Soley, Faith Nelson,
Geoffrey Philp, Kei Miller, Marlon James, Oku,
Jean Binta Breeze, Linton Kwesi Johnson, Kwame Dawes,
Bob Marley, Peter Tosh and Mikey Smith,
too numerous to celebrate.

For she who laughs the revolution
champions the voices
of a new nation

to laugh the revolution
laugh the revolution,

My friend, mentor, journalist,
feminist, raconteur, icon,
the Honourable Dr Louise Bennett-Coverley.

Fowl Pill Bruk Nes

SHIRLEY MASSEY

In Jamaica, some women who lack self-esteem and are not satisfied with their physique seek to enhance it by taking hormone-filled tablets used to fatten broiler chickens.

Maisey run cum here – mi got tory fi tell yuh gal
Weh yuh tink mi jus hear ova di FM sterial?
Wah Docta seh di young gal dem – weh a teck fowl pill fi get fat
Mus top "now" before deh fine dem self a Dovecot
Cah all those who are taking it – they are slowly dying inside
Cah inside a dem a tear dung – wussa dan any lanslide
Mi wah know how di hell – dem know seh fowl pill can teck
Mi noh know wah meck fedda noh pring out a sum a dem neck
Everybody deh run jassle fi dis unessissary big bat-bat
A who weh neva born fi fat – eh neh gi dem weh deh wah got
Soh because a dat
Di sinting gi dem likkle bottom an big top
But di one dem weh eh gree wid – a dem got Bat-Bat
As yuh si dem a come – yuh cah si di false fat
Too red yeye man – cah contented wid wehdeh got
Wid soh gut big before dem – lakka any punching pilot
I neva si a more cruel and wickid ting like dis – from I was born
Di poor fowl deh cah get nun fi teck – di manager affi lock dung
Bess Dress farm
Cah di fowl dem need it – to increase deh weight
But dem yah young gal dem – deh orda eh all by net wait

Imagine sinti weh meck fi fowl eh – human been got eh a teck
But di bastard deh neva know – it did ago gi dem side effeck
Mi hear seh – all tree gallon a wawta dem a drink a day
At dat rate – sum a dem noh soon tart lay
Resident a pay water rate a cah get none – now tell mi if dat noh hard
Gal dem a drink to much wawta man
An a shorten fi di people dem a deh yard
Water Commission shud visit those people a double deh water rate
And if dem don't want to pay
Cut off deh water an meck deh drink deh urinate
Saykadat di farma dem a cumplain – seh deh cah get nun fi gi dem fowl
Dat deh got eh eena a bat-bat – deh pah treet a roul
Ah lef di poor fowl dem fi suffa
While dem out deh a get bigga – heavy an tough-fa
Well das all mi cahseh – gud luk to those who don't want to stop
Because "slowly dying" mean anytime now deh cah drop
Soh if a mi apart – dem cah buy out every fowl pill
Cah mi know mi nah teck nun – soh ano mi it ago kill

Adina

DEANNE KENNEDY

One day I had too much tings tuh do,
Den de telephone ring, and Adina get through.
I say "I hanging my tings on de line,"
She say "Fuh trut? I jus' bring in mine,
'Cause I get outta bed at half past four,
Dust de ornaments, sweep de floor,
Soak de washing, den rest my knees
By sitting down and shelling out
Uh bushel uh peas."

And she moving and she grooving,
And she going and she coming,
Is de people like Adina
Dat is keep de world running.

Den she say she have plenty rice tuh pick,
She already reap a breadfruit with a six-foot stick!
Dat was *after* she wring de chicken neck –
It in lime and salt, it aint season yet –
But the pumpkin peel and slice and dice,
And soon she starting the peas and rice.

And she moving and she grooving,
And she going and she coming,
Is de people like Adina
Dat is keep de world running.

And if you playing malicious and look in she kitchen,
She alone in dey – nobody else cayn pitch in!

She got two stoves running – one alone cayn do –
Fuh pork, beef, macaroni pie, fish and coucou!
Especially when all de family come down –
Fuh de weddings and wakes, and she turning 'round.

And she moving and she grooving,
And she going and she coming,
Is de people like Adina
Dat is keep de world running.

And when she done cook de very last dish –
She gine clean an' bone nearly ninety-five fish –
And now it bright and before it rain,
She gine down de road tuh cut sugar cane,
Den tek de hard coconut she uncle sen'
And grater up de coconut fuh coconut bread!

And she moving and she grooving,
And she going and she coming,
Is de people like Adina
Dat is keep de world running.

If any coconut cake left,
She gine mek sugarcake
Tuh sell at de school at Lunch an' Break –
'Cause she still got uh little space lef' in de tray –
Doah she did mekkin' tamarind balls since yesterday.
And wen all uh dat done, she gine catch de bus,
Buy the groceries and still avoid the four o'clock rush.

And she moving and she grooving,
And she going and she coming,
Is de people like Adina
Dat is keep de world running.

Come six o'clock, my girl goin' tuh "Class",
Cause she tekkin' uh diploma an' she doing "Housecraft".
Call it "Home Economics" or "Food and Nutrition" –
Adina is de one who should be doing de tuition –

And she back by seven fuh midweek church,
'Cause wen tings tuh plan, dem is call she first.

And she moving and she grooving,
And she going and she coming,
Is de people like Adina
Dat is keep de world running.

Last year she get uh pick, and she went tuh Miami –
She could lecture we ministers on handling dey money!
She get four bedspreads hold in de hand luggage,
And she fill up ten barrels with extra baggage!
And because she house getting renovate,
She buy back door, front door, roofing and gate!

And she moving and she grooving,
And she going and she coming,
Is de people like Adina
Dat is keep de world running.

She handling de pressure, she handling de sugar,
De doctor stop she from getting any bigger.
Dem shoulders support friend, husband and child,
And dem legs forever travelling de extra mile.
I doan know anudda body dat could be any finer,
And I render thanks fuh de ones like Adina.

And she moving and she grooving,
And she going and she coming,
Is de people like Adina
Dat is keep de world running.

Is de people like Adina,
Is de people like Adina,
Is de people like Adina,
Is de people like Adina dat is keep de world running.

Exilia

DONNA P. HOPE

She came to this place to understand
loneliness
Stranded in a desert of urban cacophony, suburban somnolence
She is lost in the midst of sound
The bitter cold, creeping on bare feet
To emprise memories
of Yaad

Trees stripped bare of life and lustre
Hang like deathly skeletons
Guarding her balcony view
Ice dripping from gnarled pens
lull her into fitful dreams

She awakes to brilliant sunlight
Rushing outdoors she is slapped
with the icy fingers of winter's
false promise
You will find no warmth here

Her soul yearns for Yaad
Brilliant orange suns raining
oceans of warmth
Ripe black faces bursting with
life's juices running down
cheeks like sweet East Indian mango

Passions overflowing in deep
belly laughs and the boom of
dancehall songs
pon di river, pon di bank
life ebbs and flows and gushes forth
in cascading waterfalls

Even alone you are never lonely ah Yaad
Blanketed in passionate embraces
resonating voices, too much bass
mix up and blenda
sharing the widow's mite
touch your fist to mine and things
are just fine

So much warmth t/here.

Bawl Woman Bawl

PAMELA MORDECAI

After a Caribbean digging song . . .

(i) Alas for who don't sing

True man give thanks him able lift
hoe machete sound two syllable
as bomma raise de tune and call

say "Baby dead on de railway line!"
and chorus sound as we pickaxe strike
"Bawl woman bawl! You baby dead!"

Dry ground is drum as we pickaxe strike
sing how dem bury de poor baby
and ground is drum as we slap we heel

entomb a next and a next baby.
For music wail in breeze and stream
on sand on stone on paging sea.

Ma say, "Alas for who don't sing
and die with music lock in him."
We wouldn't live but we raise a tune

to move we foot else we tumble down
fetch water scrape up wood to burn
scratch de dutty to raise a crop

we walk to drink we walk to eat go hospital
to die or drop so tank you Jesus for we feet
we moving dem until time stop.

(ii) Toy boy

Look how much time Ma tell me
is trouble me courting
anyhow me give de pikni
toy gun to play wid.

That All Saints' Day morning
a late Halloween parcel by post
arrive with a broad smiling ghost
trailing down to one side

and a skull and crossbones
with a wide warning grin to the next
"Is him father!" me flare. "God know
is a man never notice this child more than so.

Now him send something come
for the pikni, you think me can tell him,
'No, son. It is yours
but you can't play with it?'"

She don't see, me don't see
when him take time and leave.
"Marcus? Come for your supper!
Wash your hand! Make haste come!"

That time him long dead on the hyena
whim of a fool-fool hysterical woman.
"Short black man in the park
with a lethal weapon!"

Ambulance pick up Marcus
him dreadlocks paste down
with black pudding blood
gainst him back

him pa toy in him hand bullet
wound in the hole of him mole
and my soul twist with dread
that my one pikni dead.

(iii) Sword on the road

Tommy Barnett was a 22-year-old black man fatally shot by police on Jan. 10, 1996, near the intersection of Bathurst Street and St Clair Avenue West. Police claimed he was unsheathing a sword.

Forward yellow red and green.
don the cape, make I-self seen
take a staff and strike a blow

for freedom, justice, peace and show
that Babylon can't keep I back
never mind I poor and black.

Jah see I take the road today
sword in hand against the fray
Jah see I chant down ignorance.

behold I-and-I do a dance
before Selassie God Most High
Lion of Judah Ras Tafari

Jah hear the iron stone assail
the sacred temple of the I.
Jah see the flood of Israelite blood

burst like a fireworks in the sky
scatter like sparks of crimson night
Jah see the I explode and die.

Still forward yellow, red and green.
don the cape, make we-self seen
take a sword and strike a blow

for freedom, justice, peace and know
downpresser can't keep Rasta back
no mind how Rasta poor and black.

(iv) If I had a hammer

Eddie Fung beat books so hard
them low him in the white people
medical program. All the same him blood

and him brain never gree with him doctor
ambition. Them burst, leave the youth
with a helmet of voices over him ears,

a roof of intrusion, no door to step
through to escape. Eddie folks never know
how to manage to take him to hospital.

Shrink form-one him, pill him up,
keep him twenty-four hour then tell him
go-long with a number to call.

Shitstem board him here, stow him there.
Eddie hate every place, land up on a grate
down Bay Street. Him don't take

de mind pills, say dem muzzle him brain,
plus street living don't suit for him love
smell fresh and dress snazzy.

Was weeks before ManLife security find
him capture the penthouse washroom.
TO best and brightest escort him

to Queen Street again. Eddie lucky.
This time a nice man take him touring
through soft falling snow to find him a bed.

When Rob say goodbye, Eddie
declare, "Reality painful sometimes, Rob
No place for me here in this world. No place here."

Rob gone off to secure meds for Eddie.
Eds feel good so decide him going for a ride.
Make a unwanted press by a girl (so them say)

as him wait for the bus. When them all
reach inside she kick up a fuss.
Driver empty the bus, call the cops.

Babylon mount the transport
approach Eds, commence to converse.
Eds hand slide in him pocket as them discuss

take out a small hammer, talisman gainst bad luck.
Babylon see the glint, leggo them rabid dog.
Dog bark over and over. Them teeth maul the youth

tear him tendon and tripe, left him dead as a dog
on the ground in the bus. Prove him right.
No place for Eddie Fung in this benighted world.

(v) Bawl woman bawl

Bawl woman bawl! We pikni dead!
in school, park, country, town, city,
dead in dem high chair, in dem bed
in dem backyard, at block party.

True say it sad for who don't sing
and die with music lock in him,
for we can't live less we raise a tune
to move we foot and struggle through,

work all night long until day clean
in farm, field, market, factory,

scrub floor, cut cane, pick coffee bean,
work till we drop to feed pikni.

And still no mind dem hunt we down
bulldoze we, choke we, batter we,
empty dem bullet in we back,
time and more time wid impunity

law is fe dem but not fe we
futile protest we liberty

Bawl woman bawl for we baby.
Bawl for we know dem won't come back.
Bawl woman bawl! We pikni dead!
Bawl woman bawl! We pikni dead!

Tooth-Ache*

RUTH HOWARD

Mi seh, a di fuss time inna mi life nuh teet ever do me so
And me pray to God dis a di laas one fi grow
Cause if mi have no more fi come like dis yah one yah
Mi really nuh tink mi cyan tek it yaw maasah
Two days ago, mi feel di teet a come
Mi feel a likkle stiffness inna mi gum
It never did a hurt me, so mi never really mind it
So it look like di damn teet decide fi spite mi

Laas night roun twelve o'clock mi wake up inna sweat
Di heaviness inna mi mout mek mi start fret
Mi go try open mi mout fi yawn
And maasah! Mi seh a so di pain jus come on

It feel so hot, mi open mi mout fi shout
And, maasah, was like dentist a draw mi teet out
It hot, it hot, it hot, it hot so till
Me'd haffi go check if mi did have no pill

Well, mi never have no painkiller, so me try fi go sleep
Mi try all kinda tings and couldn't get no relief
Mi lock mi yeye, mi open dem, mi cover mi head wid di sheet
But wid all di toss and tun mi tun, mi coulda still feel di teet

*Jamaica Cultural Development Commission 2016 Creative Writing Competition Gold Medal winner and Best Writer Overall winner.

Everytime mi spit or swallow, a piece'a pain lick mi jaw
An mi feel tormented caw mi cyaan open mi mout fi holler
Di pain all pick up speed and sound and start fi beat like drum
A so di tears dem start flow, and di teet jus a go "budum"

Mi head start hot mi, mi mind start reel
Mi couldn't tek it at all
Mi siddung up inna mi bed
Hold mi head, and start fi bawl

Only hope dem teeth yah gimme wisdom
Cause if dem suppose to mek mi wise
After all weh mi go through laas night
Maasah God know seh mi done pay di price

Thelma's Precious Cargo*

KWAME DAWES

She was bringing fried fish, festival,
banana, dumpling, roast corn,
sweet sugar cane, nicely peeled and cool
when the plastic-gloved customs officer
squinge up him nose like him smelling
his upper lip decide to
break every fruit
gut open the fish, spilling all that white flesh
and sweet fried tomato all over the counter.

Say him was searching for drugs
searching for disease
from this great-grandmother with
centuries springing in her eyes
who come just to catch a sight
of the children she never met
and who might grow up without
the grounding of stories she been
carrying all these years

But Thelma never panic before
no child, she simply gather the ruins
and then spread her bandana –
flaming red with yellow light –

*First published in *Resisting the Anomie* (Fredricton, NB: Goose Lane Editions, 1995).

on the blue stale carpet in a corner
and she place every injured offering
on the shimmering surface

Thelma light a red candle and draw a circle
round the feast like a prayer
and then she invite the people them
who line up to face the plastic-glove man
to come sit with she and her grandson
who smiling like he can't stop all this time
and eat a good sunrise meal
no fuss, just this laughing in her eyes

And them drink off all the sweetsop juice
lace with a little Appleton fire
and them eat that food like communion
and when them was finished
Thelma say a prayer and whisper
a little forgiveness to the bwoy with the gloves

And them calmly wobble through the customs
clean as a priest before service
with all the drugs and disease
swimming and singing in them belly
walking like that into the sweet Canadian air
warm as ever and ready

And Thelma tell the story again and again
and end it with the last sweet lines

Child, them shoulda follow we to the toilet
the day, for some of them seed find soil
and see the tree them there still.
Africa people been carrying them possessions in them shit
forever. Precious cargo, child, precious cargo

And man we couldn't stop laugh.

Di House

DELROY McGREGOR

Me memba when me mada an me fada woulda
cuss dem one anada from mawning till evening
bout who did a sleep wid di tenant who live
downstairs, who did a hide money unda mattress,
an who neva want fi pay di school fee fi di pickney
dem. Me memba when me big sista get pregnant
wid har fuss pickney an me bredda staat cuss har
bout him money weh a go missing from him bedroom
draw, me mada staat cuss har bout di food weh deh dun
in a di kitchen cupboard, me fada staat cuss bout har
brassiere and panty weh she eva deh show in a di house.
Me memba how people dung a Marline shop would
a stop talk when me reach, dem woulda meck up
dem face like dem smell shit and start meck noise
like a bag a mosquita when me a walk way. Me memba
di witchcraft weh did a gwaan. Yes man, di duppy weh hol'
me an mi mada dung pon di bed, di pretty, pretty bottle dem
we woulda find in a di garbage bin beside di gate,
di red candle dem unda di step in a di front yard.
Me memba nuff mawning mi mada would a bawl out
di blood a Jesus is against yuh from har bad dream dem.
Me memba di pastor weh come, come bless di place two
time in a di evenin and di dead scent in di house
when me bredda teck sick.

Licky Licky

KEMAR CUMMINGS

Listen mi, missis, all now mi still cyaan believe.
All now mi cyaan believe how one taxi fi so tief!
To think seh mi can let smaddy samfie mi so.
Mi head must tough like one piece a beef.

One day, missis, mi guh an pawn miself Downtown,
A stan pon bus stop fi wait pon taxi man.
When mi see di bwoi a come up to mi, bold an straight,
Mi couldn' wait no longa di way how mi tan.

"Lady, come let mi fly yuh home inna mi car."
"But, sar, mi nuh see nuh red taxi sign pon di back."
"Nuh worry, miss, when mi see di policeman dem,
Dem seh dem nuh care if it white or black."

Lawks, missis, mi couldn' wait nuh more.
Suh mi pile up myself wid di people pon top
A people weh move so till di door coulda hardly shet.
If di door neva shut den right out all a wi woulda drop.

Mi haffi squinge up squinge up side a people,
Di amount a people weh load up inna di one car!
"Driva," mi seh, "carry mi straight to Red Hills."
"Yes, mam. Yuh soon reach fasta dan a shooting star!"

Den di car tek off like one likkle pocket rocket.
Mi seh – di car zoom straight down di road.
"Driva," smaddy seh, "yuh gwine crash wi up before wi reach?"
"No, man," di bwoi seh, "yuh safe when mi drop off mi load."

Di car swerve lef; di car swerve right.
Di car weave in an bob outa traffic.
Braps! Wi cut cross a car. *Braps*! Wi cut cross corna.
Di car fly like it a move pon automatic.

One time, as soon as di bwoi see police car,
Him tek fright an cut cross lane.
When wi hear siren, him put di car into gear
An drive straight off di road like aeroplane.

Lawd, wi heart and foot did inna wi mouth,
Di way how wi a swerve from side to side.
When wi reach one corner, wi nuh hear nuh more
Siren afta di bwoi back inna one gate fi hide.

Den di bwoi drive off again guh pon Red Hills Road.
Di car jim-screech to a stop by di kerb.
Mi squinge past people to come outa di car
An step up to di bwoi who look like him smell di herb.

"How much fi di ride?" mi ask di bwoi.
"Just give mi five bills fi di likkle drive."
So mi tek out all di likkle bundle a cash
Mi have in hand to count out di five.

Him look pon it, him look pon it so till.
Den guess wha. . . . Di bwoi just reach out an grab
Almost di whole wad a cash an drive off!
Mi frighten! It like mi likkle heart get stab!

Mi just cyan cyaan believe it all now.
All a mi inna one piece a poca ova di sinting.
If di police eva see him again, mi really hope
Dem draw baton to give him a piece a buffing an biffing!

Miss Joyce Mongrel Dawg

RAUL A. DAVIS

Miss Joyce have a likl teefin mongrel yu si,
Mi warn him ow much taim.
But if mi go tek sinting an claat it dung,
Dem wudda charge mi fi murda crime.

You cyaa tell har nutn bout har mongrel,
She tek Jeezas aafa di cross.
She rada chat peepl bizniz,
Bout fat cow an dead haas.

Guess who teef Sista Punny May white fowl dem?
Nuh di same likl brute!
One week afta Maas Jaspa ketch him ina him grung
An bruck him front foot.

But a nuh white fowl alone him teef,
All Jankro, Babble Dove and Duck.
Him all teef yellow from outa egg,
And all now di shell no bruck!

Him teef shuga, him teef butta,
All butcha bone an meat.
How him get paas a man wid so much shaap cutliss,
Ongle Gad know how him dweet.

Jump chruu window and pick door lock,
Miss Joyce dawg briezn yu si.
Want fi go lie dung wid fi mi likl one.
But she no ready fi pikni.

Aunt Inez know him love him belly,
So she put paizn inna di bread.
You lick him dung, him bounce right back,
What a haad dawg fi dead.

Mi go tek faas an try inchravene,
A who tell me fi open mi mout . . . ?
Di rock stone dumplin ooman dash lime pon mi,
An tell mi fi kirout.

Anyway, police station deh bill dung a square,
Suh Miss Joyce mongrel dawg free paypa soon bun.
Wait . . . unu did tink a real dawg mi a talk bout?
Di teefin dawg a Miss Joyce teefin mongrel Son.
A YaYai!

A Brief Response to Miss Joyce Mongrel Dawg

But unu si mi dyin chrial doe Eeeee?
What a shame an disgrace!
Call fi mi likl bway mongrel,
No mek mi put yu ina yu place.

Him neva jump chruu nobadi window,
Or pick nobadi door.
If she did a pay attention to fi har bizniz.
She woulda know seh har husband deh give har bun, wid sore-foot
  Leonore.

Fi mi likl bway laptose inkalarant,
So iz lie! Him no nyam egg.
An him woulda neva teef di entire fowl,
Just maybe just one a di leg.

An him cyaa get paizn,
Cause him nuh wanga gut!
A nuff more tingz mi know bout da ooman deh yu nuh,
But mi a try kip mi mout shut.

An shi brite an outa aaada,
A call my dumplin rockstone . . .
She need fi go lawn fi cook cawnmeal parij,
An tap gi ppl cawnmeal pone.

Plus Fimi likl bway wid fi har likl gyal . . . ?
Yu mean likl Miss Gungu Cawfi Walk
Wat aatta claps and judgementation,
If leaf and riba bank kudda talk.

Mi want one a dem put dem han pan him again yu si,
A hell an powda house!
A woulda carry dem hair and finganail,
Go right roun a Mada Mouse.

So tinkin toe is very tink!
And gungu peas nice and shelly!
But mek dem touch mi bway again,
And dem see how wata walk go a punkin belly.
A YaYai.

Abeng in Beijing

fabian m. thomas

Battle-ready
In black, green and gold
Warrior-runner
Usain bolted
Ahead of the world
From Sherwood Content, Trelawny
This 6′ 5″ sprint anomaly
Stamped his sunshine-bred supremacy
Shattering red, white & blue ascendancy
It was bound to spark controversy
An some almshouse chat from the IOC
Oh I see
The real issue is
How dare he?
Dis lickle black bwoy
From di land of wood & wata
Him too outta arda
Now dem waan test wi yam an cassava

Beating his chest
Like a kumina drum
Usain
Took it to dem
Then danced barefoot
While the world watched
He danced for us

In a language they did not understand
Like the abeng of old
They could not decode
Bad mine a go meck
Some a dem explode
Oh say can you see?
Dem cyan chat to wi
Did you see the untied lace?
Dem a go tiyad fi si Usain face
Hol' on, my bad
Let me correct what I said:
Dem a ago tiyad fi si
Di back a Usain head!

My Chinaman Jump to the Riddim of Jah

JEAN LOWRIE-CHIN

(To the beat of "New Day" by Sons of Negus.)

It was a new day
Precious day
When my Chinaman jump
To the riddim of Jah
With a one-foot shuffle
And im eye to the sky
And im locks semi-knot
Jus' a shake and a fly

And it grieve me to know
That a man with a gun
Abuse him and rob him
Nearly shoot him for nothing

But the man with the gun
Couldn't know that my man
With a mother and a father
From a Far East land
Coulda move to the beat
Of the Rastaman
And jump to the riddim of Jah.

'88 Storm

CHRISTOPHER ALLEN

Storm a come an everybody a busy up demself.
Dem a baton dung door an winda
an a buy everything off a supermarket shelf.

Chat-people-business Audrey put block pan har roof
fi di zinc dem no blow off.
An although me have a crocus bag wid sand
a di bottom a me door, me kudd'n help but laugh.

Me cyaa wait fi see guinep tree giggle
like him get ticklish, an cocanat tree ben an touch har toe.
What a hell an powda house an belly full
when dis ya breeze start fi blow.

Me jus siddung a my winda wid my grocery list
a wait till di wata flood out Maas Garfield shop.
But me change me mind when me see Mabel tiefin son
a try tip toe go roun di back.

Somebody bawl out, "Tief! Tief!"
him frighten an get a rahtid drop.
Is the same sound breadfruit mek
when it fall pan house top.

Me never yet see my distric so lively,
even di rusty zinc dem pan Frank roof a dance an sing.
Dem bus out
big market woman laugh a play Brown Girl in the Ring.

Miss Julet tired old house just find it age paper,
it duck an dodge all kinda debris.
It make one big split an splash up dutty water
like it a play dandy-shandy.

When storm come a Jamaica, is always a sight to see.
Everything whe no have wing tek flight:
pig, puss, dog an yuh neighbour teevee.

Mi Dear Sista Sandy

SEAN C. HARRISON

(What a piece a crasses yuh come an' lef' pon wi'!!)
When deez few lines reaches yuh, mi hope yuh is in di bes' of healt'.
But mi cyan seh di same fi some ah wi who dengue did dung ya ah pelt.

Now, mi nevva know yuh fi be dat kine a person:
Before yuh come wi did have dem. But now di' moskitta problem worsen!
Ah tell yuh, situration nevva nice at all.
Yuh can imagine how dem likkle sumpn' mek big man haffi run a' bawl?

Afta' yuh visit, mi an' mi co-workers ah talk 'bout di scenes roun' wi community,
How fi a moment wi haffi wonda if it was some big birtnight paaty.
Whole heap ah everlastin' bunfire
Wid' people a wave tree branch an' smoke pan like dem was welcomin' di Messiah.
It was nuttin' more dan dem trying to keep di plague at bay.
But dem nuh bite up, bite up di whole a wi kin same way!!

Ah tell yuh, not even di good, good Reverend dem nuh spare.
No sah, dem moskitta deh jus' nevva care!
She come outta har van di Sunday fi guh a church.
An' when dem swoop dung pon har she almost haffi run een back.
In har own words she say, "Sean, it was a personal attack!"

She seh she remin' di Lord one day dat inna di good book Him did seh
Him wouldn' mek di plagues of Egyp' come back weh wi deh.
But mi nuh know if Him nevva remin' har back seh moskitta wasn' one ah dem.
How she could a figat dat an' she a big, big reverend?!

Anyway, Tanks be, when di govament step in an' launch ah all out campaign,
Tings inna di country was nevva really quite di same.
'Cause, bless dem heart, afta di moskitta man dem come
Dem tek dem foot inna dem han' an' mos' a di likkle wretch dem haffi run!!
But while dem a kitta mi hear one a dem tun roun' an' seh,
"He who bites and runs away lives to bite anodda day."
But mi an' yuh know seh weh dem a talk 'bout was nuttin' but faat,
For moskitta lifespan is very, very shawt!!

Who coulda afford repellant nevva really feel di pinch,
(Although it more feel like a shock, yuh couldn't tell which was which)
Mi was suh glad mi nevva haffi shat myself nuh more box,
Or deh a mi yard dress up inna long sleeve shirt an' ol' time bobby socks.
For mi did swear seh kill mi dead, mi wasn't gwine res'
Anyweh it deh I did haffi fine di nes'!!

Mi sista, finally, I am makin' an' appeal.
Di cards are on di table. So let's mek a deal –
If yuh comin' back, (which yuh might, but unda anodda name,
Though yuh seh right now yuh nuh have nuh travel plans all di same)
Jus' carry likkle rain an' some cool breeze fi wi inna yuh hand.
If ah dat nuh muhyuh bring from farin wi will tek yuh as wi gues'
But please, please, nex' time nuh carry those strikin' long-mout' pes'!!

Tek care fi now Sandy an' mi ah tell yuh now, mi gawn.

Yours truly,

Yuh likkle bredda Sean

P.S. Mi dyin' trial nuhbody evva si?
One a di crasses nuh jus bite mi!!

Oiii, Driva!

SIHLE ATKINSON

Oiii, Missa Taximan!
Me did tink yuh seh one an drive!
Now me come een a di cyar
An yuh still a look five?
Oiii, Driva!
Try come pull up de front seat.
Cause me leg dem lang, an if dem damij
yuh nah pay f'eet!

Oiii, Missa Taximan! A who yuh tink a ride a back?
Memba seh a Papine me a go – a jus' two second dat!
Oiii, Driva! Come tun up de radio fe me deh.
Dem a report pon di teefin man weh dem chop up Satdeh.

Oiii, Missa Taximan! Two cyaan wol a front!
Yuh neev'n have no cushion deh so, an my batty bone blunt!
Oiii, Driva! Yuh tink a Dover raceway yuh deh?
Me waan reach eena one piece, suh slow dung me seh!

Oiii, Missa Taximan! Mek me chaaj me phone likkle bit.
Ten percent me have an it a go dung faas 'cause a bad battery
  eena it.
Oiii, Driva! Wah mek yah fan ar dung so?
Yuh nuh see how she big? A pon di cyaar top she a go?

Oiii, Missa Taximan! A foo fa tyah dat a screech?
Fe yuh? No sah! One stop a de light when yuh reach!

Oiii, Driva . . . memba me bag dem eena di back
Yuh fenneh if me hegg dem tun ova, choo yuh tink yuh deh racetrack.

Alright, Missa Taximan! Jus rest dem a grung, y'hear?
Me did squeeze up to much, so-comes me could'n tek out me fare.
Aahhhmm, Driva. Know seh me day a get from bad to worse?
Nuh badda cuss . . . nuh badda cuss y'hear? But it look like me lef me purse.

Di Jril a di Ting

ANNIKA SIMONE ROWE

Di jril a di ting. Di jril a di ting
Di jril a di ting. Dok wen yu ier di ring
Di jril a di ting. Di jril a di ting
Di jril a di ting. Dok wen yu ier di ring

Put yu an pan yu ed an ed fi di tiebl
Di jril a di ting. Dok wen yu ier di ring
Kip kaam, duohn panic ar ron frantik
Di jril a di ting. Dok wen yu ier di ring

Di jril a di ting. Di jril a di ting
Di jril a di ting. Dok wen yu ier di ring
Di jril a di ting. Di jril a di ting
Di jril a di ting. Dok wen yu ier di ring

Lisn fi di bel an den yu rispan
Dok, kova, uol stan ina doorjam
Den di nex step a ivakyuwieshan
Muuv aadali, nat ina kanfyuzhan

Di jril a di ting. Di jril a di ting
Di jril a di ting. Dok wen yu ier di ring
Di jril a di ting. Di jril a di ting
Di jril a di ting. Dok wen yu ier di ring

Mek shuor set yu asembli ieria
Lain op uu a siefiti manita
Tel di chuut yu nuo di ivakyuwieshan ruut

Di jril a di ting. Di jril a di ting
Di jril a di ting. Dok wen yu ier di ring
Di jril a di ting. Di jril a di ting
Di jril a di ting. Dok wen yu ier di ring

Kom agen jain di chrend
Praktis di jril
Siefiti kom fos, preparieshan a di ting
Di uol ailan fi du di ortkuiek jril

Di jril a di ting. Di jril a di ting
Di jril a di ting. Dok wen yu ier di ring
Di jril a di ting. Di jril a di ting
Di jril a di ting. Dok wen yu ier di ring

Cat

ANN-MARGARET LIM

(*In memoriam and imagined in the voice of Miss Lou.*)

Careful-up yuself Mary,
bout dance, innna dem ya judgement days
wey anybody can get catch inna shootout,
braps so, an' die.

Why, just last night inna Nannyville,
stone t'row from wi National Stadium,
dem interrup' di wake wid a barrage a shots:
brudups, braps, bradadaps!

An' Mary, according to de cops,
de casualty, drop dead pon him back,
was a cat.
No name, no alias, like "feline",
"deadly", or "Miss Patsy one eye
scratch-up scratch-up, puss."
No outstanding mark. No, none ah dat,
jus cat, missis, jus' cat.

Me know, Jamaican people love drop leg
an' prance.
Me was one a di bigges' leggo beas'
when it come to dat.
But yu no si how mi tan ah mi yaad
an keep miself quiat now-a-days?

Yu nuh si whey de happen to de cat?
Ay yi yi!

Black

LATTECHA WILLOCKS

Black!
Insecurity
Talk low
Cause dem 'fraid a wi.

Wait
Membaseh a wi
Have the trait
Fi mek all a wi.

Tek di bait
An put up wid ih
Tek di faith
Loose yuh history.

Den demseh
Dem own all ah wi
Pan di boat
Dem chain all a wi.

Africa
Doan belong to we
Start a war
Den tief up di ting.

Sell you fren
Den go pan you knee
Serve a man
Weh we nevah see.

Black!
Right now yuh si
Open up
Space fi all a wi.

One drop
Dat is all you need
Fake tan
Or dread locks or weed.

Fake but
Learn fi twerk wid wi
All this time
Still a tief wi tings.

Meanwhile
We doan like what we see
When di glass
It look back pan wi.

Now dem sell
All di bleach wi need
While dem buy
Wi sun sand and beach.

But Jah know
Wi tiad you see
Everyday
Is a fight fi wi.

Help me sah
Nuh imprison me
Fadah gone
'im nevah help fi grow mi.

But doan fret
A nuh you me mean.
A nuh you
Do these things to me.

Dat night
Mi come home yuh see
Reach mi door
An' me have me key.

Dat man
Tek mi dignity
An' BLACK!
Dat was all me see.

Puss and Dawg Luck

ALECIA MARIA SAWYERS

(Translation: Lazy puss hear Beenie Man "Ol Dawg Like Me" ah play pon di radio . . .)[*]

Ernie Smith had no idea
that *that* nonchalant feline sitting on
the tear-up mat was going to get
the fright of a rhatid lifetime.
Apparently, this puss that took
the moniker "Cool Cat" way too personal,
figured that the hardest thing
its eternity involved, was perfecting "suave".

Respectfully speaking though,
"thinking 'bout who is who and what is what"
could never have sounded like
a deliberate, progressive occupation of daylight hours
so the fact that this creature
was attempting a career of
what could only be chalked up to blasted laziness,
seriously made the damn puss only deserving of
a bitch lick, or such the like.

---

*I have been trying my hand at what I call "skewed SJE": a kind of homage to the language in which Patwa and English have a casual mix. I find this represents the way many Jamaicans speak. Writing this poem in Jamaican Creole only would lose nuances.

It surely got away with killing time
for more time than was allotted to cats
by the gods of the four-footed,
for years later, it was still doing
its yawn and stretch ballet,
not once having the opportunity to use
another of its nine lives.

———

Beenie Man probably had no idea that his "old dawg" status
could ever transcend human species
and drive the fear of "god" turn backways
into an animal for which
the true meaning of his lyrics had no intent.
That pensive puss that had taken a rare break from its mindless musings,
tuned its condescending ears to the offerings
of a jarring stereo one day,
and its eternity was suddenly skewed,
destiny derailed.

The news "reporter" was oddly musical
but the news byte was clear:
the passionate desire to "have them inna twos and threes",
understood by the puss as an attack on its kind,
screamed a possible twist of fate –
not to mention the admission of being "wild already, believe you me" –
this "dawg" was definitely on the prowl!

Suddenly, "taking in today's vibrations"
and "taking it free and easy",
the only life skills acquired by this puss,
became the very detriment of its existence.
Utopia interrupted now required talents

unique to one two-footed Bolt,
and he could not be the needed transporter:
he entertains nothing with fur.

Coward man and sound bone
sounded applicable to the Count of Cool,
and its relocation was quick and permanent:
a limb barely bearing both its weight and
its discovery of altophobia.
And the owners of the house that had
the mat that sat the cat,
shook their heads
after several unsuccessful sardine coaxings,
thinking it had to be the work of a duppy or a gun-man.

Fever Grass

MEL COOKE

I am in Houston with a bag
Of cut up cut up green grass
Feeling a black shadow of TSA uniform which asks
Exactly what it is I am declaring I have to declare

He does not know what fever grass is, truth is
Neither do I, di pickney dem mek drink it up
Now the man who carry it fresh cut
Jus' that it grow pon roadside, it scratch back at cutlass
An' it tek down temperature

So him sen' mi likkle furda
Is July an I hope is also April one
Cause de glove de nex' uniform a stretch pon it han
Could neva be fi mi – is for the grass

Same question, same answer, but this one ask
"Do you mean lemon grass?"
No, I say in mi mine
Is fever grass: in Jamaica lemonade mek wid lime

A smell and a list confirm fever grass
Has been transformed into lemon grass
By Southwest Airlines
So is free to enter

It even ketch instant accent
An ah learn a lesson
What America sell as flavour an' scent
To Jamaica, is free medicine

Gum Bwile

LISA GAYE TAYLOR

A gum bwile teck mi last week Thursday
And dis one ting was fi real
You couldn't imagine di 'mount a pain
And agony mi feel
It lick me and it lance me
And it tun me upside down
Till me bawl out oh shakalaka
And start speaking inna tongues

Den everybody in mi district
From country and from tung
Start gimmi herbal remedy
Fi cure mi swollen gums

Miss Mattie from down di road
Sey cool yu heart deh chile
I will gi yu di prescription
Dat will sure bring down di bwile
Jus bwile up some salt water
And gargle fi a while
Three time a day before each meal
And yu problem gone mi chile

Surely enough me try it
Caa Mattie sey it was di cure
But when Friday do come
Mi gum jus hot mi likkle more

So Friday afternoon mi call mi fren
An tell har bout mi plight
An she sey dat is not a problem
A peg of garlic cannot right
Old Man Charlie hear and sey
Those solution not di link
Nuttin no bring down a bwile
Mi young fren
Like some young paw paw leaf milk

Ben sey use charcoal, coconut shell
Or gargle with baking soda
Sue sey use hibiscus leaf
Or fruit a di palm tree
Meck yu better

I think I know di solution
I think I finally find di cure
Early Monday morning
A meeting di dentist at di door

Walk Good and Good Duppy Walk wid Yu

ALMA MOCKYEN

Ay-ay-ay Aunty Roachie
I tell you mah
after de air full to the brim wid nuff words,
de rain, in a torrent of tears wash the dutty-tough asphalt
for a clean ride on her last trip to Park
under a Constance-Hollar-kind of "Flaming Poinciana" evening
kotch up pon a blue-blue sky
misty like the ocean she cross from de crosses for better.

The hills them look down unmoved by the notes of the a capella
choir
torturing the hymns of the official funeral.

Den after dat,
the wreaths, expensive and "fantabulous"
throw down like gauntlets,
tek on Missa Death, challenge him slap ina him yeye . . .
(though destined to dust, same way, like everything dat moment).

Imbedded in the beauty of de fragrant bouquets,
she sleep 'side her sweetheart,
leaving de mud and de slush of the August evening
of the land that loved her, a love she returned.

And the "Flaming Poinciana" sigh
seeing the slates put into place by de mason-man-dem
doing them best to seal de sorrowful "goodbyes"
for a lady who did always laugh loud, sing loud, and chat . . .

A Rasta drummer drum a personal salute, unscheduled, and the radio stations run them commercials, back to back, without a stop as scheduled.

(Jack Mandora . . . life dat)

Ice Cream Sundays

SCHONTAL MOORE

Ole Sundays are remembered,
when I sit, quietly, and cast my
mind's eyes backward,
to places of tenement yards . . .

Of children playing, mothers
cooking, dogs prowling, fathers
looking,
for feminine company; younger,
sweeter, fresher, he believes, than
the settled lady at home, working
damn hard
every ole Sunday.

Bling, cling, ring.
Doubled wheels bring sweet
nutty buddy coated chocolate bars
wrapped over in sugary
scheming delights of cream.
Squealing away the ice of a pained
childhood . . . motherhood,
This ole Sunday.

One man trading treats for glitter;
The other trading trusted hearts
for honey and worthless money.

So, new Sundays come to me
with scented flavours . . .
Always of red, cherry red,
to blot out mother's menstrual
pains,
and of pineapples yellow to exorcise
thorns of words and pricks
of sorrows, and of
golden sunshine ripened
Julie mangoes,
To crust over mouths and to keep
their words from condemning
the living.

On this new Sunday, I throw my
net upon the waters between
the open spaces of brown-faced cones
to haul to me that which was stolen,
but which is no longer frozen.

To redeem a lie, a life of a family
worth fighting for,
even if you are not here to
see it . . .

This rainbow Sunday, thawing
and melting this heart of old.

Mi and di Tief

AISHA SMITH

Mi heart did a boom flick an do karate chop inna mi chest
When mi hear di two tief dem a climb come ova mi fence!
One a dem did a talk bout how him aggo climb pon di roof
Di odda one ask him if him is a idiat or a fool
Yuh see,
Mi son did build mi one pretty likkle house
three storey high
Suh dem deh tief woulda need fi grow wing fi reach up suh high!
Mi listen to dem cuss and realize seh dat mi is quite safe
Cause two a dem brain nuh mek one
Suh dem woulda neva reach inside a mi place!
Dem bring one ledda, but it did too short
Di man dem did even walk wid shovel and pitch fork!
If mi neva did see dem wid mi own two yeye mi would a tink a lie
Puppa Jesas watch dem a dig up mi nice anthurium!
Mi waan fi cry!
Den dem go weh and come back wid saw fi cut di grill
Mi see hammer and even drill
Smady mussi obeah dem two yah
Cause dem nuh have no luck
Di head a di hammer fly off, di drill
did need current and di saw guh bruk!
Dem get cross now and start fi climb
Mi think dem woulda really mek it inna mi room dis time!
Mi hear one say, “Bredren mi still cyaan reach”
Suh mi open di window and shout

Shhhhhhhhhhhhhh!
Mi a try fi sleep
Di two man dem drop offa di side a di house like dead fly
Den dem start fi run fast fast like nuff duppy deh a dem behind!
Yuh waan see dem a run wid dem foot inna dem hand
Di only ting dem do correctly tonite is dem escape plan!

Bruce Ghost

MAXINE J. BROWN

Is long time Ena husband Bruce did dead
But she say she still feel like him in har bed
Every night when she 'bout to go to sleep
She hear a nasal voice call out . . .
Eeeena, Eeeena,
Wey mek you bury me so deep
Miss Ena feel is time she have smaddy
Fi rub har hands and har two foot dem
But Bruce won't give har any peace
Everytime har new guy come around
Di bed jus a shift so up and down
Di warner lady down the road
Di one dem call Mother Mattie-O
Tell Miss Ena fi wear red draws at night
So she, Bruce and the bed can stop di fight
But when time come fi do what di Mother sey
Is pure Old Spice she smell in har room
Miss Ena, look round and start fi think
She memba sey Bruce did love di colour red
And him used to splash on nuff Old Spice – kill him dead
So she decide fi go fi pink instead
And douse har room with KhusKhus oil
She know seh Mass Bruce no like the pink
And him say the Khus, Khus smell well stink
So Bruce no badda come no more
And her new guy now free fi walk through the door.

Matches Shoes Box

ANTONIA VALAIRE

Me deh yah in a tangle
Father left me when me two year old
pon d shiny concrete,
only left a TV
after Andre plea.
Him left the place so hollow
You cudda hear roach eardrum a beat.

Mumma bawl cah a three bwoy pickney
and one gal she fi fen fah
And shame and disgrace would a mad har
And life dutty tough.
Hella hard fi one without nuh help
Neighba dem nuh much better,
cause all whey u nuh have dem want.
Dem eye a green and orange
So we dey ya a taggatagga.

Me sidung under a tree an ole reasoning
with Bredda Shorti.
The man back tough you si!
From eye deh a knee
him nuh wear shut
And the old tegereg
would a never dare bite him
But a me dem surround
like Pharaoh plague,
di Portmore national bird.

So yes me dear
After twenty-five years me puppa draw him ole bruk self
a claim fifty-fifty share fi wah him never build
Pay light or wata,
Much less the vagabond land tax
Send letter from some lawyer
A chat whole heap a legal terms,
Me nearly piss cross the room
And me eyes them swell up like any bull frog
Sadness and pain riddle me body.

Old crocodile tears full a ball room
Sympathy fi such an old man
heart so wicked.
Fi me mumma pray
Like weeping Jeremiah
And me say it nah guh so
So me contact fi me lawyer
whey me meet a one award ceremony
Cause me did inna the poetry fever.
When we hear the price me start fi bawl and wail
me nuh know whey me a go find
The ham leg to this almshouse drama.
U see me dying trial?

Wooiii, a how karma a treat we so?
Christmas fi nice but is Santa nightmare,
Nimrod tales from the crypt
Lawd a massy me just fed up.
Belly button fi drop out anytime soon
Me fi dey yah a enjoy likkle home
Whey Manley promise in 1980s fi civil servants
If a never fi it, we would a under tree
or in a bush a squat
A batter and batter,
Now me heart bleed fi this travesty.

But see we yah, God merciful eeee
And we come a far way
from the concrete echo wall to some nice furnishing
And some extra bathrooms and bedrooms
Kitchen and thing
roof nah show belly and a swim
but can run off now like stream.

Yuh know more time you grateful
but troubles and trials could hang the undertaker
Me mind run wile
Me heart boom so fast under the pressure buss pipe
Suicide is not an option, but me brain rackle.
What a dilemma we find we selves inna.

Justice delayed is justice denied, dem say
So me wah act fast because me wah my day in court
But not even the first dollar me have
And tax increase and cost a living pon high.
Dollar a swim and drown
Call the highway patrol as robbery in full bloom
Like any hibiscus.

And we so dead and numb to this exploitation
That we in colonization in a reverse
Till a hole on to masa frock tail
All when she fan we off in Windrush
off the Queen's English.
We prefer disown we patwa fi belong.
So me dey yah write this ya piece
even though me kibba heart bun
And despite me ina tango and limbo
So as me end this ya tory, pray fi me
And next time we talk again soon.
So walk good.

Queenie Queenie and Colonial Empire

LILLIAN ALLEN

A whole year de people dem spend a fix-up and a prepare fah her Royal Imperial Majestic, the Queen of England to visit the town of St Jago de La Vega, the second largest city on the island of Jamaica. In this little town de people dem wuk hard an make de La Vega a pleasurable place fi them and them family and near-family cause anybody deh bout is family.

Not nuff industry of employ except the textile mill, miles up a Ariguanabo near Bog Walk. An' there was Caymanas Sugar Estate factory on the road to old Port Henderson, with marble statue of Admiral Lord Nelson standing in fa de Queen and conquest. Yu wooda did lucky if one of yu distant relative or even third cousin removed did get a job dey. An yes, the coveted Alcan job a Linstead. If you or family member get dat job, yu done dead and find yu self a heaven. Dat there was red golden. But it sad how dem dig up the ground, whole side a mountain, mash it down, strip up Massa God earth, then mush it up with caustic soda, and move wey de poor likkle venda dem.

Dem tek wey wha dem want and sen big fat tanker shipload to Canada and America to refine (an doan get mi started on that, like we only good enough fi soso dirt and not refinement!). Dem leave the mountain valley of caustic soda sludge, a constipated red river bringing sadness and ill-health. Otherwise is soh soh penny hustling, hand to mouth work at Record Office, or fi the more tapanaris dem with connection, wuk a Parish Council. Prison, yes; warder work, police, hospital, school teecha, learn trade, rum shop, dry-good store, haberdashery, small grocery, or wuk at the market or cemetery – Number Five Bawling Ground. Days wuk, domestic, any little ting.

Hand mi down recycle, pull an stretch, one-one coco. Every mikkle mek a mukkle and every mukkle mek a mite. Day in day out. One-one coco full baskit.

In the town, little Delveena, nine year and swish young was a pickney wid a tough constitution, trong like a harse, full of sheself wid a mine of har own. She an' her friend dem couldn't understand wey all the fuss was about dis ya visit and why when dem have so much gazillion people in the world, heroes and sheroes who do so much for human kind, so many who do kind things for dem neighbours and others, so many nice nice grandmothers and aunties, that dis one ooman, the Queen, was getting so much attention.

All the likkle pickney dem inna the town of St Jago de la Vega was well versed pon the Queen, her Empire and her riches. De pickney dem was made to practise day in day out on how to behave in front of royalty. These pickney dem was no fenke fenke pickney. Dem was haughty and use to run up and down inna hot hot sunshine plenty. But none a dem eva stretch to the limits like them was the day the Queen of England came to visit Jamaica. Imagine all the pickney dem inna the broiling tropical sun all day ah wait fi get a glimpse of the Queen of England as if she couda did save dem soul.

Sun set an sun rise, people wuk an pot bwoil. Dem no wait, dem no hurry, time run come in front of dem to bring this day. Blaaps! The poor likkle pickney dem did scrub down, cleaned behind the ears and under dem arm and scrub double in hidden creases. All dem poverty and lack of opportunity fi a bright future covered up under the sheen of shine up shoes, powdered faces and impeccably starched and ironed uniforms. Criss an not a crease.

Dem herd di pickney dem like cattle and put dem pon show fi mek di Queen know dat she loyal subject dem will forever be reproducing likkle loyal subjects, if she doan object that is.

Dis ya visit was the biggest sinting de town ever see. Di biggest sinting the whole island ever see, fi dat matter. Joe Blowwow who sell scrapses meat reduce im price. Miss Diana sweep up har yard and tie bow pon the guinep tree. Miss Meeme spend two days straight without a drop a sleep and mek grata-cake like it did a go out a style. Even at the Chinaman shop dem spruce up di place and a give wey free sweetie to di school children dem. Everybody dress up dem house or one room like is Easter and Christmas in one. The nice nice tablecloth, chenille spread and bleach clean curtain wey only see the light a day fi very special occasion, proudly displayed to welcome the Queen. De way everybody dah gwan, yuouda did think sey a Christ a cum again.

Buzz, buzz, buzzing. De worl was a buzz buzzing; Britannia. "Rule Britannia, Britannia, rule the waves and Britons never, never shall be slaves!" This sentiment drill into every likkle pickney and inna every woman and man in di country fi a whole year. Rule Britannia! Well, well, Mother Thelma did sey dem a trow dem wud pon Black people, cause if dem invent slavery and dem will never, never, never . . . not one or two but three "never" be a slave, then a who fi be di slave?

For the entire year in the town of de la Vega, the word Britannia ruled supreme and was a rallying call. Britannia was represented by her stately self the Queen, England, the Empire, and the universe.

Hurried, harried, hassled, and whipped into shape – that's how it ouda did look to you if you did see how dem pack dat town square overflowing with school pickney, all in line and formation more orderly than the Eleventh Battalion of the Queen's very army. All this by eight a.m. sharp that morning. All to dutifully await the visitation of her Imperial Majesty Queen Elizabeth the Second of England. Bacchanalia throughout the town that day. Military band, police, and Boy Scouts groups march up and down through the streets. Hundreds of little British flags waved everywhere. Big flags were on every flagpole in schools, prisons, churches, and public places. And choruses of "Rule Britannia" could be heard every whey yu turn.

It was said that from dem hear the word "go" over a year ago, the ole solider man dem deck out demself inna full uniforms wid dem ribbons, dem buttons, dem sashes and dem medals, and dem practise march up and down and around the town five nights a week. Dem talk story and tell bout soldier life and wartime happenings. Dem was like survivors of Battleship Galactica Star War attack and now awaiting accolades from the Divine leader of the universe, though nuff nuff ah dem never see no war business, ongle the uniform.

People rush to finish tidy up dem house before the sun come up. Dem bring out the cup an' saucers dem nevah touch fi years, just in case. Nuff a de church people dem recall scriptures an de Easter song about Zacchaeus that goes, "Now Zacchaeus was a very little man and a very little man was he. He climbed up into the sycamore tree for the Saviour he wanted to see" (repeat chorus), for the Saviour he wanted to see. And as the Saviour passes by he looked up in the tree, and said, "Now Zacchaeus, you come down, I'm coming to your house for tea. I'm coming to your house for tea." Oh lordie, lord!

The route dat the Queen was to take was all fixed-up. Bruk-down fence, mash-up wall, and some yard wey never cleanup ebber get fix-up. Everybody was given freebie government paint and material to do repairs and all the neighbours worked together with even the government man dem giving a hand to do a splendid facelift job. The way the place look refreshing it mek some people remark, "Mek dem government man couldn't help we out just fi wiself sometimes. De ongle time dem do something fi wi is when dem waan wi vote or dem waan show aff to foreigner!"

Don't get it wrong now, is not everybody did feel subjected to the Queen. Nuff people gather round and backstab she. Dem wonder out loud why, if she is the richest woman in the world and control so much wealth and riches – why she sending only so-so sympathy to the poor in her Christmas message, when all she have to do is to get up offa some of that cash?

A group of Rasta man led by Bongo George and Count Roots draft up a letter wey sey

"The reason the Queen have up so much money is because she tief up the treasures of Africa and nuff other countries, and tief up people land wey dem own and live pon continuously long before she or anybody she know or related to was ever born" . . . and dem demand that she give the monies, treasures and lands back.

But when dem tek the letter to the authorities to ask it to be delivered to the Queen, dem arrest every single one of dem wid signature pon the letter and threaten Bongo George and Count Roots with the cat o' nine. And dem never let the Rasta man dem outta jail till the Queen was safely out of the Caribbean. And when dem finally let dem out, dem dreadlocks cut off clean clean, and the officials give dem each a likkle paper bag wid dem personal souvenir of the Queen's visit. Each bag have een some tough red an' white sweetie, Union Jack stickers, and pictures of the Queen and the Royal family.

Thousands lined the street with the motorcade on its way. The pickney dem wait patiently from way before eight o'clock in Massa God mawning. Dem bear up like highly trained troopers. Dem couldn't even talk or go pee pee. As soon as yu hear a likkle susu, a big mouth teacher wouda did yell out, "Be quiet, please! Respect for the Queen!" The pickney dem just strups dem teeth and stan up dey wid de patience of Job. For hours dem packed together inna the blazing sun, though not as tight as bodies pon a human cargo ship.

When twelve o'clock come, it was like the sun was full of vengeance. If it couda did talk a pure blirdeets it oulda did sey. Instead the sun blazed down mercilessly pon the pickney dem. In the meantime, the teacher dem oulda spell dem one anada off and go rest off inna the shade, wey dem sip likkle Kool-Aid sweetened wid brown sugar. Officials of pure so-soh big time, full belly man dem sit reverentially pon the platform that was built specially for the occasion by the undertaker carpenter son, Walley. De man dem siddown stiff and obedient, well pleased with the world. Only intermittently dem ouda fan flies and whisper kindly to each other like dem feeling a magic.

Bam! At 11:30 a.m. the sun claimed its first victim. The nine-year-old Delveena just couldn't tek it no more. She was the first to hit the pavement. An' then a wave of fainting spell see dozens of shiny Black children been taken into the shade and fanned, smelling sauced and bay-rummed.

The blazing sun was the only someting that showed no sign of tiring. Everybody look wilted. Even the flag stap flutter pon the flagpole looking thirsty fi wata. By 12:45 even the most diehard loyalist was starting to becoming irritated, albeit with a slight stoicism. But they were not nearly as irritated as irate parents proudly watching from the other side of the town's square who declared, "The Queen didn't care a hoot bout dem pickney dem wey a bun up inna the boiling heat" because, as soft-spoken Dina reasoned out loud, "If it was fi she pickney, Prince this and Princess that, she oulda did have servants a fan them an' hold umbrella over them head!"

At 1:30 p.m. a small breeze fluttered through the crowd. Tensions eased, and before you could sey, "Jack Mandora, mi nuh choose none", a woo of excitement went up to welcome the Queen. It was like magic. A beautiful angelic wave-like chorus of woos floated up over the gathering of ten thousand dutifully gathered subjects. And then there was silence . . . and confusion. What was supposed to be the Queen appeared in a white convertible without crown, throne, horses or foots-men. A person who appeared to be the Queen waved tiredly with one hand. Slowly.

Children turned and searched each others' eyes, in confusion to see and asking, "Where is the Queen?" There were no clues to signify that this tired looking white lady with a waving hand was the Queen. The pickney dem strain dem neck while the Queen was in full view, still looking, still asking, "Where is the Queen? Where is the Queen?" People start to strups up dem teeth, vex soh till. After all dem preparations and excitement the Queen didn't even have the courtesy to show up in her crown. Bad enough she didn't bring any of the postcard looking guards in front of Buckingham Palace, and not even one of Princess Anne's dress-up horse.

The boiling sun eased its persistence . . . and King's House, the court house building, Parish Council and Record Office with the Rodney statue part, threw a gentle shadow like a sign that the universe and Jah know that de pickney dem couldn't tek the heat nuh more.

The convertible carrying the Queen and her motorcade came to a stop right in front of the platform full of politicians, government officials, dignitaries and rich people. All the man dem pon the platform get up in unison and give the Queen a serious salute. The Mayor with a necklace look like straight outta Compton presented the Queen with a key to the town. "Strups strups", an' "struups up" was heard all around; people say dem was going home that night to change the lock pon them door.

In the shade by the side of the platform away from hordes of uniformed very tired school children, Likkle Delveena was recovering from her faint. She looked up and saw an ordinary looking white person. She asked to make sure. "A dat the Queen? A she dat? A de Queen dat?" The teacher standing beside Delveena shuss her down to indicate for her to be quiet and then replied with tremendous excitement, "Yes that is she. That is wi Queen!"

Delveena eased herself up from where the teacher had put her to rest. She looked around from left to right, at all the other pickney dem and all the other nuff nuff people who dress up demselves like dress puss, she looked at the tapanaris people dem pon the platform, then darted to the convertible that carried the Queen. She stood beside the convertible, the Queen still waving to the crowd. Likkle Delveena put her hands pon kimbo, push out her chest and shouted, "Look mi prettier than de Queen!"

A loud cheer went up in the town's square. The teacher strode embarrassingly and grab Delveena, and she hauled her to the back of the platform where another teacher held her to the ground. The Queen didn't even blink. She just kept waving her arm in slow motion as she looked straight into the crowd. She seemed disinterested and fatigued, growing tireder by the second. Her waving arm moving even slower through the thickness of the tropical heat. Within moments her motorcade drove on. The Queen had come and gone, just like that. Braps!

In the meantime, Delveena escaped the teacher who was holding her to the ground. She ran out into the crowd. The crowd went wild with cheering her. They lifted her up in the air. The other school children jumped around and clapped and tussled jokingly with each other forgetting their dozens of rehearsals on how to vacate the square in an orderly manner. Teachers yelled for order and quiet without effect. The authorities came over the loudspeaker calling for quiet and order. People carried on with their chatter and jovialities as if an inside damn had broken loose. No one paid attention to the high-pitched calls for quiet and order that continued over the public address system for some time. A festival atmosphere erupted.

Afterwards, the town buzzed with festivities, thousands more little British flags and pictures of the Queen appeared everywhere. Souvenirs of American-made British sweets, and pens, pencils, and exercise books made in Japan were being distributed freely. Not long after, a light dusk came and brought a dreamy atmosphere. There were big questions on everybody's lips. The questions and answering became a game. Someone would take on the role of the questioner in a group and the whole group would prove the answer. It was done kinda sing-songy with a beat.

"Did you see the Queen?"
The answer: "Which Queen?"
Then: "Was she big or was she likkle?"
The answer: "She was likkle with mukkle an' mettle!"
Then: "Was she wrong or was she right?"
The answer: "Who cares. She showed some life!"

The nine-year-old Delveena was unofficially crowned "de la Vega's little queen" and was nicknamed Queenie-Queenie. After a year of anticipation and preparations, the Queen of England, Her Imperial Majestic Royal Elizabeth de Second had come and gone. Somehow her status had slipped, forever. It was no wonder that the fate of her empire would follow suit.

Goodnite

LINTON KWESI JOHNSON

siddung pan varandah in yu wheelchair
shame-a-lady now growin at yu gate

yu dawtah dem baid an powdah yu
put yu inna nappy like baby
children a run up an dung out a road
dem lawftah is music in yu ears

yu is a big girl now in sandy rivah
baidin andah rose apple tree

2
siddung pan varandah in yu wheelchair
in di calm evenin atmosfare

no heaviness a hawt no worryin tawt
jus a peaceful feelin deep widin

flowahs in yu gawdn please yu eye
a ripe julie mango drap a grung

bird pan litepost a sing a late sang
yu a wandah wat tomarrow agoh bring

3
siddung pan varandah in yu wheelchair
tankful fi di likkle cool breeze

arthritis mek yu bone dem betray yu
no bittah tais lingah pan yu tongue

battalions a cloud mawchin yandah
di weary sun soon gawn to bed

di lite a fade fawce in di twilite
time a draw near fi seh goodnite

Nativity*

LASANA M. SEKOU

Culture is Self

. . .

& love for so to stop all
the foolishness & cussing we oan vict'ry
& behaving like we ain got no folks
                &
                tales

& acting up stupid stupid
like we forgetting something
& how we tun in chameleon knights
with Ma'tinus on the porch in Agrément
grandchildren like halos lighting on his knee
to hear him hum twilight awake
& tell we story 'bout Bo' Nansi/& Brer Rabbit
depart guerrilla lore
   like mother sparrow
   to the mouths of babes
pass on cassava meal to outfit new flamboyant
armour/
keep we cleverer
      to outwit the mighty
causin "the day the leaf falls in the water

---

*© Lasana M. Sekou. Excerpt from *Corazón de pelícano – Antología poética de Lasana M. Sekou / Pelican Heart – An Anthology of Poems by Lasana M. Sekou*, ed. Emilio Jorge Rodríguez (Philipsburg, St Martin: House of Nehesi Publishers, 2010), 320–21.

is not the day it sinks"
mek José say "Love and Labour Conquer
All
Things"
mek we race
jinnal & tallawah
like Miss Lou cunny jamma oman
scratch dungle heap for phoenix to come out
laugh open we self
when Paul on the road to de-mask us
balance Tantie Merle basket on we heads
& Dominica woman wid sweet tongue balancing
Banana labour pon she head
pass by the reevah^^^^^^^^^^^^^^forthnighting
down de heel to load the boat by the sea
call morning up from sleep & everybody
clap Joby Bernabé hands
hands akimbo
& say:
buh eh eh, boo, we got grace nah, *oui!*

Slavery in Reverse

EMILE GRANT

I watched *Roots* as a child
I learnt from it
Unforgettable – the rape of our daughters

I watched *Roots* as a man
I couldn't stand it
Unforgettable – the gang rape of our sisters

We sing about mental slavery but what do we mean
Are we enslaved by "two-year-old", "fresh vegetables"
"twos and threes"

The music we love
Now a tool to enslave
Why are Michigan & Smiley
No longer the rave

I seldom listen the dancehall of today
Is Romaine's "Dutty Man"
Leading the way?
We need a change and we need it now
Netanya's generation needs the know how

Olivia, Peter, Andrew
Hear the children's cry
For our culture has gone awry
Transformation! or kiss Vision 2030 goodbye

Bleachface is now a ward of the state
Not one lyric
Allow to escape

Our forefathers watched helplessly
As black daughters suffer
Now our sons prey on their sisters as if
Their lives do not matter

Louise witnessed colonization in reverse
Lovely rhythm and words so kind
Artists please
Free our minds

Pastor

SUSAN LYCETT DAVIS ("DR SUE")

But a wha' wrong wid Pastor doh eh
Him really dey pon fire today!
Whateva him a say seem fi a burn hot fi true
Cause not a soul seem able fi sit dis yah sermon through!

Mi see Sista Jean pop a poco move
Den round di corner a sleepyhead Joel dat a ketch di groove!
Den Pastor mek mistake go beg choir sing again
Whoooh . . . di congregation caan stop shout amen!

Den as if dat no enough
Brother Mac jump up and start rant some stuff
Before we know Pastor start fi implore
Thou shall not do dat no more!!!

Mi no know wha "dat" waz
But is like him was a talk to me
Mi say before Pastor coulda done implore
A mi dat dung pon di floor!

Every word Pastor say just reverberate inna me being!
Mi undertand it was quite a scene
When mi come back to, cause mi was inna a trance
Everybody round mi dey pon fire, a drop, a cry and a dance

Mi still no know a wha did wrong wid Pastor today
But mornings like these, me glad me neva gone way
Cause when Pastor de pon fire, all we do a pray
And thank God fi another blessed day!

Evelyn's Wisdom

SONIA S. WILLIAMS

1.
I in't pick muh teet'
I jus' do wha I had to do

I send de boys when I coulduh send dem to school
I did a membuh of de Parish Church

I send de children evah Sunduh to Sunduh school
so de priest know we face

causin' de vestry got de powuh
if you want a pick, you gotta get your name pon de list

you can't wait pon heaven.

2.
Now as for de girls . . .
Iffin dere was a place to sen dem, Uh-woulduh-sen-dem

Yuh haf-to-haf money to pay fuh de girls;
as you well know, in dis-place girls does serve.

Just keep dem outtuh-de-family-way
uh girl does only get pregnant once

after dat – she is woman.

3.
De youngest kin stitch
I send she to learn how tuh cut

She can mek anyting.
What-a-way she look like Princess!

Me front room-a-full-up wit' clawt'
& me heart-a-full-up wit' pride

how she set she mind pon de task!

4.
De other one says she wants to go to Ingland
she can't tek it nuh mor! So I gi' she me blessing.

She gone.

5.
& de piece-uh-man just bout de place
planting he cassava stick dung in evah hole.

It aint only now it is evah since, some tek root and done grow.
Yuh tink I don't know? Me eyeballs see de fruits dem drop.

To God be de glory!

6.
I raise muh children wid dese two hands
dey int nuffin, dat dese two hands can't do.

I tek-in a little washing. I do a little cleaning t'ree times a week
fuh de madam in de big house, I even help lay bricks in de
  Anglican church.
As long as dere is flour, sugar an' dese hands, my chil'ren good!
I mek sweets and sell from muh tray!

I throw a little su-su, when meeting turn come
I add on a little piece pon de house.
God don't gi' yuh no more dan you kin bear.

7.
Yuht'ink I does look fuh he pay slip?
De rum shop got a new coat a paint.

You int see it?!

No More "Smalling Up" of Me*

JEAN WILSON

No more meekly saying "yes"
When my heart is screaming "no"
No more taming of my feelings
So my power won't show
No more hiding my exuberance
From disapproving eyes
No more watering down myself
So my spirit won't rise.

No more "smalling up" of me
Pretending I am not here
No more running from the music
And the spotlight's glare
No more living in this prison
Barricaded by my fears
No more turning and retreating
In the face of new frontiers.

Even as I am speaking
I am taking shape and form
Harnessing my powers
Like a gathering storm
There's no obstacle so bold
As to dare stand in my way
I am taking back my life
And I am doing it today.

---

*First published in *No More "Smalling Up" of Me* (Kingston: Ian Randle, 2003).

Use My Tongue Wisely

MARLON HENRY

Dear God, although my visits to you may not be so timely
And mi often talk di wrong ting . . .
when mi know fi do it rightly

Gossiping, back-biting, leak secrets weh friend confide mi
I pray for self control . . . So mi can use my tongue wisely

The tongue is a mighty thing an mi nuffi tek it lightly
It hold LIFE and DEATH, the power fi define or defile mi
So everytime mi bout fi use mi mout' mi a beg yu remind mi
Fi have some self-control and use mi tongue wisely

Even when mi tink da yute/girl deh nuh like mi
And mi find out all di tings weh dem chat behind mi
Or the teacher weh mi think a fight mi and always a try style mi
Help mi kibba mi mout' like Liza and use my tongue wisely

Jesus mi pray yu have mi back, plus front an stay side mi
Always be near fi care and plus bless mi an guide mi
Instead o criticize . . .
help mi sympathize kindly
And give me the control to use my tongue wisely!

Jamaican Women

QUEWANA COLLMAN

Mi aunty, mi uncle, mi neighba, mi fren, heh!
Come mek me tell yuh bout Jamaican women,
They are hardworking, dem full a strength,
Dem love di bling bling and di excitement,
Weh mi seh? EXCITEMENT!

Jamaican women are industrious,
Although some a dem, you cyaa really trus,
But nuh worry bout dat, just leave it to God,
A him a di true and di Almighty one.

Anyways mek mi tell unuh a secret
One day this man, him name Jeremiah,
Him cheat pon him wife, she name Gloria,
She cook di food, she clean di house, she do di laundry,
She gi him six pickney and him a bawl, Mi sorry,
SORRY? RUN HIM!

Jamaican women are so powerful,
Although dem look weak, dem strong like a bull,
Dem liff up di block and help build di house,
And when yuh check a stack, di man throw dem out??!!
DEN TELL MI NOW, DEN NUH WIKIDNESS DAT?

Mi seh Jamaican women are so beautiful,
Dem look remarkable and so wonderful,
Suh don't you worry and don't get stressed,

Because Jamaican women, you are truly blessed,
Mi seh Jamaican women, you are truly blessed,
Mi seh Jamaican women, you are truly blessed,
Yuh blessed, yuh blessed, yuh blessed, yuh blessed!

Mi Name Jamaica

OWEN BLAKKA ELLIS

mi is a lickle island nation
pon di world map mi look like a speck
but any time mi name get mention
it get recognition an respeck

people smile wid admiration
dem stan up an clap an cheer
sometimes dem grumble condemnation,
or swell-up wid bad-mind an fear

dem cyaan andastan ow
wan country weh young an poor an small,
can taak so loud an waak so proud
an stan up so strang an tall

mi dance to any beat selecta play
an join inna every song dat sing
mi come een like air or water
cause mi inna every lickle ting

media, litricha an academia
new discovery, science an racket
if a egg me haffi inna di red
an if is jacket me inna di packet

inna music, dance an drama
wid brains an beauty me claim di fame
inna every field an form of sport
di whole worl know mi name

yes, a mi name Jamaica
nu badda judge mi by mi size
mi lickle but mi tallawah
an mi come fi claim di prize

Chanting Down Babylon

ALEXANDRIA MILLER

PREFACE

> Bring in all Rastas, dead or alive.
>
> —*Prime Minister Alexander Bustamante*

On 11 April 1963, during the Holy Week of Easter and less than a year after gaining independence, the Jamaican government waged a war against Rastafarians across the country, known as the Coral Gardens Massacre.

After a fire was set to a local gas station and eight people were killed, including two police officers, the government rounded up, jailed, and tortured hundreds of men and women across the country, scorning them for their Black Nationalist beliefs and dreadlocks; they were seen as an undesirable national threat to the budding independent nation. Police and military raided communities, arrested Rastas across Jamaica, and even cut off their locs, a symbol in Rastafari of physical and mental strength.

Although the following story is a work of fiction, the story of Rasta women, in the wake of the Coral Gardens Massacre, has since been less often depicted. This short story is dedicated to the sistren who resisted, but whose stories have not been told.

WATA MORE DAN FLOUR

The word was out. Bustamante wanted all Rastafarians brought in, dead or alive. All the Rastas across the country were in a panic. Some ran to their houses, some ran to their mothers, others to the temple. But one thing was for sure; if you had locs, you were not safe. Balli P knew this was true, and his empress, Tanga, knew they needed a plan to survive. They sealed their bond just two years ago, but they had known each other since primary school. Balli, five years her senior, grew up as a sort of big brother to Tanga, looking out for her when her older brothers and cousins weren't around. They had grown so close in Tanga's last three years at the University of the West Indies, despite the four-hour drive between Kingston and St Elizabeth on weekends. Tanga and Balli were soulmates after all.

Police raids were getting bigger and bigger as youths from Coral Gardens to Alligator Pond flocked from cities to the dense bush in the outskirts of town. Di dutty babylon had already killed Ras leaders Rudolph Franklyn, Carlton Bowen and Clifton Larman. Now they were targeting leaders across parishes. Balli P was the most revolutionary in Black River. He was a skilled farmer, opening his garden to anyone in need. He reasoned with local youths, warning them about "politricks", all while guiding them to the teachings of His Imperial Majesty. Although he was no more than twenty-six himself, he helped bring up a new generation of Rastafari.

Scaling down Spur Tree Hill's spiralling road or leaving Negril's sea-foam green waters, people flocked in droves to visit Balli P. The police targeted him first when they ventured out of St James. Tanga, on the other hand, would not let that happen.

One night in early September, just after Tanga's birthday, Deputy Corporal Melbourne stormed into their home. Tanga sat out on the back veranda smoking a spliff and getting a jump-start on breakfast. As she removed the ripe fruit from its skin and let out a calm puff of smoke, the police kicked down the front door.

"Weh di bloodclaat likkle stinkin Rasta deh?"

The entire bowl of fresh ackee crashed onto the concrete and rolled down the porch.

No Craven A in sight, the ital ganja burned a hole in Tanga's skirt.

"Yuh dutty jancro. Unno need fi come outta mi yaad an' go suck unno madda."

"Cooyah, di likkle gyal tink seh she a big ooman! Alright den, come mek we treat yuh as such. Mi a go ask yuh one more time. Which part Balli P gone?"

Tanga tried to run as four officers grabbed hold of her.

"Unno favour mi batty. Jah Jah know babylon soon fall. Jamaica a capture land and unno, unno a no better. Bun fyah to all yuh who nuh follow Rastafari."

"Hmmmm gwaan chat yuh likkle wench. Mek wi chop off yuh ol' stinkin natty an' haul yuh down-a Bellevue, a mek dem foo-fool chat deh."

"Alright, alright. Mi nuh know which part him gone. Him gone from long time. Him lef mi pon mi earthstrong and neva come back."

Melbourne stood in disbelief. "An' yuh still love him suh? Woiii! Mek wi faaward a di next place mi boy. All a dem Rastaman wutless nuh blow wow."

The police left Tanga's home, laughing all the way till they went to the next Ras compound down the street. Despite her brave face, Tanga was shaking inside. She now knew they were watching, and she and Balli P had to be more careful. Balli was sitting right there in the house. He heard everything, blood boiling as he listened to them disrespect his wife but following the pact they had made. He sat idle and powerless. They had gotten word four days ago from Bobo Jerry, an elderly Rasta from Lacovia, that the police would be on their way.

On her birthday, after dancing in the moonlight for what could be the last time, Tanga wrapped Balli P in their spare mattress and secured his new hiding place with four metres of rope. It was the best they could do with such little time. He was close to his love, and yet still out of sight. For the next three days, Tanga sat virtually motionless next to Balli P in the folded mattress.

They reasoned for hours, on the works of Garvey, on their hopes and dreams, on their repatriation to Selassie's home. Tanga fed her king through the small opening where the mattress' two halves came together. She took the lessons of Empress Menen, wife of Emperor Selassie, very seriously. She mixed him spirulina for strength. And the full meals! Tanga was the best cook inna di scheme and always made sure Balli P was well fed. She fed him roast breadfruit, callaloo, dumpling, yam, and banana. She had to keep him strong, especially if they needed to go on the run.

The next morning, Tanga headed to the local market. Stocking up on extra vegetables, she bought triple of everything, more than usual. With Balli P out of the garden, supplies ran low. She bought cho-cho, yellow yam, golden Scotch bonnet peppers, June plum, jackfruit and soursop. Tanga stumbled out of the downtown market; she had more bags than she could carry. And as she looked around, hailing all the women in sight, it dawned on her that other of Selassie's dawtas had just as many bags. The market was almost clean out of food, a rare occurrence for Jamaica's breadbasket. All Rasta men were in danger after Coral Gardens, and all their women protected them.

Tanga hailed everyone in sight, "Wah gwaan Sista? Yea mon, mi deh yah. Jus a cook up likkle soup fi di evenin' yah. Mek everyone know seh di Sistrens' Circle a gwaan ova Independence Park tonight. Jah know, we nuh have a reasonin' in a good while."

The Sistrens' Circle was a small gathering for all the empresses in Black River. They met at Independence Park in the centre of town. They vented, they chanted, and they even traded handmade soaps and jewellery.

Because of gender politricks, Sistrens' Circle was a joke among local authorities. "Yea man, trade di likkle cookin' recipes before wi haul unno down a station," police officers often mocked as they passed Independence Park.

"Cookin' a di least! We a chant down babylon!" they always responded defiantly.

GOAT DEH SWEAT, BUT LONG HAIR COVER IT

Sistrens' Circle was buzzing. All of the women wondered why Tanga had called this sudden meeting, especially when Ras gatherings were so dangerous, even among women.

"Dawtas, mi dawtas! Wi have nuff business fi chat inna di evenin' but wi haffi flex like nothin' a gwaan. Zeen? Lay out di likkle bead dem. Fol' up di fabric and chop up some herbs. Di Circle cyaan look a-ways," Tanga instructed.

The women stood bewildered. What was Tanga talking about? What was so serious, so urgent that needed to be discussed right then and there?

"Mi know wi nuh waa too chat 'bout Coral Gardens. Worse, wi nuh waa chat 'bout weh di man dem gone, but wi haffi deal betta dan dis. Nuh difference wi a deal wid, wi haffi unite," Tanga reasoned.

At that moment, a sudden lull ran over the band of women. They became pensive, reasoning with themselves. Then, an uproar began. The questions shot at her from all corners.

"Weh yuh seh?"

"How wi fi do dat?"

"Mi cyaan deal wid di almshouse right ya now. Mi jus waa tek care a Ras Fire!"

"Weh 'bout di pickney dem? Mi cyaan dead an' leave dem. Who a go raise mi pickney?"

The women shouted over each other, completely forgetting that they shouldn't be drawing attention to the park this late in the evening. Tanga started, "Woiii, woiii, listen mi! Imagine if wi did mek a set plan? Wid nuff cooperation, wi coulda protect the king's men and watch ova di likkle yute dem as one."

"Alright, what's the plan den?" said Iyesha, empress to local carpenter Junior Wendell.

"Wi cyaan live ere, dat a one. Di plot ova Vineyard sweet. It deh right ova di river. If wi all move 'round deh suh, an' move di man dem inna di swamp, wi coulda watch ova dem, yuh zeen? An' no babylon a go ova deh. Di alligata too nuff an' only wi alone know how fi deal wid dem."

Tanga was onto something. She looked at the women's faces and decided to take a vote. "If dis a di plan, shout I and I."

Independence Park rang out, "I and I . . . I and I . . . I and I . . . I and I." Everyone agreed, almost in perfect harmony. The plan was set then. They would all spend the next week gathering their belongings and next Sat'day would tread the short journey to Vineyard.

The day had finally arrived. After a week of moving across town with trepidation, constantly watching over their backs to make sure no one noticed as they moved the men down to Vineyard one by one, the empresses, their children and their kings were safely in their new compound. Tanga had chosen Vineyard strategically. The area was dense with bush, safe and secluded; if the police ever tried to capture them, their approach could easily be heard over the silent emerald waters. Even better, Vineyard could only be entered by boat on one side. There was no way dem babylon boys from Kingston knew how to deal with no alligata. Only real country people knew how to do that.

Most important of all, Vineyard afforded them an uninhibited connection with nature. As Rastas, they believed in oneness with the earth. Being out in nature allowed them to better livicate themselves to Jah Rastafari.

Every morning, empresses woke up in Vineyard, gave thanks to Jah, and started off their day preparing meals for the camp. "Ital is vital," the women rang out, as they steamed cabbage and pressured peas for stews. By day, they cooked, sang, rejoiced and even held classes for the children about their African roots.

The women sent food to their partners sequestered deeper in the Black River swamps by tying pots to mangroves. At night, they went into the swamp hideouts to be in each other's embrace. The first to be together were Tanga and Balli P.

"Big ooman, yuh don't even know how long mi wish fi hol' yuh tight!" exclaimed Balli.

"Mi know, love. Yuh natty flash like Anansi a crawl pon mi. Yuh alone mek mi grin."

"Hmm, wi safe out ere fi now, mi wife. How tings a gwaan pon di next side a camp?"

"Know seh dem nuh too bad. Di pickney class a gwaan good. Mi neva tink a myself as a teacha, but afta mi see how di lessons dem a gwaan, mi woulda love fi teach."

"Eeehn? Tun up suh? Wa else?'

"Yuh know, a big reasoning woulda do dem some good. Jus fi talk out all di downpression dat a gwaan. Di sistren dem need it, Balli. Dem strong like Empress Menen but dem still need fi reason."

Balli P kissed his teeth, "Nuh seh a word Tanga, dat a di least. Round dem up, just before midnight tonight."

Rasta reasonings were especially important to their survival at the new settlement. It was how they would come to overstand life, downpression and their faith. Balli P, as the most revered Rasta in Black River, would start it off.

As Tanga poured tea for the camp, Balli P took the first smoke from the large coconut chalice and bellowed, "JAH RASTAFARI! It nuh easy fi mi start dah reasonin' yah knowin seh wi bredda dem out dere a suffa. Di politician dem wrong, my yute. How dem jus pick up a soulja? Fi wa? True seh him hair loc an' dem waa white tourist money? Dem nuh overstand, dis a nuh a physical appearance ting. Wi loc cause it mek wi strong. All a wi energy come outta ere," as he patted the top of his head, "Wi natty a wi energy, fi keep wi body strong. Look ere, since nun a wi woulda safe if it neva fi di sistren dem, wi a go leave dah one fi dem. Tanga, mi empress, hol' di reasonin mi wife. Yuh is a true queen, yuh have di grace of Omega."

"Yeah? Balli, yuh sure?"

He nodded in agreement and took another puff from the chalice before passing it around.

"Alright den, mi a try pencil out di state o' Jamaica. Jamaica is a black island, a Black independent nation, and dem a try kill wi off as black people. Fi wa? Fi build Half Moon Bay Hotel? Dem a seh wi cyaan walk up and down free pon fi wi own land, a land weh babylon carry wi pon inna di first place. Dem a tell wi seh pride inna wi blackness is crime! Is not right! Wa kinda foolishness is dat?!"

"Yes mi sista! Talk di truth!" Di sistren and bredrin dem roared in agreement. Everyone had gotten a puff of the chalice by now, and a cloud of smoke surrounded them as Tanga continued to reason in the Light of Jah.

"Mi seh Jamaica a capture land!"

"Bam, bam, bam." Their voices mimicked real guns as Tanga's one line touched a corn. "Wa wi fi do, Tanga?"

"Wi follow His Imperial Majesty an' Prophet Garvey. Wi go back to Africa. Africa is di ancestral land, nuh dah land yah weh Columbus come pitch pon like fly an' hand ova fi di Spanish. Africa is our repatriation, wi rightful place inna di world. Wi mus' tek up a next commission an' faaward home."

Tanga's truths had riled everyone up, so much so that they didn't even realize how loud they'd gotten. Just as they took the last puff from the chalice, they saw police boats bearing down on them from the swamp's only exit.

TROUBLE NUH SET LIKE RAIN

The entire Vineyard camp scattered, terrified of being captured. They tried to grab their earthly belongings, but the police had seized their boats and there was nowhere else to run.

"Di swamp, run down inna di swamp," Tanga yelled frantically.

"Tanga, yuh deh ere. Mi did 'ear seh a yuh did a run di show. If yuh deh-ya, Balli P cyaan too far." It was Corporal Melbourne's voice.

By this time, it was almost five in the morning. With all the cheering for Tanga, apparently some fishermen making their way seaside heard all the noise and alerted the police.

"Dutty bwoy Balli P, come out now or mi a tek Tanga fi miself," Melbourne shouted.

Balli P swooped in from nowhere, grabbed Tanga and darted further into the swamp. Vineyard was in disarray. Police grabbed and tortured the men and women alike, their wails dissipating over Black River. They were outnumbered and had no chance to fend for themselves.

As Balli P and Tanga made a run for it, Balli P suddenly realized he had dropped the garden trowel Tanga had given him for his twenty-fifth birthday. The trowel, he told everyone, was the reason he was the most skilled farmer in Black River, for it was Tanga's love that bought it for him, and a bit of that love poured into every crop he touched.

"Tanga, mi haffi go back fi it."

"Balli, dere's no time fi dat! Wi mus' go now!" Tanga hissed.

Balli P turned around anyway. Tanga followed, hoping that the sooner they found the trowel, the sooner they could make their way to safety.

Just when Balli P saw the trowel reflecting off of the morning sun, he heard the click of a gun cocked to his head.

"Mi get yuh now, yuh likkle wasteman," laughed Corporal Melbourne.

Tanga turned around and saw Balli P on the floor, Melbourne snickering as he pulled out his handcuffs. "Let him go! Mi seh let him go right now!"

"Likkle gyal, move yuh rass. A man business dis, yuh cyaan do nothin."

Tanga pulled a pistol from her sack, cocked it and repeated, "Mi seh let him go right now!"

"Weh di blouse an' skirt?" Melbourne replied in disbelief. "Yuh nah go dweet." Corporal Melbourne could not take Tanga's small frame seriously. He and Tanga were at a standoff and Balli P was caught in the middle.

"Put di revolva down before mi kill yuh off too," Melbourne warned.

"Tanga, baby, weh yuh get di gun from? Tanga, mi will be alright, jus put di gun down." Balli P pleaded.

"No big man, yuh an' mi a return to Zion. Melbourne, let him go!" Neither of the two backed off.

BOOM!

A single gunshot echoed across the swamp. Vineyard went silent. Tanga's sobbing filled the swamp and emptied out into the river. "Balli, mi love yuh."

Louise Go a Country

NADIA L. HOHN

(*Time: 1920s/1930s Jamaica.*)

It was the last day of school and Louise could not wait to visit her Grandma in St Mary. Mummy helped her pack the grip with clean frocks, frilly socks, and fine shoes, plus a basket of June plum, mackerel and hard dough bread.

"Goodbye, country Bibs," Mummy said. Louise waved to her on the platform as the train pulled out of Kingston station. It was many stops to Highgate, St Mary. When Louise arrived, Grandma gave her a huge hug. Uncle Cornelius picked up Louise to seat her on the donkey. "Hold on tight," he said, handing Louise the grip to hold.

"Please Uncle, let Grandma take my place. This road is too hard and hilly for her," Louise said.

"A forget you forget ah 'ere so me bawn," said Grandma. "Me have me two 'trong leg dem fe walk up dis ya hill. I cyan manage." She walked proudly, leading the way with Uncle Cornelius leading the donkey with Louise placed on it, trying to keep up. Grandma asked Louise about Mummy and school and the conversation took a turn.

"There's going to be a Dinki," said Uncle Cornelius.

"What's that?" she asked.

"De neighba dead. Me gwine host de nine night," he said.

"What's . . . ?"

"Dat's not a place fe pickney. Dem drink and dance and wail. You city pickney will frighten," Grandma said.

"It's an African tradition. All are welcome," Uncle Cornelius said.

Grandma kissed her teeth.

After dinner of oxtail and stew chicken, rice and peas, salad and ginger beer, Louise rinsed all the dishes at the standpipe. Then she put on her housedress and brushed her teeth. Grandma and Louise kneeled at the bed and said their bedtime prayers and even lay side by side on the single bed that they would share during the holidays. It was not long before Louise began her quiet snore. She did not hear Grandma get back up, close the door or leave the house.

Dooo-doot dooo-doot dooo-doot dooo-doot . . .

Louise's eyes twitched. What was that sound? The strange rhythm stirred her from her sleep. Louise tossed and turned but it was useless.

Quietly she crept out of bed, tiptoed through the kitchen, and looked out the window.

In Uncle Cornelius's yard, there were people wearing all white, the men with slacks carried torches, the women with long frocks danced and whirled and wailed.

Mi dis a come sah
Mi dis a come sah
Me no want no boderation, oh.

The wailing voices, the slow heavy beats that made her want to cry but also tap her foot. Louise had never heard anything like this before. It went on and on. Her heart beat fast.

She opened her grip to take out her pencil and notebook and she came back to the window where the bright moon shone and tried to remember the words of the song until her head dipped, her eyes grew heavy, she yawned and crawled back to bed and fell asleep in the empty bed so she barely heard when Grandma opened the door and crawled into bed beside her as the sun began to light her room.

The next night, ivory domino tiles banged on a table. And the next night, Louise heard a different sound. One night it was the tambourine. One night it was uncontrollable boisterous laughter. Another night it was deep startling cries. And still another, it sounded like a pastor preaching in church. Another night, it was the delicious smell of spicy jerk chicken and pork and pots of curry goat and corn soup. Louise wrote down the sights and sounds.

On the ninth night, the stomping feet of the mourners filled with wails, tambourine, and fife.

Tarry me, me nana, Tarry me o.
Country man a dig hole fe bury me . . .

The curiosity could not keep Louise inside the house any longer. She became bold. She wanted to know more. So she put on her slippers, slowly opened the front door, and tiptoed outside toward Uncle Cornelius's house where the people in white stepped. Louise hid behind the trunk of a mango tree brushing the mosquitoes from her face but he spotted her. "Come, Louise," he called.

"You scared?" Uncle Cornelius asked.

Louise shook her head "no" but jumped, startled, when she saw the bushes move. "Duppy," she shrieked.

No, it was Grandma.

"Come here," she said. Louise thought she would be dragged home and punished. Instead, Grandma linked Louise's arm and steered her to march in step with the others. They sang and danced until their voices croaked, until the faint rays of dawn peered over Blue Mountain peaks.

Most of the days in St Mary were hot and sticky. Each afternoon, Louise wanted to do nothing but lie down while the sweat stuck to her skin. But she helped Grandma cook in the evenings and tidy in the mornings. At night, she combed and plaited her grandmother's soft white hair. And Louise listened to the stories and songs on those moonshine nights under banyan tree. Grandma shared the tales of the African ancestors who toiled these lands to bring about sugar cane and coffee with their sweat and blood. She shared the stories of a curious little spider man called Anancy who always outsmarted everyone to live again and tell another tale.

The days grew shorter and soon it was time to leave St Mary, the hills, the donkey, the Dinki and her sweet Grandma. Louise was sad but the drum rhythms were still in her chest and new songs now played in her head. She hummed and tapped them as she sat on the train to keep them close to her heart.

And years later, when she remembered that school break in the countryside with her Grandma, the last one in fact, water came to her eye.

Soun de Abeng fi Nanny

JEAN "BINTA" BREEZE

Nanny siddung pon a rack
a plan a new attack
puffin pon a red clay pipe

an de campfire
staat to sing

wile hog a spit grease
pon machete crease
sharp as fire release
an er yeye roam crass
ebery mountain pass
an er yeas well tune to de win'

an de cricket an de tree frog
crackle telegram
an she wet er battam lip fe decode
an de people gadda roun
tune een to er soun
wid a richness dat aboun
she wear dem crown
pon er natty platty atless head

an ebery smoke fram er pipe
is a signal fi de fight
an de people dem a sing
mek de Cockpit ring

an de chant jus a rise, jus a rise
to de skies
wid de fervour of freedom
dat bus up chain
dat stap de ceaseless itching
of de sugar cane

We sey wi nah tun back
we a bus a new track dutty tough
but is enuff
fi a bite
fi wi fight

an ebery shake of a leaf
mek dem quiver
mek dem shiver
fa dem lose dem night sight
an de daylight too bright
an we movin like de creatures of de wile
we movin in a single file
fa dis a fi we fightin style

an de message reach crass
ebery mountain pass

we sey wi nah tun back
we a bus a new track
dutty tuff
but is enuff
fi a bite
fi wi fight

life well haad
mongs de wattle an de daub
eben de dankey
a hiccup
in im stirrup

for de carrot laas it class
so nuh mek no one come faas
eena wi business

dis a fi we lan
a yah we mek wi stan
mongs de tuff dutty gritty
dis yah eart nah show no pity
less yuh
falla fashion
home een like pigeon
an wear dem number like de beas
but wen yuh see er savage pride
yuh haffi realize
dat
wi nah tun hack
wi a bus a new track
dutty tuff
but is enuff
fi a bite
fi we fight
dutty tuff
but is enuff
is enuff

so mek wi soun de abeng
fi Nanny

SECTION 4

ENGAGING IN A QUARREL WITH HISTORY

In this section, writers examine Miss Lou's work as an activist who challenged the legacies of colonialism and highlighted the beauty, contradictions and extraordinariness of ordinary Jamaican life. Her work championed Jamaican culture and consistently placed it at the top, making it central rather than marginal. Nonetheless, Bennett's work was not merely blind adoration of Jamaicans or its culture, as she offers critique, interrogates and asks us to be self-reflective.

The contributions capture the many facets of Miss Lou's revolutionary zeal. She had the audacity to question the status quo at a time when society dictated that a woman's place was in the home, and in a manner that enabled the majority of Jamaicans "to get the message".

Colonization in Reverse

LOUISE BENNETT

Wat a joyful news, Miss Mattie,
I feel like me heart gwine burs'
Jamaica people colonizin
Englan in reverse.

By de hundred, by de t'ousan
From country an from town,
By de ship-load, by de plane-load
Jamaica is Englan boun.

Dem a pour out o' Jamaica,
Everybody future plan
Is fi get a big-time job
An settle in de mother lan.

What a islan! What a people!
Man an woman, old an young
Jus a pack dem bag an baggage
An tun history upside dung!

Some people don't like travel,
But fe show dem loyalty
Dem all a-open up cheap-fare-
To-England agency.

An week by week dem shippin off
Dem countryman like fire,
Fe immigrate an populate
De seat o' de Empire

Oonoo see how life is funny,
Oonoo see de tunabout?
Jamaica live fe box bread
Out a English people mout'.

For wen dem catch a Englan,
An start play dem different role,
Some will settle down to work
An some will settle fe de dole.

Jane says de dole is not too bad
Because dey payin' she
Two pounds a week fe seek a job
Dat suit her dignity.

Me say Jane will never find work
At de rate how she dah-look,
For all day she stay pon Aunt Fan couch
An read love-story book.

Wat a devilment a Englan!
Dem face war an brave de worse,
But I'm wonderin' how dem gwine stan'
Colonizin' in reverse.

"Pedestrian Crosses"

Sites of Dislocation in "Postcolonial" Jamaica*

CAROLYN COOPER

Long before the term "postcolonial" became fashionable, Jamaican literary critic and poet Edward Baugh, in his classic 1977 essay "The West Indian Writer and His Quarrel with History", stated that "[w]ith the possible exception of Wilson Harris, the writer who exhibits in his work most acutely, at an explicit, theoretical level, what I am calling the West Indian quarrel with history, is Derek Walcott".[1]

Baugh's querulous trope evokes a contentious disengagement from colonial discourses of margin and centre, periphery and metropole. Furthermore, at that time, the "West Indian writer" was immaculately conceived as male. This presumption engendered yet another quarrel with history, specifically with patriarchy.

Like the Guyanese novelist Wilson Harris and the St Lucian Nobel laureate Derek Walcott, Jamaican icon Louise Bennett engages in her own quarrel with history, most appropriately articulated in her discredited mother tongue. Upward social mobility in Jamaica requires the shedding of the old skin of early socialization: mother tongue, mother culture, mother wit, and the feminized discourse of voice, identity and native knowledge.

---

*A version of this article was first presented as a plenary lecture, Association of Cultural Studies Crossroads Conference, the University of the West Indies, Mona, Jamaica, 2008, and later published in *Inter-Asia Cultural Studies* 10, no. 1 (2009): 3–11.

1. Edward Baugh, "The West Indian Writer and His Quarrel with History", *Tapia*, 20 February 1977, 6.

Conversely, Bennett's choice of language and subject matter for her poems and dramatic monologues, which most often focus on working-class Jamaican life, privileges nativist aesthetic values rooted in the particular sociopolitical contradictions of Jamaica's colonialist history.

As an aspiring poet in the 1930s, Bennett assumed that her exclusive models were the English Romantic poets; her ambition was to "express [her] thought and whims in dulcet poetry".[2] But responsive to the explosive sounds around her, Bennett soon abandoned dulcet poetry for dialect poetry. Like her literary role model, Claude McKay, Bennett was to discover a native, dualistic, oral/scribal aesthetic, grounded in both Jamaican popular culture and her formal training in theatre. Mervyn Morris, Jamaican poet, literary critic and editor of Louise Bennett's *Selected Poems*, describes the genesis of her first dialect poem thus:

> One day she set out, a young teenager, all dressed up, for a matinee film show in Cross Roads. On the electric tramcars, which were then the basis of public transportation in Kingston, people travelling with baskets were required to sit at the back, and they were sometimes resentful of other people who, when the tram was full, tried to join them there. As Louise was boarding the tram, she heard a country woman say: "Pread out yuhself, one dress-oman a come" [Spread out yourself, a dressed-up woman is coming]. That vivid remark made a great impression on her, and on returning home, she wrote her first dialect poem "On a Tramcar" which began:
>
> Pread out yuhself de Liza,
> One Dress-oman dah look like seh
> She see di li space side-a we
> And wan foce herself een deh.[3]
>
> (Spread out yourself Liza
> A dressed-up woman looks as if
> She's seen the little bit of space between us
> And wants to force herself into it.)

2. Quoted in Mervyn Morris, introduction to *Selected Poems*, by Louise Bennet (Kingston: Sangster's), iv.

3. Ibid., iv–v.

This literal spreading out of self is an evocative metaphor for the irrepressible survival instincts of Jamaica's dispossessed who refuse to be squeezed out of existence. The amplitude of the body becomes a figure for the verbal expansiveness that is often the only weapon of the politically powerless; tracings and other forms of verbal abuse are essential armaments in class warfare. The well-dressed young woman who is not permitted to sit among the market-women, at her convenience, must know her place; she cannot violate the social space that the ostracized market women have come to claim as their own. Verbal confrontation on the public transportation system in Jamaica continues to be a popular safety valve for ventilating social frustration.

From a quite different class perspective, Louise Bennett's humorous poem "Pedestrian Crosses",[4] first published in the *Star* (16 March 1955, 7 col. 3), vividly documents the frustration of an exasperated motorist complaining vociferously about the trials of negotiating around pedestrians who are not at all familiar with the protocol of using newly established crosswalks. The pedestrian crossing, designed to enable safe passage across busy streets, becomes a site of potential misfortune for both pedestrians and motorists.

In an ironic reversal, it is the motorist, not the pedestrian, who is represented as the victim at the crossing. Indeed, the title of the poem, "Pedestrian Crosses", proves deceptive since "pedestrian" alludes to the crossing itself, not to one who is crossing.

> If a cross yuh dah-cross,
> Beg yuh cross meck me pass.
> Dem yah crossin' is crosses yuh know!
> Koo de line! Yuh no see
> Car an truck backa me?
> Hear dah hoganeer one deh dah-blow!
> Missis, walk fas' an cross!
> Pickney, cross meck me pass!
> Lady, galang an mine yuh business!
> Ole man, meck up yuh mine

4. Louise Bennett, *Jamaica Labrish* (Kingston: Sangster's, 1966), 74.

Walk between dem white line!
Wat a crosses dem crossin' yah is!

Awright, galang noh mah!
Weh yuh tan up fah sah?
Oh dem know one anada, ah se!
Dem a-meet, dem a-greet,
Dem a-kiss, wat is dis!
Dem a-tun back to-gedda, eehee!

Now me chance come at las',
As dem cross ah gwine pass,
Ah mus beat dah ole-ooman to dis!
By de hook or de crook –
Lawd, one police a-look!
"Pass on, lady, your right of way, Miss."

From de Eas' from de Wes',
Like a plague, like a pes',
Dem a-come one by one, two by two,
De crossin a-stop we from pass meck dem cross,
But nutten dah-stop dem from cross meck we pass,
Dem yah crossin is crosses fe true!

(If you're crossing,
Please cross and let me pass.
These crossings are really a cross, you know!
Just look at the line! Don't you see
All the cars and trucks behind me?
And just listen to that hoggish one blowing the horn!

Miss, walk quickly and cross!
Child, cross so that I can pass!
Lady, go along and mind your business!
Old man, make up your mind,
Walk between the white lines
What a bother these crossings are!

Alright, move along, ma'am!
Why are you standing still, sir?
Oh, they know each other, I see!

They're meeting and greeting
They're kissing, what's this!
They're turning back together, ah ha!

Now my chance has come at last,
As soon as they've crossed I'm going to pass,
I must beat that old woman to it!
By the hook or the crook –
Damn, a policeman is looking this way!
"You pass, milady; it's your right of way, Miss."

From east and west,
Like a plague, like a pest
They're coming one by one, two by two.
This crossing is stopping us from passing so that they can cross
But nothing is stopping them from crossing so that we can pass
These crossings are really and truly a cross!)

Louise Bennett destabilizes the somewhat convergent meanings of passing and crossing; to cross is to pass in opposite directions. She affixes precise class values to what is now represented as diametrically opposed trajectories: the pedestrian wishing to cross obstructs the motorist wishing to pass. In the Jamaican vernacular the compound word "cross-pass" literally means "a cross-path; a place where paths cross; a crossroads", as defined by the *Dictionary of Jamaican English*.[5] At the intersection between crossing and passing is a contestation over rights.

Appropriating Louise Bennett's witty poem, I deploy the trope "pedestrian crosses" to signify discourses in contemporary Jamaica that unsettle received wisdom about cultural politics: what is "high" and what is "low", who is powerful and who powerless. I foreground the irreverent perspective of "walk-foot" people – pedestrians – who subvert the usual power relations between themselves and motorists by claiming the right to be in the way.

The pedestrian crossing becomes a site of confrontation or, in the Jamaican vernacular, "run-jostling", where refusal to walk between the

5. F.G. Cassidy and R.B. Le Page, *Dictionary of Jamaican English*, 2nd ed. (1980; reprint, Kingston: University of the West Indies Press, 2003).

white lines, or even to walk quickly across the road, becomes an affirmation of subaltern control of the public sphere. The pedestrian crossing metamorphoses into a catwalk on which masquerades of power are grandly staged. In that moment of suspension of privilege as the motorist is forced to wait until the pedestrian casually crosses, or not, Bennett asserts the authority of power from below.

The trope "pedestrian crosses" also signifies the mundane aggravations that do accumulate and eventually explode in full-scale class war. Much to the mystification of Louise Bennett's frustrated motorist, the pedestrian's seemingly urgent business of crossing the road becomes far less important than attending to social rituals. The pedestrian crossing is thus transformed into a space for intimate socializing – "dem a kiss, what is dis" – forcing the motorist to accept his/her temporary powerlessness.

Jamaican pedestrians are notorious for ambling across roads with a studied indifference to traffic. Their manner suggests that they are daring motorists to knock them down. I, myself, have often asked careless pedestrians, "You have spare parts put down at home?" In that moment of seeming human vulnerability at the crossing, where the contest between metal and flesh would appear to be decidedly in favour of the machine, it seems that Jamaican pedestrians presume that they are divinely protected against accidents. All evidence to the contrary, they affirm an entirely unfounded faith in the goodwill of motorists.

This seemingly naïve conviction of protection at the crossing may have its genesis in a fatalistic worldview, of African origin, that is confirmed in the Jamaican proverb: "Man born fi drown cyaan heng" (If it's your fate to die by drowning, you can't die by hanging); or in this context: "Man born fi dead inna im bed can't get lick down dead by car" (If it's your fate to die in your bed, you can't be killed in a car accident). Indeed, there are no "accidents"; it is all fated.

More than half a century later, Bennett's poem remains current, as illustrated in a newspaper article by Mark Beckford.[6] Beckford reports his

6. Mark Beckford, "Motorists' Role in Protecting Children Raises Questions", *Gleaner*, 8 February 2008, D6.

conversation with a traffic warden, Joyce Thomas, stationed in downtown Kingston at a pedestrian crossing that serves three schools:

> Thomas takes up her position at the crossing in the afternoons between 1:00 p.m. and 2:30 p.m. to assist the children in making their way across the busy thoroughfare. She has been in the job for nine years and has several complaints about the behaviour of children, parents and motorists who she has to control on a daily basis. "Some children use it, some children just run across, teacher, parents and children. Most time me just stand up yah a do nuttin" (Most times I just stand here doing nothing). . . .
>
> The conversation was broken, though, as Thomas blew her whistle and raised her blue and white wooden "STOP. CHILDREN CROSSING" sign to assist a group of children across, some licking their fingers from their afternoon snacks.
>
> "Them suppose to group up, but it's hard to get them to group up because the parents don't listen and they don't listen. See there!" [They are supposed to cross in groups but it's hard to get them to cooperate because the parents don't listen and neither do they. See what I mean!], she said, as several children dashed across the street several metres below the pedestrian crossing. Thomas also blamed motorists for failing to obey instructions and said drivers of sport utility vehicles are among the most uncooperative.
>
> "When you signal them to stop they don't. They have their cars tint up and the windows wind up, and they on the cell phone. They not listening and they don't want to stop" [The car windows are tinted and wound up tight and they're on the cell phone. They don't pay any attention to me and they don't want to stop].[7]

What Thomas here underscores is the contempt in which she is held as a mere traffic warden. SUV drivers on cell phones symbolize obvious class privilege. But as Thomas exasperatedly admits, even those "walk-foot" children and parents who would not ordinarily be defined as "privileged" also violate the codes of the pedestrian crossing, thus undermining her fleeting authority. Teachers, too, themselves authority figures, disregard the traffic warden who is reduced to impotence:

7. Ibid.

"Most time me just stand up yah a do nuttin." Like a statue, the traffic warden is a symbol of petrified road codes that have lost all currency in Jamaica.

Language is a primary site of dislocation in postcolonial Jamaica, as illustrated in "Pedestrian Crosses". The Jamaican vernacular is the spontaneous heart language of the majority of the Jamaican people. Conversely, English is the language of propriety, respectability and restraint. The vivid difference between the seemingly subdued performance of my English translation of "Pedestrian Crosses" and the vibrancy of my rendition of the Jamaican original is not a theatrical device deployed to prove my point. Rather, the differences of rhythm, tone and temper articulate the way in which language actually functions in bilingual Jamaica.

The motorist in "Pedestrian Crosses", whose frustration is passionately expressed in the vernacular, strikes a dissonant note in English to sarcastically express enforced chivalry under the watchful eye of the policeman:

> Now me chance come at las',
> As dem cross ah gwine pass,
> Ah mus beat dah ole-ooman to dis!
> By de hook or de crook –
> Lawd, one police a-look!
> "Pass on, lady, your right of way, Miss."[8]

There is a world of difference between that disparaging "dah ole-ooman" (that old woman) and the excessively polite "lady". The motorist's forceful intention of beating the old woman in the contest between passing and crossing is conveyed in the Jamaicanized English idiomatic expression "by the hook or the crook", which is defined in the *Oxford English Dictionary* as "by any means, fair or foul".

But the foulness of the motorist's intention is mediated by the fair language in which right of way is ceded to "dah ole ooman", now elevated in English to the status of "lady" and youthful "Miss". In the subjugated consciousness of the motorist, English is the language of unwilling compliance to authority; Jamaican is the language of evasive abuse. The

8. Bennett, *Jamaica Labrish*, 74

ideological equivalent of the policing of the pedestrian crossing is the regimentation of language identity in Jamaica. English often becomes a cross for Jamaican speakers who have not been taught the language efficiently and struggle under the burdens of its many idiosyncrasies.

In the construct "Pedestrian Crosses", Bennett cleverly puns on "cross", both monolingually and bilingually. The English "crossing" transmutes into "cross" which the *Oxford English Dictionary* defines in a figurative sense as "[a] trial or affliction, viewed as to be borne with Christian patience". This is the same sense of the word in the Jamaican vernacular. The *Dictionary of Jamaican English* defines "cross" as "a misfortune or adversity; often in the plural". Bennett's artful, multilayered pun – crossing/cross/crosses – enacts the equal value of English and Jamaican, thus dislocating the imperial language from its pedestal of superiority.

In her dramatic monologue "Jamaica Language", Bennett argues humorously, through the persona of Aunty Roachy, that just as the pedigree of respectable languages like English is never in question, Jamaican should be recognized as a legitimate language.

> My Aunty Roachy seh dat it bwile her temper an really bex her fi true anytime she hear anybody a style we Jamaican dialec as "corruption of the English language". For if dat be de case, den dem shoulda call English language corruption of Norman French an Latin an all dem tarra language what dem seh dat English is derived from. Oonoo hear de wud? "Derived." English is a "derivation" but Jamaica Dialec is corruption! What a unfairity! We derive too![9]

> My Aunty Roachy says that it really angers her whenever she hears anyone disparaging our Jamaican dialect, dismissing it as a "corruption of the English language". For if that's the case, then they should describe the English language as a corruption of Norman French and Latin and all those other languages that they say English is derived from. You see that word? "Derived." English is a "derivation" but the Jamaican Dialect is corruption! How unfair! We are derived too!)

9. Louise Bennett, "Jamaica Language", *Yes M'Dear: Miss Lou Live* (Island Records, ICT 9740, 1983), quoted in Vivien Morris-Brown, comp., *The Jamaica Handbook of Proverbs* (Mandeville, Jamaica: Island Heart, 1993).

Louise Bennett's poems and dramatic monologues, performed in the Jamaican vernacular, lucidly articulate a politics of displacement that decidedly turns colonialist history and ontology on its head. Like Baugh's trope of the quarrel with personified history, Bennett's conception of revisionist history is derived from a body of rooted knowledge/theory that valorizes contestation as liberatory. Reverse colonization engenders a querulous reclamation of the self from historical discourses of powerlessness.

At the "cross-pass", caught between the compelling demands of motorized upward social mobility and the grounded intimacy of the kiss of greeting, Caribbean people often choose to take it easy. For proverbial wisdom warns that "foot cyaan swear fi pass" (the foot can't determine its path). Vivien Morris-Brown, compiler of the *Jamaica Handbook of Proverbs,* explicates this enigmatic proverb thus: "Do not be too quick to swear against going to some place, or doing a certain thing. Nobody knows what the future holds."[10] Here, "foot" becomes a decidedly pedestrian metaphor that encompasses even the most gas-guzzling of SUVs. For it is the authority of volition that is contested in the proverb, not the efficacy of the mode of transportation: "engine cyaan swear fi pass". The shared vulnerability of pedestrian and motorist to the indeterminacy of fate is the great social leveller.

Louise Bennett's "Pedestrian Crosses", a seemingly transparent poem written in the marginalized Jamaican vernacular, authorizes complex readings that illuminate the slippery nature of cultural politics in contemporary Jamaica. Louise Bennett takes on the crosses of the masses of the Jamaican people – the devaluation of our mother tongue and our consequent alienation from formal literary discourse. Her creation of articulate, self-confident personae who step into the crosswalk with assurance is, ultimately, a political decision. At the crossroads between oral and scribal discourse, between English and Jamaican modes of self-representation, Bennett chooses to affirm the dislocating authority of pedestrian knowledge.

10. Morris-Brown, *Jamaica Handbook*, 58.

The Truth Must Reveal Itself

KLIVE WALKER

May 30, 1954, was the wedding day of Louise Bennett and Eric Coverley in Harlem, New York City. At their reception, they posed for the photographer, acting as if they were about to cut the wedding cake. Louise appears in that image as an attractive, full-figured woman, who looked younger than her thirty-four years. Her fitted dress hugged her curves.

She didn't project what became the familiar body language of her performance alter ego. In those photographs Louise shared nothing with Miss Lou, the persona who performed her stories, recited her verses and sang the Jamaican folk songs she treasured. There were no gaping eyes. No dramatic facial gestures. No pastoral outfit.

Six weeks later she was on stage at the Village Vanguard, a New York nightclub famous for showcasing folk singers, great jazz musicians and gifted calypso singers, such as Roaring Lion from Trinidad and Harry Belafonte, the matinee idol, Broadway actor and recording artiste, born in Harlem and raised between there and Jamaica. Louise stood as if at attention on the Vanguard stage. She wore a roomy full-length skirt and a short-sleeved crew-neck blouse. The wrap around her skirt is a plaid fabric known as bandana. It blushed red with traces of white and yellow. She sang into a microphone installed on a tall stand.

At the Vanguard, she wasn't promoted as Miss Lou. She was billed as "Lady Louise Bennett of Jamaica – Famous Calypso Singer". Maybe in a moment when ska and reggae didn't yet exist, "calypso singer" was a convenient description for a mento artiste, when the world assumed all music from the English-speaking Caribbean was calypso.

UNDERSTANDING LOUISE

Is it possible to separate Louise from her Miss Lou persona? Those two very different images of her – one at her wedding reception, the other at the Vanguard – suggest it is. Distinguishing between them is a way to explore a better understanding of Louise's art and life.

Several generations of Jamaicans know about Miss Lou's prominence in their homeland's culture from the 1940s through the 1970s. They know her as a ubiquitous performance poet, griot and comedian from her radio show *Miss Lou's Views* and her television programme *Ring Ding*. Some may remember her as an actress in Kingston's popular Christmas pantomimes over the same thirty-year period. They are aware too, of her massive contribution to the use of Jamaican language as something legitimate.

What about Louise? How well do we really know *her*? She was the writer, recording artiste, folklore researcher, playwright and actress. She wrote many pantomimes. Books gathering collections of her poems and stories include *Jamaica Labrish* and *Aunty Roachy Seh*. Though her theatre work involved a significant portion of musical comedy, early in her career she featured in dramas, among them *Upheaval*, Frank Hill's story about the 1938 island-wide labour revolt, and *Deep are the Roots*, a play about race in the American South.

Her radio career first soared in the diaspora. She was a regular on BBC's *West Indian Guest Night*.[1] On New York City's WWRL, she contributed to the landmark radio show featuring an African American woman, Alma John, as host.[2] Louise was successor to Una Marson as a pioneer Caribbean woman broadcaster in England, except she extended her seminal accomplishments to both sides of the Atlantic.

That's a dizzying scope of work for any artiste, but her extensive yet varied resume doesn't end there. She became the first Jamaican singer to record popular music a few years before her nation's recording industry

1. Denise deCaires Narain, *Contemporary Caribbean Women's Poetry: Making Style* (London: Routledge, 2002), 56.

2. Mervyn Morris, *Miss Lou: Louise Bennett and Jamaican Culture* (Oxford: Signal, 2014), 19.

emerged.[3] Her recordings on London's Esquire label and New York's Folkways Records surfaced in the early 1950s. It was on Folkways that she released her debut album *Jamaican Folk Songs*.

Then there was her activism. When her homeland was still a British colony, her persistence to write and perform using the Jamaican language was revolutionary, as poet Edward Baugh confirms.[4] In Jamaica's anti-colonial movement during the first half of the last century, Louise was possibly the only recognized female icon. Her contribution to Jamaica's women's movement was significant. She became island supervisor for the Jamaica Federation of Women in 1950.[5]

Louise was more than Miss Lou and, at the same time, she was her alter ego's performance heartbeat. Louise was the serious artiste and activist.

She was born in Jamaica just over a century ago, on 7 September 1919, in the guts of the colonial era when everything African – skin colour, hair, culture, religion and language – was identified as bad, negative, sub-human, a time when Jamaicans of African heritage, like her, were subjected to escalating levels of mental slavery. Louise resisted this tsunami of brain-washing.

She said: "The thing is I never had a feeling of inferiority. . . . How can everything be bad about people? When people say: 'She have bad hair and dat one have good hair' my mother always said: 'There is no such thing as bad hair or good hair, it's just different types.' So I said to myself, the talk is not bad either."[6]

Miss Lou's performance was immersed in the folklore of kidnapped Africans and their descendants. This focus was one of the reasons she rose to prominence in her homeland as a jocular grassroots folk hero. Louise, the serious artiste, paid an enormous price as a writer whose

3. Herbie Miller, "Louise Bennett and Popular Music" (unpublished essay, n.d.).

4. Mervyn Morris, "On Reading Louise Bennett Seriously", *Jamaica Journal* 1, no. 1 (1967): 69–74.

5. Morris, *Miss Lou*, 17.

6. Lilieth Lejo Bailey, "Jamaican Writers: A Chat with Louise Bennett –1992", *Island*, 24 July 2015, https://theislandjournal.com/2015/07/24/jamaican-story-telling-a-chat-with-louise-bennett-1992/.

verse and stories on the page reflected the people's language steeped in African retention. Her published works were dismissed by Jamaica's cultural elite as secondary to those working in English. The literary journal *Focus* refused to include her narratives and poems and she was ignored by the Jamaica Poetry League.[7]

Louise explained why she was stubborn about navigating this unforgiving journey for so long: "One reason I persisted in writing in dialect, in spite of all opposition, was because nobody else was doing so and there was such rich material in the dialect. Our people – the people I keep studying and portraying, they have such a wonderful sanity and clarity in their language."[8] She adds: "My main thing is to get people to respect the language."

In Jamaica today, only English is formally recognized, but there are campaigns to establish the language of the people as official and to ensure it is taught in schools. These commendable efforts, for obvious reasons, associate closely with Louise's pioneering contributions, sometimes to the extent that it reduces her legacy to just legitimizing the language. That approach undermines her multi-faceted artistry. When she received the 1972 Norman Manley Award for Excellence, the citation read: "To separate the actress from the folk-researcher, and the poet from both, is convenient, but unreal. For in one Louise Bennett . . . the three are in perpetual interaction."[9]

Any attempt to understand her should calibrate a careful balance between her artistic craft and her promotion of the language, so that the former doesn't become secondary, or worse, get lost. Her genius resided not just in her ambition to "get people to respect the language", but in the process of how she achieved it. She used the talk as lifeblood for a variety of artistic mediums. That's how she was able to reach the widest audience and create enduring work. Louise the researcher, Louise the artiste

7. Mervyn Morris, "Remembering Miss Lou", *Caribbean Beat,* November–December 2006, https://www.caribbean-beat.com/issue-82/remembering-miss-lou#axzz618UVNhEF.

8. Renata Papke, *Poems at the Edge of Differences: Mothering in New English Poetry by Women* (Gottingen: University of Gottingen Press, 2008), 107.

9. Morris, *Miss Lou,* 31.

and Miss Lou the popular entertainer intersected in a delicate juggling act where each persona complemented the other. In reality, during the colonial era, those personas didn't exist in harmony.

There was a tension between Louise the devalued artiste-writer and Miss Lou the popular performer. That friction was tempered only by the mid-1960s when poet and scholar Mervyn Morris penned "On Reading Louise Bennett Seriously", the first positive academic appraisal of her writing.

Louise and Miss Lou differed in their artistic motivations. How could Louise be serious while Miss Lou seemed concerned with laughter and fun? This was the paradox posed to her in the late 1960s.

ANGRY

Dennis Scott, then a young local poet and playwright, interviewed Louise in Kingston, Jamaica, in 1968. He asked, "Is your work angry?"[10] She paused before answering, thinking through a response that would have been different had the question been posed twenty-five years earlier, in a hostile, colonial climate.

Louise's discussion with Scott took place in a time of Black Power, of Rastafari's increasing profile, when embracing African heritage became the natural thing for many young people to do, a time when the people's language was much less disparaged, when artistes in music, literature and theatre used this language as a way to rebel.

At the time of the interview, Louise was a middle-aged woman one year away from her fiftieth birthday. Her cautious answer reflected her stage in life and navigated two very different moments in history. She said: "Not obviously. Not obviously angry." Her response was clear. Anger was a driving force behind her work. She teased out an understanding of why people under intense oppression use fun and laughter to numb the pain of their suffering: "Most of the time that we laugh, it is so we don't weep."[11] That was why Miss Lou seemed like the opposite of angry.

10. Papke, *Poems*, 107.
11. Ibid., 106.

Miss Lou recited Louise's anger with precise comic timing through performances that were often joyful and buoyant. How can a comedian be angry? Gifted comics typically craft their jokes by mining tragic circumstances. The themes for much of Louise's poetry and stories were no different. She wrote about Rastafari being violently removed from their commune in "Pinnacle". She meditated on the life and death of outlaw Rhygin in "Dead Man". She considered independent Jamaican women in "Bans o' Woman" and was passionate in her defence of the people's language from its elite critics in "Bans o' Killing".[12]

The traditional songs she adopted as her staples are immersed in hardship, pain and even death: "Judy Drownded" discusses a woman's death by water. "Linstead Market" tells the story of a higgler stressing she is unable to attract even one person to buy her ackees. Louise wrote about the daily grind of being lower-class, poor and black and its often dire consequences. Miss Lou performed those stories, verses and songs with humour that was like the nervous laughter of someone under severe pressure.

Louise was crystal clear about her intentions. She says: "I found a medium in which I can pretend to be laughing." She was even aware some of her audience would get the joke but lose sight of the social commentary: "This is true. Many people do miss (the serious social content). They prefer to pretend that it's all in fun. And I don't mind, I go along with them. As long as I myself am sincere in what I am doing, I feel that the truth of the thing must reveal itself to the right people."[13]

AUNT JEMIMA

Miss Lou dressed in the style of noble market women. In the 1940s, this salt-of-the-earth fashion choice may have represented some kind of cultural, if not political, statement. The 1960s, when she talked to Scott, was the age of dashikis, Afros, dreadlocks and miniskirts in Jamaica. Her bandana outfit, then, morphed into something pastoral. It was something

12. Louise Bennett, *Jamaica Labrish* (Kingston: Sangster's, 1966).
13. Papke, *Poems*, 107.

existing on a spectrum ranging from folk artefact to quaint nostalgic indulgence.

There are those who claim to adore Louise but treat her work as the object of a curious sentimental past. They are seduced by the nostalgic pull of the Miss Lou character. They see Jamaican language of the colonial era as a cute and funny artefact that should be rolled out on special occasions when, in its time, it was more like the dancehall talk of the day. They seem oblivious to the idea that Jamaican language is a dynamic, living, breathing thing, adapting as it confronts social upheaval, political change and the transitions of the nation's popular music.

The dub poetry album *Woman Talk* features Louise performing "Dutty Tough", not in the mento style it was written for but in a halting somber dub approach synchronizing with the reggae rhythm percolating underneath it.[14] It's fascinating that when artistes from the generations that succeed Bennett voice her work, many of them seem unwilling to give it any kind of contemporary or updated treatment.

Others insisted Miss Lou's wholesomeness, her humour and her traditional costumes, coincided with the look, if not the core of the African American Aunt Jemima stereotype: a maid associated with defending or deferring to the racist establishment. They suggested Bennett was no revolutionary. Mervyn Morris, in his 1964 essay about taking her writing seriously, describes this attitude toward her: "By many people she is regarded more or less as a joke; a good high-spirited joke, but, in the end only a joke."[15]

In the colonial period it was the upper classes and the literary elite who demonstrated this demeaning observation of Miss Lou. The poor, the sufferers, the working people easily shared a kinship with her. Several decades later, there appeared to be a strange inversion of how she was perceived by different social classes and different generations in Jamaica. Now, the upper classes seemed to embrace a vision of her as a safe, passive, comedic Miss Lou, decked out in bandana and frozen in a time

14. Various artists, *Woman Talk: Caribbean Dub Poetry* (Vinyl LP Heartbeat Records, 1986).
15. Morris, "On Reading", 69.

warp of a distant colonial past. They separated her from her experience as overlooked writer and angry revolutionary.

Some contemporary critics with origins in the grassroots, like Ishawna and Tanya Stephens, have taken Miss Lou's bandana costume and her role as champion of the language as hollow reasons for why she should be remembered. When Stephens was challenged to go back to school to learn about Miss Lou, she issued a devastating response to her challenger and to those among Miss Lou's supporters who lead the nation's education institutions: "I don't know if Miss Lou is being taught in school here."[16]

ESSENCE

Several questions emerge from Stephens's pushback: Do we really have a collective sense of the essential factors for why Louise is such a significant cultural figure? Is it more than just her persona as a colonial-era performer, dressed in bandana promoting the Jamaican language of the day? What about her contributions as researcher, writer, playwright, actress, recording artiste?

There has only been one attempt at a biography of her. Mervyn Morris's 2014 book *Miss Lou: Louise Bennett and Jamaican Culture* is an important if concise consideration. It crafts a great framework for something that can place a magnifying glass on some important aspects of her biography which he summarizes or mentions briefly – something considering her place in Jamaica's social and cultural history and taking a deeper dive into her relationship with the diaspora. Louise, in many ways, remains a shadowy figure, a partial sketch folded neatly into her carefully crafted Miss Lou persona. Louise should be the subject of biographers and historians, in addition to English professors.

Her contributions should be observed through the lens of a sixty-year career spanning the Great Depression, the rise of Marcus Garvey, the birth of Rastafari, the gestation of the local women's movement, Jamaica's

16. Tanya Stephens's video on Instagram: "'Miss Lou Didn't Liberate Me' – Tanya Stephens", *Loop News*, 17 July 2017, https://jamaica.loopnews.com/content/video-miss-lou-didnt-liberate-me-tanya-stephens.

political independence, through to her exploits in the 1990s. It must include her impact and legacy in London and New York during the 1950s.

What about her time in Toronto? She lived in that city for twenty years. It's where she died in July 2006. Toronto was her home away from home, a place where she was still active as an artiste at least up until the 1990s. It's the city not shy about gifting her with mainstream attention and accolades: from an honorary degree awarded by York University to her appearance in a television bio-doc about her in Frances-Ann Solomon's *Miss Lou: Then and Now,* to downtown Toronto's Harbourfront Centre naming one of its three room venues Miss Lou's Room, which offers an exhibit about her.

Louise's influence on and encouragement of especially Toronto poets and playwrights of Jamaican heritage like Lillian Allen, d'bi young anitafrika, Trey Anthony and Michael St George is an indication of her interest in encouraging talent in the diaspora. Her contribution to the forging of Caribbean communities outside the region has escaped most of those attempting to document her life and work. Her significance as a Jamaican figure of the Caribbean diaspora, though not detailed here, is a crucial feature of her iconography.

UNITY

Like all meaningful, long-lasting relationships, the one between Louise and Miss Lou existed not just in tension but in unity: Her full figure matched her commanding sense of purpose in performance. Her wide-open eyes underlined a stubborn assurance and steadfast optimism. The laughter rippling through her artistry shaped the survival of a young nation's true self on its journey toward redemption. The Patwa that erupted from her mouth, on rapid, still echoes the streets of Bloomsbury, Harlem and Scarborough. Her bleak narratives glided and often soared on the wings of a seductive humour. Her defiant voice shifted easily in all its code-switching glory from the abandon of her mento Creole to her breathy proper English.

Shifting Bodies and Missing Commodities

Louise Bennett on the Impacts of World War II on Working-Class Jamaicans

DALEA BEAN

Civilian writers were key participants in the Caribbean wartime literary landscape, with many leaving behind a rich and often overlooked archive of poetry. Goldthree's assessment of the wave of poetry during and after World War I highlighted the ways in which they used literary devices as a means of "public claims-making" and how they capitalized on an active political environment.[1]

Similarly, Bean examined politically motivated poetic expressions during the post–World War II debate for women's franchise in Jamaica. The importance of poetry in this instance is summed up by Bean thus: "through poetry, women visibly forced a renegotiation of their relationship with the colonial authorities and discredited *a priori* assumptions of masculine power and privilege".[2] World Wars I and II therefore became critical contexts for the emergence of subaltern literature to express opinions, demand rights, contest ideas and solidify bonds of struggle.

Louise Bennett's wartime poetic repertoire can be comfortably situated in this rich context of wartime literature emanating from the Caribbean from soldiers and civilians alike. Her war poetry engaged in public

1. Reena Goldthree, "Writing War and Empire: Poetry, Patriotism and Public Claims-Making in the British Caribbean", in *Caribbean Military Encounters*, ed. Shalini Pury and Lara Putnam (New York: Palgrave Macmillan, 2017), 49–69.

2. Dalea Bean, *Jamaican Women and the World Wars: On the Front Lines of Change* (New York: Palgrave Macmillan, 2017), 137.

claims-making and offered a necessary renegotiation of working-class people's relationship with colonial authorities; but much more than this, they solidified Bennett as a national mouthpiece for Jamaican working class reactions to the not-so-distant international conflict. These voices were often silenced by the sensational European wartime news reports and the clamour of upper- and middle-class war work.

Scholars such as Adisa have examined Miss Lou's role as a national spokesperson and advocate for nationalist sentiments after Jamaica gained independence.[3] However, even before 1962, Bennett had humorously and thoughtfully reflected the views of the common folk. In short, "Louise Bennett was an indefatigable social commentator"[4] and she presented the war as an important affair on which Jamaicans had every right to comment. The expression of these views in nation language also separated Bennett's work from other poetry of the time, which was not only written in standard English but also used European cultural markers to explain Jamaican wartime phenomena.

For instance, in a rant against Jamaican men who refused to answer the call of Empire, *Gleaner* contributor "Chimps" (*Daily Gleaner,* 13 April 1916, 11) borrowed lines from the patriotic Scottish song *Scots Wha Hae* to illustrate the dangers of shirking masculine duties:

> Who will be a traitor knave?
> Who will fill a coward's grave?
> Who's so base as be a slave? –
> Let him turn, and flee.

Chimps condemned the unmasculine behaviour of local deceitful knaves/unscrupulous men who, as able-bodied Jamaicans, refused to respond to their country's call. In contrast, Bennett used Jamaican language and concepts to voice her opinion on men who shirked military duty in the piece "Solja Bwoys":

3. Opal Palmer Adisa, "Culture and Nationalism on the World Stage: Louise Bennett's Aunty Roachy Seh Stories", *Global South* 4, no. 2 (2010): 124.

4. Mervyn Morris, *Miss Lou: Louise Bennett and Jamaican Culture* (Kingston: Ian Randle, 2014), 78.

Mac whe meck you dah-siddung home
An nutten wrong wid yuh?
Afta yuh na baffany bwoy!
Go jine govament to!

One can imagine the embarrassment of the proverbial Mac as he is reprimanded (in his own tongue) by an authoritarian matriarch for wasting his able body at home rather than joining armed forces.

Reading Miss Lou's wartime poetry can be equated to reading the news of the day, but with a heavy dose of comedic relief. She left no stone unturned in her quest to comment on the major happenings of the war and, specifically, its impact on Jamaican life. Her publication *Jamaica Labrish* includes twenty-two poems which were originally published in local media, primarily in the *Gleaner*.[5] The poems situated Jamaica squarely in the midst of World War II and served to educate the public about the course of the war as well.

All of the poems are written in nation language, which was a deliberate act of literary subterfuge. According to Nwankwo, "writing in Patois was a political act, intended to counter what [Miss Lou] saw as an irrational and unfair devaluing of a language she saw as emblematizing and metaphorically embodying the tremendous capacity and creativity of the Jamaican people".[6]

I will unpack two themes from seven of Miss Lou's poems: (1) the war's impact on access to commodities, and (2) trends in employment and migration. These themes were undergirded by Bennett's treatment of the "isms": racism, colourism, sexism and classism in the wartime colonial milieu. The poems reviewed from *Jamaica Labrish* include "War-Time Grocery", "Rice Gawn", "Soap Vacation", "Recruit", "Tan a Yuh Yard", "Solja Bwoys" and "De ATS".

5. Louise Bennett, *Jamaica Labrish*, with notes and introduction by Rex Nettleford (Kingston: Sangster's, 2005).

6. Ifeoma Kiddoe Nwankwo, "The International Engagements of Working-Class Jamaican Women: Listening to Louise Bennett and Her Routes Women", *Meridians: Feminism, Race, Transnationalism* 15, no. 2 (2017): 416.

"RICE GAWN": THE WAR'S IMPACT ON ACCESS TO COMMODITIES

During World Wars I and II it was clear that subjects of warring nations far from the trenches, hostile seas and invaded airspaces were not excluded from the deleterious effects of modern warfare. While Panikar[7] and others have dubbed the wars as "civil wars with the European community of nations" rather than world wars, the position of the belligerent nations as imperialists meant that the fate of the world was inextricably linked to the course and outcome of the conflicts.

Jamaica reeled from deficiencies in imported foodstuffs as authorities imposed quota restrictions on imports and as trade ships gave way to battleships. The shortages severely affected the price of basic goods. Wheat, rice and flour were in short supply. Bennett's poem "Rice Gawn" humorously gave persona and agency to the staple, blaming the price control authorities for tampering with the prices to control the purchase of the precious commodity and causing rice to disappear. An excerpt reads

> Authority control all price,
> Dem teck off an put awn;
> Authority go fas' wid Rice
> An Rice get bex and gawn!
> Rice sey, sence dem confine her, sence
> Dem put her eena cage,
> Sense dem low rate her prestige,
> She noh want no patronage.

Bennett goes further to ask curry goat, stew beef, and other meats which are traditionally paired with rice what they will do without their trusted partner, subtly hinting that other indigenous staples will have to replace the foreign delight. In "Soap Vacation", the shortage of imported washing soap is lamented as clean clothes became the newest casualty of war and Bennett more explicitly considers home-grown options to launder clothes. She explains:

7. Quoted in Melvin Page, "Introduction: Black Men in a White Men's War", in *Africa and the First World War*, ed. Melvin Page (London: Macmillan, 1987), 1.

Ackee-skin and ashes is me
Dutty clothes dem only hope
For me hear Pooto dah tell Jane
Sey dem meck good washin-soap.

The poem does not end with much hope for these alternatives but speaks to the resilience of Jamaican women who will stop at nothing to ensure that their families' clothes are kept clean.

A constant thread in Bennett's work is the extent to which she wove a tapestry of policy and implications on the common Jamaican. Her extensive and deep understanding of the strategic moves of the pricing authorities did not hamper her ability to creatively explain the implications of the disappearance of rice or soap on Jamaican households. In so doing, Bennett not only educated the populace about the inner workings of colonial economic policy but offered laughter as a coping mechanism for the hardship and uncertainty that the war produced.

Her own preference for rice in her meals is also made clear in the work when she made a plea to the authorities to bring back rice, signalling her commonality with readers who longed for rice to return to the shelves. She also joined with her characters in lamenting the loss of cleaning agents. In so doing, Bennett used poetry to cement bonds of hardship and struggle among all Jamaicans and branded herself as part of those besieged by wartime constraints. Reading these pieces also offers a peek behind news as reported in print media of the day, which often focused on macroeconomics and on strategic wartime decisions. Bennett's poetry tapped into the micro-realities of everyday people and therefore offers ethnographic evidence of hardship and modes of survival.

Importantly, the shortages of foodstuff heightened racial tensions as Chinese shop owners were accused of profiteering and adding additional hardship to black working-class patrons. Indeed, in the aftermath of World War I and in 1938, prior to the outbreak of World War II, anti-Chinese riots occurred as a result of the perception that shopkeepers were exaggerating the prices of staples for their financial gain.[8]

8. Howard Johnson, "The Anti-Chinese Riots of 1918 in Jamaica", *Caribbean Quarterly* 28, no. 3 (1982): 19–32.

So despised were the Chinese during World War I that the Parochial Board of St Ann noted on 4 October 1917 that the Chinese "are the cause of many bankruptcies, vagrants and paupers".[9] There is no doubt that Bennett was influenced by these prevailing anti-Chinese sentiments. She castigated the Chinese shopkeepers (or "Queeze-Y'eye" as she calls them in "War-Time Grocery") for various misdeeds in retail trade including pairing commodities in demand with those that were hard to sell:

Cornmeal an flour dem married,
Sal'-pork and mackerel to,
Ef dats de way dem gwine carry on
Wha poor people dah go do?
An nutten hu't me, all dem do,
Dem don't even know shame,
Anytime you call dem dung bout it,
Is poor war get de blame.

Ironically, while Bennett's treatment of Chinese shopkeepers in this piece is racism-adjacent, she boldly decried the classism that many shop owners practised by giving special concessions to middle-class patrons who gave them steady and reliable business. As she expressed:

Queeze-Y'eye ooden sell me one small tin
O' "School-Bwoy" dis mornin,
An lickle after Miss Pam servant
Go buy bout four big tin!

The fact that Miss Pam was able to send her servant placed her above the working-class patrons among whom Bennett identified. In her estimation, the Chinese were obviously refusing to sell to some in order to afford others small luxuries.

Bennett therefore engaged in multiple layers of commentary as she made an appeal for the poor of the country who were not merely facing wartime hardship but a specifically Chinese-induced burden. She discarded political correctness and favoured representation of the black

9. Victor Chang, "Lessons from the Past: Chinese-Jamaican Relations" (lecture delivered at the Chinese Benevolent Association, 2017).

working-class sentiment over "rogue" shopkeepers who many believed held the public to ransom. Interestingly, this poem is punctuated by frustration over the profiteering by shopkeepers rather than the usual humour which graced other wartime pieces. Her anger is evident from the first line ("Ah bex so tell ah kean talk!") and does not wane through the piece, suggesting that anger was as important as humour in pieces that lobbied for social justice and equitable treatment.

"RECRUIT": TRENDS IN WARTIME EMPLOYMENT

Maas Joseph tun-foot nephew,
Aunt Jane twis-mout Uriah
Miss Tamachigarookoo son,
Dah-goh a 'Merica!

Bennett wrote about the movement of commodities and had much to say about the journeys of bodies in service to the war effort as well. Many of her wartime poems excavated the issues of wartime oversees employment for ordinary Jamaicans (as the excerpt from "Recruit" illustrates), the transformation of some from civilian to soldier, and the elevated status afforded to ordinary Jamaicans through their service and movement overseas.

Notably, however, Bennett's commentary on Jamaican service to the war effort, particularly to the United States after they entered the war in 1941, often mocked the men who were catapulted into soldiering, many of whom were not ideal candidates. She levelled critique at sexist policies which recruited socially debilitated men over women, noting in "Recruit":

De man dem dah-get all the break
De worl' noh lebel mah,
Ebery lickle boogooyagga bwoy
Dah-goh a 'Merica!

Bennett was keenly aware that the war created opportunities for employment, adventure, travel and other "betterments" from which women were routinely sidelined. Undoubtedly, gender discrimination was evident in wartime labour polices and recruitment drives. Men were favoured over women for wartime employment. As Bean indicates, even in cases where women were able to secure local wartime employment, wage disparity between men and women was great.[10] Bennett loathed such gender injustice, a stance that positioned her among the nation's proto-feminists[11] of the 1940s and 1950s. She made little effort to separate the soldiering and civilian opportunities in her poetry, uniting both under the canopy of spaces from which women were missing. As she expressed:

It bex me fe see how de man
Dem dah-get whe soh quick
And it teck soh long fe sen weh
Po' ooman as domestic
We gal did tink it was a war
Of a break we gwine get
We fix up fe action, but not
A gun noh fire yet

Bennett was evidently following closely the stirrings in the early 1940s about implementing a scheme for wartime domestic work for Jamaican women. In the United States, there was a marked shortage of domestic workers and it was estimated that up to twenty-five thousand Jamaican women could be used to fill the gap left by American women engaged in war-related jobs. This notion was supported by various bodies, including the Jamaica Chamber of Commerce and the newly formed quasi-capitalist political party, the Jamaica Democratic Party.[12]

Perhaps the most vibrant supporter of the wartime migration of Jamaican women was Amy Ashwood-Garvey. As president of the short-lived,

10. Bean, *Jamaican Women.*

11. Proto-feminism is a term used to describe those who exhibited a feminist perspective and agenda prior to the coining of feminism as a philosophical position in the Western world in the 1960s.

12. The Jamaica Democratic Party was an upper-middle-stratum political party which strove for an ideological middle ground between socialism and capitalism which characterized the People's National Party and Jamaica Labour Party respectively. The party supported universal suffrage, a bicameral legislature and an executive committee as proposed by the Legislative Council majority. Colin Palmer, *Freedom's Children: The 1938 Labor Rebellion and the Birth of Modern Jamaica* (Chapel Hill: University of North Carolina Press, 2014).

but ideologically forward-thinking Jag Smith Party, which was launched in 1943, Ashwood-Garvey was among the major challengers of the male-oriented bias in wartime labour recruitment and was a staunch supporter of the scheme to recruit female domestic workers to the United States.

Bennett's clever wartime symbolism of the proverbial gun not firing to let women have a chance at domestic work schemes served as not only a historical record of the discrimination but a call to action on the part of officials in real time. Indeed, she ended the poem with faith that "ooman day wi come at las". While women's day did come through service to the British Army, mainly in the Auxiliary Territorial Service, the scheme to employ civilian women as domestic workers remained a pipe dream of Ashwood-Garvey and Bennett alike.

J. Edgar Hoover, then director of the Federal Bureau of Investigation, was disturbed by Ashwood-Garvey's plans as he surmised that any success in importing Jamaican workers would have bolstered the influence of the Universal Negro Improvement Association on blacks in the hemisphere.[13] His interference killed the plans. Locally, the People's National Party cautioned women against running into a scheme which would possibly result in them facing racism and other atrocities in American homes. Amy Jacques-Garvey, Marcus Garvey's second wife, was also wary of Ashwood-Garvey's "latest racket . . . to take domestics servants' money, letting them believe that she can influence legislation in America to admit thousands of them in the USA".[14]

Jamaican women's historical entry into the British Army through the Auxiliary Territorial Service (ATS) was also of interest to Bennett. This is evident in her piece "De ATS". Over the course of World War II, over six hundred Caribbean women served in the British Army in England, Canada, Washington, DC, and in their respective island homes. Trained as soldiers, these women epitomized the bonds of Empire and challenged gendered colonial paradigms of military service. Bennett's piece focused very little on the impressive development of women being allowed to

13. Fitzroy Baptiste, *War, Cooperation, and Conflict: The European Possessions in the Caribbean, 1939–1945* (New York: Greenwood, 1988), 24.

14. Tony Martin, *Amy Ashwood Garvey: Pan-Africanist, Feminist and Mrs Garvey No. 1, or A Tale of Two Amies* (Dover, MA: Majority Press, 2007), 174.

serve in armed forces, however. Instead she comically and mockingly highlighted that joining the ATS was a means to an end of snagging a foreign husband.

> But you know de right reason why
> Me want go to Englan?
> Ah tink is time a sekle dung
> An get a good husband.
> Soh me wi help de war, an ef
> De war shoulda help me
> Fe get married, me husband can
> Gwan fight fe him country.

Bennett's impersonation of a typical member of ATS is mainly comical and not supported by first-hand accounts of their reasons for joining the war effort, which included gaining exposure and adventure, and acquiring educational and employment opportunities.[15] However, Bennett's interpretation is perhaps evidence of the lack of seriousness that was accorded to ATS women's actual role in the war as a result of their gender.

While Bennett's work on male soldiers highlighted the dangers of battle and the joy of bravery, her thoughts on female soldiers highlighted the prestige of marriage and presented women as opportunists who were on a personal mission rather than being the empire's saviours.

Shifts in gender roles manifested by the wars were also evident in Bennett's poetic commentaries. In the piece "Solja Bwoys", Bennett embodies the persona of the influential woman tasked with encouraging men to offer their bodies to Empire:

> Me never want yuh fe go weh
> Me never want yuh loss;
> But me conscience a-bite me, as
> De Solja dem a pass.

Bennett's sentiments mirrored the local movement during World War I to conscript women to enlist men for service. Women featured prominently in the leadership of recruitment drives as "the war era did facilitate

15. Bean, *Jamaican Women.*

the expansion of elite women's civic roles and working-class women's value to the colonial order as intermediaries between men's bodies and the Empire's needs".[16] Numerous appeals were made to women of the working class to encourage their able-bodied men folk to be recruits for the Jamaican contingent. Women were portrayed as all powerful in this regard. The *Gleaner* editorial (17 May 1917, 8) explained: "The women of Jamaica can make their husbands, their brothers, their fathers, their lovers, do almost anything they please. They can shame the men into greater patriotic activity."

Such positioning of women continued during World War II, with women once again being entrusted with seeing to the Empire's need for soldiers from the colonies. Bennett's poem can be compared with an extract from Rose DeLisser's 1915 poem, "An Appeal" (*Daily Gleaner*, 26 October 1915), which noted:

An appeal from the Throne! Ah, you women,
Be strong in the hour of strife;
Never hinder your men that are willing
To stake all for honour and life
It is better to know they are fighting,
For that which is dearest and best
Than to see them home playing the coward,
In a languorous ease and rest

Both DeLisser's and Bennett's pieces have verses which shamed men into serving while conferring dignity on a militarized woman who encouraged her man to serve. However, Bennett's imagination went further than DeLisser's through the use of nation language and Jamaican worldviews. She reminded any man fearing death and injury (and by extension any woman that harboured similar trepidations) that no harm could come to him if that was not the way he should die:

Noh fraid fe bum or poison gas,
Noh fraid fe sword or knife,
Ef yuh fe dead wid coco-bey
Gun-shot kean tek yuh life.

16. Ibid., 88.

In Miss Lou's post-independence writings and performances, Aunty Roachy emerged as an alter ego and medium through which she steered her Jamaican audience through the minefield of being African descended people in an English dominated cultural milieu. As Adisa points out, she functioned as a prophet and guide to the nation.[17]

While Aunty Roachy did not feature in Bennett's wartime poetry, her role as a guide is evident from the early 1940s. Bennett was versed in the details of the war and was deliberate in what she chose to highlight to educate the populace. She was also not timid to change her mind about current affairs. In "Tan a Yuh Yard" Bennett clearly expressed her analysis of the poor conditions of farm workers in the United States during the war. She urged Jamaicans to avoid the scheme, despite her earlier belief that such schemes were golden opportunities for working-class Jamaicans, as is evident in "Recruit". She warned:

Win yuh mine offa foreign lan'
Koo how some o' de man dem
Run back come home like foreigner
Did set dem bad dog pon dem!

De same sinting wey sweet man mout
Wi meck him lose him head,
Me read eena newspapa sey
Two farm-man meet dem dead!

Close to fifty thousand men were employed in this scheme between 1943 and 1945, but reports of low wages, poor working conditions, racism and untimely deaths under various tragic circumstances were often carried by the *Daily Gleaner*. Bennett used her platform to remind locals that all that glittered overseas was not gold, as a counter-narrative to prevailing views that "going to foreign" was the only way to build a meaningful life. She was keen on nation building and implored Jamaicans to "Lef 'Merica Alone" with all its indignities meted out to the black worker.

17. Adisa, "Culture and Nationalism", 127.

CLOSING REMARKS

Through comedy, irony and satire, Bennett's pieces weaved a tapestry of the hardship of working-class Jamaicans during the conflict and examined the ways in which these bodies capitalized on wartime opportunities to better themselves and their families. While doing so, she undertook racial and gender analysis and constantly reminded her audience that World War II collided with colonial rule, racism, sexism and classism to create multiple jeopardies for black Jamaicans.

However, she also invited her readers to laugh; not merely to make light of many serious issues, but to survive the war's multifaceted effects. As Nettleford reminds us in his introduction to Bennett's *Jamaica Labrish*: "an uprooted poor but proud people are primarily concerned about surviving, having found themselves alive".[18] Bennett was nothing if not proud and invited her people to react to the war with pride as well, in order to survive its tight grip on their bodies, bellies and consciousness.

18. Rex Nettleford, introduction to *Jamaica Labrish*, by Louise Bennet (Kingston: Sangster's, 2005), 22.

Miss Lou

Organic Intellectual of the Jamaican Masses in Her Examination of Racial Politics

AJAMU NANGWAYA

Louise Bennett-Coverley, affectionately called Miss Lou, was a cultural worker and organic intellectual who sided with the African Jamaican labouring classes. As such, it was inevitable that her poems addressed the matter of racism or white supremacy and its manifestations in the lives of the African majority in Jamaica. It could be argued that race and class served as the backdrop to her commentary on the lives of the wretched of the earth, even when she was not explicitly examining race, colour and/or racism. The preceding assertion is so because racism as a system of oppression mediates, in part, the experiences of African Jamaicans.

MISS LOU AS AN ORGANIC INTELLECTUAL

Miss Lou's embrace, articulation and promotion of the culture and language of the African labouring classes in Jamaica placed her in the ranks of Antonio Gramsci's "organic intellectual" category as a member in good standing. In Edward Said's words: "Gramsci saw [organic intellectuals] as directly connected to classes or enterprises that used intellectuals to organize interests, gain more power, get more control."[1] The organic intellectual might serve the oppressive forces, for example, the capitalist class, or she may advance the interests of the working class or other oppressed groups.

1. Edward Said, *Representations of the Intellectual: New York* (Vintage Books, 1996), 4.

In the Gramscian sense of the intellectual, Miss Lou fulfilled that function in society because she was "connected either with the production or distribution of knowledge".[2] I have a strong preference for Gramsci's conceptual approach to the person who serves as an intellectual because it is grounded in the social function that one carries out in society. One is not necessarily an intellectual on account of being certified by a university.

An instructive and revealing aspect of Miss Lou's role as an organic intellectual for the African Jamaican sufferers is the fact that she had a choice of staying loyal to the petit bourgeoisie and serving as a gladiator for the capitalist political and economic elite. The reward for conforming to class expectations can be seductive: "The system will give you a nice house, a front lawn, a car, a reasonable bank balance. They will say, 'Sell your black soul.' That is the condition upon which you exist as a so-called intellectual."[3]

However, she rejected the implicit entreaty to serve the interests of the local African and coloured petit bourgeois elements who were being apprenticed into the art of neocolonialism under the rubric of internal self-government. Miss Lou's action foreshadowed the exhortation of Frantz Fanon in encouraging the racialized national middle class in the Global South to use the knowledge and skills gained in colonial institutions of higher learning for the liberation of the people.[4]

Additionally, Miss Lou's action was in alignment with the Guinea-Bissau nationalist leader Amilcar Cabral's call for the *revolutionary* petit bourgeoisie to commit class suicide by rejecting its class aspirations, developing a greater degree of revolutionary consciousness and becoming one with the masses.[5] Ian Boyne, late journalist and public intellectual, wrote a thoughtful assessment of Miss Lou's national contribution and revealed her preferential option for the oppressed: "She accepted our language, our stories, our ways of seeing the world, the indigenous forms of our culture, when 'polite society' deemed them scornful and inferior. She

2. Ibid., 9.

3. Walter Rodney, *The Groundings with My Brothers* (reprint; Chicago: Research Associates School Times Publications, 1990), 62.

4. Frantz Fanon, *The Wretched of the Earth* (New York: Grove, 1961), 150.

5 Amilcar Cabral, *Revolution in Guinea: Selected Texts* (New York: Monthly Review Press, 1969).

never craved authentication and validation from the middle and upper classes. She stood her ground, nurtured in excellence in all she did and the middle and upper classes had to 'bow' to her and rise to her heights."[6]

Miss Lou's body of work, as reflected in the theatre, oral presentations, community development work, publications, radio, television and writings, highlights a cultural worker who functioned as an organic intellectual, faithfully serving the needs of the African Jamaican masses. As someone who spoke truth to power, Miss Lou held up a mirror to Fanon's "wretched of the earth" in order to encourage them to transform their ideas and behaviours to advance the struggle for social transformation. It should not be surprising to anyone that many of the social issues that were tackled by this cultural worker and organic intellectual are still with us. It could not be any other way, since the Jamaican labouring classes are still confronted with anti-African racism, patriarchy, class exploitation, neocolonialism and imperialism.

By highlighting and analysing a selection of her poems and a monologue, we will see the extent to which Bennett used the proverbial bully pulpit to draw the people's attention to topical and relevant issues, affirm her role as an organic intellectual and attempt to raise the people's political and social awareness.

EXPLORING RACE, THE COLOUR LINE AND A CRITIQUE OF WHITENESS

Race is a social construct deployed by racially dominant groups to serve goals that perpetuate their power and influence. Despite race being a social fiction, it has affected the racially marginalized for five centuries of European global domination. Race and racism were used as ideological tools during slavery to mask and justify the economic reasons behind the extraction of labour power from enslaved Africans to further the interests of the capitalist class in Europe and the Americas.[7]

6. Ian Boyne, "The One and Only Miss Lou: True and Still Unspoilt Icon", *Gleaner*, 3 August 2003 (available at http://louisebennett.com/wp-content/uploads/Miss-Lou-97.pdf).

7. Rodney, *Groundings*, 25; Eric Williams, *Capitalism and Slavery* (London: Andre Deutsch, 1964), 7, 18–29.

The racialization of Africans as morally, intellectually, socially and religiously inferior, and the attendant assigning them a degrading status in society, constructed the illusion of a self-evident truth. This racialization accompanied Africans into the Emancipation period and the present neocolonial era, with some modifications based on class status. As an organic intellectual, for Miss Lou, racial questions would have had to be a topic of reflection and intervention.

The issue of internalized racism and intra-African conflict over colour differences are interrogated in her poem "Colour Bar":[8]

Sir Lyle eena House o' Commons
Dah-talk bout "colour-bar"
But right eena Jamaica we
Dah-have big "colour-war".

Po' Sir Lyle hooda shock fe know
Dat de colour fight dung yah
Is not wid black and w'ite, but wid
Red nayga and black nayga.

Some o' de red-kin nayga feel
Soh bex dat dem noh w'ite
Dat dem start fe cuss black nayga,
An soh dem ketch a fight.

The poet and organic intellectual demonstrates her awareness and knowledge of the manifestation of the anti-racism discourse in imperialist Britain, and the added layer of white supremacy in the colonial outpost of Jamaica. Racism was the order of the day against African Caribbean immigrants by white British civil society and the state, despite the former being there to help with the post–World War II reconstruction of the country. It was a "black and w'ite" racial conflict in Britain, but to the astonishment of the poem's narrator, the "colour-war" was between "Red nayga and black nayga" in Jamaica.

We are looking at a situation of internalized racism wherein the lighter-skinned Africans believed that the visible presence of some level of white

8. Louise Bennett, *Jamaica Labrish* (Kingston: Sangster's, 2005), 282.

genetic inheritance elevated them to near-white status. However, from the perspective of the narrator, the racially deluded person is simply a light-skinned African person (red nayga) and not even a "Jamaican white" such as the Lebanese/Syrian.

Miss Lou also addresses the subject of a character using the social resources accorded to whiteness to negotiate her way in white supremacist United States in the poem "Pass fi White".[9] The main character is racially categorized thus: "Her family is nayga, but / But dem pedigree is right." Despite her racial classification in Jamaica as an African person, the young woman was in the centre of world imperialism passing as a white person:

> Miss Jane jus hear from Merica –
> Her daughter proudly write
> Fi seh she fail her exam, but
> She passing dere fi white!
> She seh fi tell de trute she know
> Her brain part not so bright –
> She couldn't pass tru college
> So she try pass fi white.
> She passing wid her work-mate-dem,
> She passing wid her boss,
> An a nice white bwoy she love dah gwan
> Wid her like she pass!

The young woman might not be an intellectual giant in the classroom but the valued commodity of whiteness allows her access to employment opportunity, the social capital that comes from being networked with white workplace colleagues and supervisors and neighbours, and a boyfriend whose resources might lift her out of working-class status. By passing "fi white", Miss Lou had the main character demonstrating that a racist and patriarchal society is not truly committed to education and hard work as a passport to the destination of a better life.

Miss Lou was critiquing the meritocracy of liberal capitalist society that trumpets hard work but allows race, class and gender constructs to

9. Louise Bennett, *Selected Poems* (Kingston: Sangster's, 2005), 113.

determine the extent to which some groups can move forward based on achievement criteria. Ascriptive measurements also rule in a society that is guided by the colour bar.

Miss Lou exposed the absurdity of global white supremacy and the socially constructed nature of race when a "nayga" young woman from Jamaica can pass as white in the United States. The ridiculousness and fiction of race were exposed by the poet when the young woman's father's experience with Jim Crow was shared:

De gal puppa dah laugh and seh
It serve Merica right –
Five year back dem Jim-Crow him, now
Dem pass him pickney white.

The father was declared a racial Other while his daughter was embraced as an embodiment of whiteness. Unfortunately, the father holds this turn of events as a matter of pride:

Him dah boas all bout de district
How him daughter is fus-class
How she smarter dan American
An over deh dah pass!

Well, she is not only passing for white, but she has herself a white partner to demonstrate the "success" of her integration into the benefits of whiteness.

In the poem "Soldier Work",[10] Miss Lou humorously and insightfully examined and critiqued the attraction that dark-skinned and light-skinned Africans have to whiteness when it comes to dating and mating. The poet bemoaned the fact that

Jamaica man out a power
Doah Government gidem raise –
Dem no got no gal fi spen it pon
For soldier is de craze.

10. Bennett, *Selected Poems*, 107.

Nayga man haffi look out fi
Gal a dem own colour
For all de brown-skin lef dem out
An gawn to white soldier.

The poet seems to be synonymously equating "Jamaica man" with dark-skinned "nayga man" and, as such, she is informing the readers that, in spite of these men experiencing a financial windfall from an increase in their wages, they cannot find the desired "brown-skin" women to wine and dine. These lighter-skinned African women are now in the arms of white soldiers stationed in Jamaica during World War II. The "brown-skin" women settled for the "nayga man" with money in the absence of racially preferred pickings. The organic intellectual is telling us about the plight of the dark-skinned woman who is at the bottom of the pecking order when it comes to desirability as the ultimate choice as mate by African Jamaican and white men. African men are seemingly left with the Hobson's choice of "gal of dem own colour".

RACE, RASTAFARI AND REPATRIATION

The organic intellectual of the masses will often be called upon to intervene in topical issues and to raise questions about the soundness of positions taken by the masses as a whole. Miss Lou presented characters in the poems "Back to Africa" and "Deares' Chief" that might have some pan-Africanists or Rastafari wondering about her progressiveness on the race question. In these two poems, the characters question the political direction of the desire to repatriate to Africa on the part of some African Jamaicans who were disillusioned by race and class oppression.

The repatriation of diaspora Africans in the Americas to the ancestral land of Africa has been a cardinal principle of Rastafari since its inception in the early 1930s.[11] Emperor Haile Selassie's coronation on 2 November 1930 was read by many African Jamaicans from the working class as the sign of the kingly redeemer who was supposedly prophesied by the

11. George Eaton Simpson, "The Ras Tafari Movement in Jamaica: A Study of Race and Class Conflict", *Social Force* 4, no. 2 (1955): 167–71.

pan-Africanist Marcus Garvey. In "Deares' Chief",[12] a poem addressed to Alexander Bustamante, Miss Lou captured the noticeable enthusiasm in Kingston for repatriation among sections of the labouring classes:

Deares' Chief, prepare yuh tempa,
Serious tings a-happen yah
Yuh falleras dah-lef yuh out
Fe Back-to-Africa!
Rememba how dem sing and shout an
Rave bout yuh? Well see yah sah
Is the same way dem dah-gwan over
De "back-to-Africa!"
Jus like how dem jump an halla
When yuh shout and weel yuh head,
Jus like yuh magnet powah
Back to Africa dah spread.

Alexander Bustamante was affectionately called "Chief" by the members of the African Jamaican working class. In the eyes of the masses, the "Chief" was a white man, and this conservative, pro-imperialist character peddled a biographical narrative that placed his lineage in whiteness.[13] Yet despite the internalized racism of many Africans in Jamaica, and Britain's concession of universal suffrage and internal self-government in 1944, this repatriation movement generated a high level of resonance and excitement. Miss Lou might be revealing here that the material conditions and the race consciousness of the people were such that the "magnet powah [of the] Back-to-Africa dah spread".

Yet Miss Lou may have reflected her own and the people's ambivalence or reservation about repatriation when she wrote:

Till Maas Sam get bex an start fe cuss dem
Ungrateful and tief,
Sey deem shouldn' rave and gwan so

12. Louise Bennett, *Aunty Roachy Seh* (Kingston: Sangster's, 2005), 195.

13. George E. Eaton, *Alexander Bustamante and Modern Jamaica* (Kingston: LMH Publishing, 1995), 53–55; Colin A. Palmer, *Freedom's Children: The 1938 Labour Rebellion and the Birth of Modern Jamaica* (Kingston: Ian Randle, 2014), 44–46.

Over nutten else but Chief
Janey sey ef we ever follow dem
Back-to-Africa fool,
Be de time po' Chief tun ruler,
Him woan got a soul fe rule!

The uncertainty around repatriation is a bit more pronounced in the poem "Back to Africa":[14]

Back to Africa, Miss Mattie?
Yuh no know what yuh dah seh?
Yuh haffi come from somewhere fus
Before yuh go back deh!

This later stanza seems to capture where Rastafari thought, if not action, is located today on the actual status of repatriation:

Ef a hard time yuh da run from
Tek yuh chance! But Mattie, do,
Sure a whey yuh come from so yuh got
Somewhere fi come back to.
(116)

The last two lines in the above stanza offer pragmatic advice to Rastafari to make the place that they are currently located liveable in order to have "Somewhere fi come back to". Miss Lou, in her capacity as a producer and disseminator of ideas, communicated a message to Rastafari about twenty years before a similar one that was allegedly said directly to Rastas in April 1966 by the late Emperor Haile Selassie: "Liberation before immigration/[repatriation]."[15]

Some people might still read Miss Lou's pronouncements on repatriation as racially problematic but when they become aware of the "divine" injunction by Haile Selassie about "liberation before repatriation", they would appreciate this organic intellectual's prophetic judgement on this matter. How many of the financially successful Rastafari reggae artistes and petit

14. Bennett, *Jamaica Labrish*, 115.
15. Leonard Barrett, *The Rastafarians: Sounds of Cultural Dissonance*, rev. ed. (Boston: Beacon, 1988), 160.

bourgeois professionals have self-repatriated to Ethiopia or Africa from the African diaspora? Not many of these economically privileged Rastas.

Miss Lou had a strong appreciation of African retentions in the African Jamaican national culture, as demonstrated in her contribution as a cultural worker. Her doubt about the wisdom of mass repatriation did not come from a colonized, anti-African outlook. As a thinker using poetry to engage in consciousness-raising, mass repatriation from Jamaica would be disruptive and unrealistic, as articulated in "Back to Africa":[16]

> What a debil of a bump-an-bore,
> Rig-jig and palam-pam
> Ef de whole worl start fi go back
> Whe dem great granpa come from.

How would materially poor African societies have accommodated so many unskilled and economically marginalized returnees without it being a social disaster? It would essentially have been the manifestation of Miss Lou's feared "debil of bump-an-bore / Rig-jig and palam-pam" – social dislocation on a gigantic scale. Eric Doumerc frames the preceding predicament thus: "In this poem, Miss Lou takes the common sense view that if everybody in Jamaica or Europe went back where their ancestors were from, utter shambles would follow."[17]

There is an additional factor that likely informed Miss Lou's outlook on mass repatriation. Her racial politics probably embraced an indigenization of the African presence in Jamaica, so there were no compelling reasons to repatriate, in spite of the "great resemblance", racially speaking,[18] between Miss Mattie and continental Africans. By declaring that Miss Mattie's "whole generation, / Oonoo all bawn dung a Bun Grung" suggested the African Jamaicans' indigenization of the cultural and territorial space that is Jamaica. In other words, the sweat, blood, tears and labour of Africans in Jamaica that built and transformed this land earned them the right to permanently hold it as home.

16. Bennett, *Jamaica Labrish*, 110.
17. Eric Doumerc, "Louise Bennett and the Mento Tradition", *ARIEL: A Review of International English Literature* 31, no. 4 (2000): 26.
18. Bennett, *Selected Poems*, 115.

CONCLUDING THOUGHTS

Many people who read or hear Miss Lou's poems, monologues, or stories might not view her as functioning in the capacity of an intellectual producing and disseminating ideas. Miss Lou was and is seen as an entertainer by many people because of her intentional and excellent ability to make us laugh at the tragedy of living in an environment dominated by social alienation.[19]

The integration of humour in Miss Lou's cultural and intellectual work enables people to laugh at the seriousness of the racial, class, gender and other topical issues that informed her poems and monologues. This capacity to "tek serious tings mek joke" is very evident among the African labouring classes in Jamaica and it is probably a survival tactic of other people who live under oppressive conditions. Instead of humour distracting from Miss Lou's place as an organic intellectual, it should be seen as a fundamental element of her work in the production and dissemination of ideas and the receptivity of her audience to the political and social messages within her poems, stories and monologues.

Many people do not see Miss Lou as a race-conscious woman as they would fellow cultural workers such as Peter Tosh, Judy Mowatt and Bob Marley. In her monologue "Jamaica Philosophy", Miss Lou expounded on the capacity of Jamaican proverbs to reflect philosophical profundity in their simplicity.[20] "Jamaica Philosophy" critiqued the racist view that the ideas in African Jamaicans' proverbs "cannot be expected to extend to abstract and metaphysical subjects" as asserted by James Stewart in 1823 in his book *A View of the Past and Present State of Jamaica.*[21]

A central part of Miss Lou's mission as an organic intellectual was the legitimation and affirmation of the intellectual autonomy of the folk philosophy of the African Jamaican masses. This organic intellectual was

19. Doumerc, "Louise Bennett", 27.
20. Louise Bennett, *Aunty Roachy Seh* (Kingston: Sangster's, 2005), 7–9.
21. Cited in Roger D. Abrahams and John F. Szwed, *After Africa: Extracts from British Travel Accounts and Journals of the Seventeenth, Eighteenth, and Nineteenth Centuries Concerning the Slaves, Their Manners, and Customs in the British West Indies* (New Haven, CT: Yale University Press, 1983), 105.

a race-conscious woman and her treatment of African Jamaican proverbs as instruments of philosophical discourse was an excellently executed response to the racist diatribe of James Stewart.

Race mattered for Miss Lou and it is the task of today's intellectuals to engage her body of work and illuminate her anti-racist political commitments. This political orientation is needed in this period of resurgent global white supremacy and its manifestation in the continued vitality of internalized racism within the ranks of the African labouring classes and even the petit bourgeoisie.

The Cunny Jamaican 'Oman and the Value of a Positive Counter-Narrative

DONNA AZA WEIR-SOLEY

Like many book lovers, I have quotes and one-liners from my favourite writers that sustain me through all kinds of crises. One of my favourites is from Sandra Cisneros's book of vignettes, *The House on Mango Street*: "Shame is a bad thing you know. It keeps you down." I want to talk about how Jamaican icon Louise Bennett's work helped me to beat back shame, to have a deep and unshakeable knowing that formal education or not, high class or low, urban or rural, black or brown, I was a person, and therefore worthy. My humanity, my intrinsic worth, was neither up for discussion nor debate.

I grew up in a little valley called 'Oman Pond, in the hilly district of Bois Content, nestled between the lowlands of Colbeck and the mountains of Bellas Gate, in Jamaica's largest parish of St Catherine. Although sexism, colourism, classism, racism and colonialism were important signifiers in my life, I knew that I could rise above them and achieve economic stability. I got the message early on that if I did well in school, I could transcend the shame of poverty most of us are made to feel in a capitalistic society. On my mother's side of the family are the McCallas and on my father's side are the Weirs; each had a self-serving narrative that I internalized as a child.

The McCallas were practical, entrepreneurial, colourist and proud; the Weirs were equally proud, religious and educated. I had Weir uncles and an aunt who were college educated; my aunt was an elementary school teacher who taught my mother as well as many of my McCalla relatives. I was raised exclusively by the McCalla side of my family. But as a Weir, I was expected to be bright, because that was the Weir story.

People literally said to me, "Yuh a Weir. Yuh must bright." It was as if my being "bright" was going to be the proof some needed that I was my father's child, since my parents were never married. This should have been odd, since my father was himself uneducated, but I only thought about that later. The Weirs were bright. That was the story told by the collective and it was my job to make it a self-fulfilling prophecy.

Even without formal education, the McCallas ran sustainable businesses – four in my childhood: two grocery stores by uncles who could barely read; a shoemaker's shop by my only middle-class uncle who lived in Kingston and employed several workers in the factory he built in his backyard, and "the garage", a car repair business that doubled as mechanic training school run by my youngest uncle on my grandmother's land. So, until I moved away from my extended inter-generational family circle, it was hard to feel shame about who I was, given that I came from people who were poor, but proudly self-sustaining.

Because my mother frequently travelled to Old Harbour, seven miles away, or as far away as Kingston, and further still to Canada, looking for work, I lived with my grandmother in my formative years.

After a physical altercation with my preschool teacher over spanking (of which I did not approve), I was kicked out of the preschool in Bois Content. That early expulsion, coupled with the fact that my grandmother was battling stomach cancer, forced me to leave my beloved Mummah in the village to live with my mother in Old Harbour.

I excelled in my new "basic" school, a one room affair which was built on "capture land" by Mrs Rickman, an English missionary. I redeemed my reputation of being a cantankerous child by learning to conform. I blossomed into a good reader. However, I missed my grandmother and would return to the village every weekend, often bringing with me the latest song, dance or even my primer lesson to teach my country cousins.

I loved performing, imitating the adults around me who told stories animatedly and in Jamaican Patwa. They were Anancy stories, bawdy "Big Boy" stories about sex, duppy stories about wandering ghosts from the Kendal train crash trying to find their way home, the UFO that followed the church sisters home from prayer meeting, fire-eyed rolling calves that were the duppies of people who were bad and went to hell, stories my sick grandmother told me about things she would manifest *after* she died, as well as my mother's stories about her life growing up as a pretty but sickly "gal pickney" who was preyed upon until she learned how to fight back.

On one of those weekends, I was introduced to Louise Bennett's poetry at a school recital at Bois Content All Age School. I could not have been more than five or six. I was quite a good mimic as a child. I learned some of the words from her popular poems by heart, even before I had ever seen a written poem by Bennett. I began listening to her in the *Lou and Ranny Show* on radio.

After I graduated from the combined preschool and kindergarten run by the missionaries, my mother enrolled me in the elementary school in Old Harbour. I was evaluated and deemed so advanced that I skipped grade one. From grade two to grade five, I was discouraged from speaking Patwa by my teachers and the school principal. We were beaten with a cane or a leather strap if we were caught speaking the way we spoke at home.

This was especially true for those "bright" students who were being groomed to pass the Common Entrance Exam. Patwa, the language spoken at home, was getting in the way of our class advancement and social mobility. As I discussed with Ifeoma Nwanko in a special issue on Louise Bennett for the *Journal of West Indian Literature,* published in 2009, the only safe way in which to speak my parents' and grandparents' language in school was to recite Louise Bennett's poetry at school concerts.

I was very attached to my grandmother and it was comforting to hear and to speak her language. I became shy and withdrawn after my grandmother died. But when I performed Louise Bennett's poetry in my grandmother's language, or a close approximation of it, I was no longer the unlucky girl who had lost her mummah. I was barefaced and bold.

Louise Bennett made an important intervention in my consciousness at a crucial age. I was just learning the relationship between being smart and being formally educated. I had thought my McCalla relatives smart enough without much formal education. I had learned mathematics from making change, weighing flour and sugar, and measuring oil for the villagers who bought groceries from my uncle Wammy's shop in 'Oman Pond and Uncle George's shop in Crawl Pass. I'm sure I also learned to read from having to learn the difference between the bags marked "flour" and "sugar" and the aluminium pans marked "kerosene oil" or "coconut oil". I knew, however, that getting an education could take me further than the village.

None of my father's educated relatives lived in the village. Some lived abroad, like my better-off McCalla relatives, and many lived in Kingston. They lived in nice houses with electricity and running water and had good jobs. I was beginning to learn that education was the way up the social ladder.

It was hearing Louise Bennett's poetry, humorous stories and proverbs recited in the language of the rural uneducated Jamaicans that I grew up around that made me "see" them at a time when I was being taught in school to discount them. And, quite frankly, the folks I grew up around did say and do things that would have made them easy targets for derision.

Despite any flaws in Jamaican folk culture, Bennett taught me that there was humour, knowledge and, most significantly, "survival narratives" to be found in it. The way to interpret those narratives for critical application was to listen to the people who spoke them. To listen actively meant you first had to respect them and to see them as people who possessed knowledge, even wisdom. That knowledge was worth something, which meant, by deduction, that the people speaking it were themselves valuable carriers of a unique culture, cosmology, language codes and systems of interpretation, subjectivity and empowerment.

Bennett taught me these lessons indirectly by being visible, vocal and larger than life. She made a career out of folk knowledge and the Patwa that carried it. In my childhood, she was a beloved celebrity and later she became a national treasure.

Later, Bennett moved to Canada and became an international sensation. She was well known in the United States and in the United Kingdom and she frequently performed to eager audiences made up of Jamaican immigrants in all three countries. The language, folk ways and beliefs of the Jamaican people, which she altered to suit her message and style of delivery, had made Bennett internationally famous. I grew to associate her with the Jamaican folk, my own rural working-class people.

Years later, while writing a dissertation chapter on her work, I discovered that Bennett was not "of" the folk as I had assumed. She was from the Jamaican middle class. Furthermore, in some of her work, she was clearly satirizing, parodying and "othering" the folk, creating pathos from their folksy ways of speaking and being. But by then the positive impact had already been made.

The groundwork had been laid for a counter-narrative that resisted interpolation. I could critique Bennett as I critiqued the folk she corrected, celebrated and laughed at, but I could not politicize or radicalize myself out of those covert, insidious and subversive seeds of self-worth she was partly responsible for sowing: worth for my language, for my people, for myself.

When I passed Spanish at the PhD level, but was struggling with French in order to qualify for PhD candidacy at the University of California, Berkeley, I had a stroke of genius. I petitioned the Department of English to allow me to take one of my foreign language exams in Jamaican Patwa, since I was writing a whole dissertation chapter on Louise Bennett's work. Sociolinguist John McWhorter had recently been hired by Berkeley and he came to us as an academic star of sorts. They consulted him and he affirmed in writing that Jamaican Creole was indeed a foreign language.

McWhorter wrote an exam for me in eighteenth-century or early nineteenth-century Jamaican Creole with recognizable elements of old and Middle English as well as, I am sure, West African language influences. I took and passed the exam and was able to move forward to the next stage of my degree. McWhorter wrote a similar exam for my friend Valorie, who is not Jamaican. My recollection is that she passed it and was moved along to candidacy also.

Bennett is far from being my only influence for the valuation of Jamaican Creole as a language to speak in, to write in, to dream in, to make love in, and to create dangerously and boldly in. By the time I went to UC Berkeley, cultural critic Carolyn Cooper was not the global icon she is today, but she was already writing a national newspaper column in Jamaican Creole, celebrating the language and making a case for its primacy in Jamaican arts, history, culture and global influence.

Opal Palmer Adisa had already published *Bake Face and other Guava Stories*, *Tamarind* and *Mango Women*, and shortly after we met at UC

Berkeley, she published *It Begins with Tears*. Before graduate school, I taught Olive Senior's *Summer Lightning* to my high school students at Manhattan Comprehensive Night High School in New York City. There was a not a single Jamaican among my students, but together we fell in love with that little gem of a book set in rural Jamaica.

While in graduate school at UC Berkeley, Lorna Goodison's poetry hit me in the gut like a Nyabinghi drum roll way up in the hills of Northern California. Michelle Cliff, Erna Brodber, Mutabaruka and Jean "Binta" Breeze were only some of the writers whose work invoked pride in my Jamaican culture and language. Their words celebrated Jamaican Patwa as a language not only useful, but necessary for explicating the complex themes and symbols of Jamaican politics, historiography, culture, survival motifs, folk wisdom and narratology.

Later, other Jamaican writers would wind their way into my developing consciousness. They spoke to me on various registers, locating themselves across the linguistic spectrum, from almost English to deep country Patwa, to ghetto youth lyrics, to urban middle-class jargon; from informal and regional-based spelling systems such as those practised by Louise Bennett to the Cassidy system preferred by writers like Ifeona Fulani and Carolyn Cooper in some works; from St Elizabethian and Montegonian colloquialisms in the west, to Kingstonian vernaculars in the east – all invoking, mimicking, celebrating, challenging, parodying, revising, and retooling the language, livity and worldview of my ancestors, as if to test me, as if to challenge me to say something, to push back. But Miss Lou was first.

In graduate school, I discovered postcolonial critics who had a stake in rescuing folk cultures and languages from colonial narratives of inferiority and alterity. Edward Said, Albert Memmi, Ngũgĩ wa Thiong'o, Edward Brathwaite, Jamaica Kincaid, Gayatri Spivak, Stuart Hall, Frantz Fanon and others created critical counter-narratives that showed the connections among language systems and codes, national identity, cultural autonomy, agency and personhood.

They, along with the creative writers and poets M. Nourbese Phillip, Paul Keens-Douglas, Merle Hodge, Grace Nichols, Dorothea Smartt and so many others, provided a pan-Caribbean and global dimension to the theories and applications of English-based Creole languages that were crucial to my developing consciousness of language as a political tool. But Bennett was the first creative writer, performer, cultural critic and critical thinker to plant the seeds of all of these connections within me.

For this subversive *Anancyism* of giving a little country girl a voice; for surreptitiously slipping me the weapons to combat shame; for granting me permission to speak in the only language that was mine to speak in, a language deemed illegitimate, not just by the external forces that directed my life, but by the authority figures around me whose sophistry I did not possess the tools to contest; for rescuing that language from bastardization and elevating it to be used in service to drama, to poetry, to fiction, to writing as resistance, to inscribing subjecthood and dignity – I give thanks to the cunny Jamaican 'oman, the Honourable Dr Louise Bennett-Coverley. In this her one hundredth year, I salute our beloved Miss Lou for whom the passing of time has only substantiated and consolidated her brilliant, bodacious, prescient genius.

The Language Quarrel in Jamaica

A Pedagogical Conversation

ISIS SEMAJ-HALL AND L.A. WANLISS

This is a meditation on Miss Lou that is dedicated to those of us who are determined to figure out what it means to teach English in Jamaica and about this long-time Jamaican quarrel with language.

Almost one hundred years ago the Jamaican pan-Africanist hero Marcus Garvey produced an educational guide for black people's upliftment. The first lesson of his "Course of African Philosophy"[1] noted the following:

> To be able to read intelligently, you must first be able to master the language of your country. To do this, you must be well acquainted with its grammar and the science of it. Every six months you should read over again the science of the language that you speak, so as not to forget its rules. People judge you by your writing and your speech. If you write badly and incorrectly, they become prejudiced towards your intelligence, and if you speak badly and incorrectly, those who hear you become disgusted and will not pay much attention to you but in their hearts laugh after you. A leader who is to teach men and present any fact of truth to man must first be learned in his subject.

I imagine that Garvey's words could be applied to contemporary Jamaica. I can only do so with Louise Bennett in mind, for she has been one of the greatest champions of Jamaica's national language, Patwa. Yet, in national spaces, the language of the everyman is not usually the

1. This is from lesson 1 of Marcus Garvey's "Course of African Philosophy", *Message to the People: The Course of African Philosophy*, ed. Tony Martin (Dover, MA: Majority Press, 1986), 2–3.

language of the elite. In professional spaces, the language of the employee is not usually the language of the employer. In Jamaican academic spaces, the language of art and the language of analysis are not usually the same. At no time did this become clearer to me than when I taught a focused seminar on the work of Louise Bennett at the University of the West Indies at Mona.

The Honourable Louise Bennett-Coverley is recognized as the confident embodiment of Jamaica's linguistic culture. Her decades of stage performances, television and radio recordings, and writings amplified the voice of a people who yearned for independence. Her stories' characters and her poems' personae speak with the voice of a people who believe that they have a unique cultural identity to be proud of. Whether orally or scribally, Miss Lou used real and fictive voices to uplift the Jamaican masses.

So, I cry, "Oh, what a sinting" to find that current local employability often hinges upon an applicant's command of English rather than fluency in the Jamaican language. And "Oh, what a calamity", I say, that a man is assumed to be "one dunce outta di ghetto or country" if he speaks in the same voice that Miss Lou used to grace hallowed Jamaican, English, American and Canadian stages. The same voice that opened doors for Bennett for more than half of the twentieth century still closes doors on ordinary Jamaicans seeking work at home or abroad today.

One can ongly himagine di piece ah confuushon that befell me when I entered the university classroom to teach Louise Bennett to upper-level undergraduate students. Knowing that Miss Lou had made it her life's work to decolonize how Jamaicans view what Brathwaite termed nation language, and knowing that I would be expected to assess these students' use of English grammar rules in how they analysed Louise Bennett, nuh mek nuh sense to me. In a class where some students were doing the double work of translating Louise Bennett from Jamaican to English in order to write about it academically, it seemed wrong. It is not that teaching Louise Bennett revealed an inherent language bias that I was unaware of; it was more that teaching her works in the Jamaican academic setting placed language inequality front and centre, revealing the hush-hush speech rules at the heart of the country's institutions.

Those who are fluent in reading, speaking or writing in multiple languages have a communication advantage. And those who can code-switch often take that skill for granted. But, for those who cannot, for those whose singular mode of fluent communication is using a language that is deemed less-than, their one tongue becomes a barrier to their success. In Jamaica, this means that individuals who cannot speak and write English well are less likely to succeed in school and in work. And despite Miss Lou and her honourable legacy, this remains the reality of language inequality in Jamaica.

As I faced students who were all old enough to vote, I became less interested in how English is taught to pre-university students and more interested in how reverence for English is taught in Jamaica. And, for the sake of Miss Lou's legacy, I wanted to know how Jamaican modes of communication were being *un*taught in schools and across society.

In the face of Miss Lou's rich catalogue of works, I considered the fact that little has changed in the fifty years since Mervyn Morris first asked readers to examine Louise Bennett's works "seriously".[2] It seemed that Morris's 1960s readers and my twenty-first-century tertiary school students both maintained a rather concrete image of Louise Bennett as the jokey-jokey-bad-talking-Jamaican-voiced stage performer. Still, I wanted to push beyond Morris's seminal essay to ask a pedagogical question: How does writing about Louise Bennett seriously complicate Jamaican students' notions of language identity and verbal belonging?

I decided to sit down with a dear friend and fellow word lover to discuss some of these questions and concerns. After a long conversation about language, identity, and how Miss Lou factors into acceptance in Jamaica, we realized that our reflection on classroom pedagogy was worthy of sharing – how Jamaica celebrates Miss Lou, yet denies the embodied voices that inspired her work. A focal point is the contention that all language arts and literature instructors ought to place her work at the centre of their primary, secondary and tertiary English classrooms. I teased all

2. Mervyn Morris, "On Reading Louise Bennett, Seriously", *The Routledge Reader in Caribbean Literature*, ed. Alison Donnell and Sarah Lawson Welsh (London: Routledge, 1996), 194–97.

of this out with L.A. Wanliss, a Jamaican dramaturge, award-winning writer, editor and published poet – and also a teacher of CSEC (Caribbean Secondary Education Certificate) English.

Traditionally, fifth form students who are, on average, sixteen years old, test for CSEC. In Jamaica, many employers require that applicants present their CSECs as a way of verifying their qualifications as high school graduates. The only two CSECs that are required for basic employment in Jamaica are maths and English.

INTERVIEW WITH L.A. WANLISS

Isis Semaj-Hall: Talk to me about your classroom.

L.A. Wanliss: I teach English at a high school and at a vocational (nursing) institution. These are two very diverse and yet connected spaces. One is a traditional space meant for high achievers under the age of sixteen. The other is a space for women and a few men who are second and sometimes third or fourth chancers, ranging from sixteen to forty-five years old.

ISH: Very diverse and yet not. Education can be so complex. Tell me how Miss Lou's work enters into your English spaces.

LAW: Miss Lou enters my classrooms as a text and also as the language/expression through which communication is explored. So, in the traditional high school I teach Miss Lou in eighth grade or second form. Miss Lou, of course, is also very popular in drama clubs across the island – just pay attention to JCDC [Jamaica Cultural Development Commission]. Miss Lou's work isn't a staple in the drama club at my high school, but it is a good and easy place for performance. This is what I mean by Miss Lou is text. It is studied and used. In this way, Miss Lou is historical text and also a performance/performer's text.

The work is historical because, for example, a poem like "Dutty Tough", which is popular and relevant, teaches the students about the currency of the time. It's a good place to begin to talk with them about the 1970s and the way goods were being "married" because supermarket items were scarce. But it's also relevant because it talks about some people's inability to make ends meet and the forever-distress of the ordinary Jamaican. And, yes, the language and expression which Miss Lou writes in and about are what I am being asked to refine in my non-traditional classrooms.

ISH: I appreciate how you've stated that point and couldn't agree more. Even in the tertiary space, for me, it feels almost hypocritical to demand that students Anglicize the language they use to articulate their understanding of a performer-writer like Miss Lou. As a dramaturge, can you tell me more about the performance aspect? Does Miss Lou's work also help your students to communicate with you?

LAW: Miss Lou's rhythm and cadences afford us a completely Jamaican style of performance which Mervyn Morris calls "Labrish". This performance style is taught to primary school performers and is seen at every Jamaica Day performance in schools.

ISH: Can you describe that performance style?

LAW: It's hands clapping, big step forward, back bent with hands akimbo. It's the same sight seen in the market, at a neighbour's fence, on an upper St Andrew verandah, in rural communities, on public transportation, etcetera. It's the "draw long bench" performance, the "tell-me-story-gyal" mannerism.

ISH: It's incredible how you just canvassed the island with your description. This performance is certainly layered by class and gender.

LAW: That's the power of performance; it engages with everything. So, at my vocational institution, when I communicate with my students there, I have a visceral experience with Miss Lou that is beyond the page. In the classroom I must look at her through her understanding of language and communication and what she was telling us honestly and humorously about the way we communicate, about the way my students communicate. Because Patwa isn't just about words. It's also about an unsaid understanding and an interpretation based on social norms and "what we spirit take", or our personal and cultural "vibrations". Because of this understanding of Miss Lou, she is always in my classroom. For example, think about the poem "Love Letter":[3]

3. Louise Bennett, "Love Letter", *Selected Poems* (Kingston: Sangster's, 1982), 73–74

As ah puts me pen to paper
An me pen-nib start fi fly
Me rememberance remember
De fus day yuh ketch me yeye!

Yuh did jus come off a tramcar,
A bus was to yuh right,
A car swips pass yuh lef aise,
An yuh tan up stiff wid fright.

Yuh jaw drop, yuh mout open,
Jus like when jackass start yawn;
Me heart go boogoo-boogoo,
An me know wha mek me bawn.

I remember it because I performed it at JCDC for Ardenne Prep. In this poem, what entertains us is the way the persona described the pain and shock. We find humour because of his expression of how he sees the woman he admires. But there is so much more going on. For example, if we pay attention to the poem carefully, we see Miss Lou's rendering of the Jamaican language of love (heart): "Me heart go boogoo-boogoo."

Here the racket of a broken-down car is the same sound of his heart racing, and he can hear it among the chaos of the tramcar and the busy street. And because we are aware of the racing heart from fairy-tale descriptions of love, we know he cares but we can also intuit from that line the fact that he too is frightened just from the sound of his heart palpitating. Two meanings in one onomatopoeic sound. This feeling which is articulated in the Patwa *boogoo-boogoo* makes sense only to Jamaicans.

The persona, through this description, reveals to us the way communication happens, which is what Miss Lou is great at reminding us of through her dramatic poems. There is a feeling that, when not easily expressed with words, we always find other ways to express our meanings. He doesn't express his fear or his care with words – he uses sound. It is left up to us to interpret the meaning of that sound. This is what I must do all day, every day in the classroom.

ISH: Your memory is impressive and so too is your performance of the text.

LAW: Thanks. I know "Love Letter" like the back of my hand because I performed it, and performance always rewinds memory. It is in this way that Miss Lou enters the classrooms. Not through barrier of words, but the barrier of sound and feeling. The students' work is to find new ways to receive the word in order to interpret it. Because if the word comes to them like a feeling which they accept, the task is for us to learn how to deconstruct those feelings as organized ideas for an exam that is scheduled nine months into the future.

And that takes us to the next stanza of that same poem:

> Do, no scorn me lickle letter;
> No laugh after me, yaw –
> Me learnin not too gran, so what
> Me cyaan spell me wi draw!

These students have found new or rather very common ways of expressing themselves that take them further from the restrictive English ways that the CSEC exams require. There is no formula in their expression. One thing is everything and meaning is not always clearly or correctly interpreted because though they *feel* "it", they can't always identify clearly what they feel. In this way, from the perspective of a teacher, I am an observer, a fake Miss Lou. Without the talent to decode, I am only able to listen to and interact with my students in the ways that Miss Lou was known to interact with and create from her community in Gordon Town and wherever she went to do her research.

ISH: So, this is how language works for your non-traditional students? Jamaican language and the body all seem to come together in natural ways. Decoding, as you say, these feelings into a single English interpretation can be challenging. Is it at all because they are further removed from the academic expectations as adult learners?

LAW: No, because this is also true of the well-trained young students. They are beginning to understand the vibe. Some, having mastered it, find it useless to be writing for so long when they "get it". They "see" or understand it.

ISH: Would it be too cheesy to say that there's a "vibe over scribe" factor to be considered when unpacking or interpreting Miss Lou's work in a Jamaican classroom?

LAW: Wow. Isis, that was cheesy. But, I guess you are right. In both spaces Miss Lou impacts my classroom because I am reminded, through my own knowledge of Miss Lou and the Jamaican people, that these students must interact with the information through the way it makes them *feel*. The way they feel about certain words or ideas is based on whatever signifier is necessary for the knowledge to be given to them and their own ability to decode and respond to the information.

ISH: I under- and overstand. It makes me wonder what value Jamaican students place on Miss Lou in 2020.

LAW: I keep playing with Raymond Williams's 1958 essay "Culture Is Ordinary".[4] So, my cheeky response is: Does anyone really think about the value of any aspect of their culture beyond the lived experience of it?

Miss Lou is as important to the students as the national heroes are important to them. She is a part of our culture and, as we know, culture is ordinary. Miss Lou, Usain Bolt, Bob Marley, not necessarily in this order, are our premier icons. Students are taught this from primary and prep school days. They understand her value as someone to be lauded. You cannot go into any primary or prep school and say the name Miss Lou and students look at you as if they are dumb. This is the brilliance of Jamaica Day. Yet, there are still a few students who can't understand her significance because the significance of the language is still lost on them.

ISH: Precisely! But is that language lost or just uninterpretable?

LAW: You know, maybe it's both. Because they understand the joy of the text as performance and a snippet of history, but do they understand the text as a place to see how we truly communicate and how meaning is given and lost in our communities? Who knows? And should children really be asked to think in this way? There are Jamaican students who love to hear Patwa but will tell you that they can't speak it. I often wonder: can they then understand the significance of Miss Lou's journey, her BBC

4. Raymond Williams, "Culture Is Ordinary (1958)", in *Raymond Williams on Culture and Society: Essential Writings*, ed Jim McGuigan (London: Sage, 2014), 1–18.

programmes, *Ring Ding,* and so on that she gave to their parents' and grandparents' generation?

ISH: It seems that this is the value that the educator brings into the classroom. Isn't that what we present the students with? Don't we bring them the critical history and lens through which to make sense of the feelings, the vibes and the Patwa? Miss Lou's work is there for us. Her archive of language awaits, no?

LAW: Yes, but we can't put it all on Miss Lou. She didn't create the Jamaican language; she wrote and spoke in it. But I see the value of her writing, speaking, performing and publishing the language of the common man. I see the value in giving us permission to talk as we feel and that gives us value as humans, irrespective of what we sound like. This is vital. This is how we begin to break down the elitist hold on Jamaica. Freeing the language was necessary as that vestige of slavery was choking so many Jamaicans and stagnating our possibility for economic, moral and social growth. We see it with Jamaicans across classes and in the diaspora. The Jamaican language and its cadences are our pride and joy; it isn't a hindrance anymore. We are masters at code switching.

ISH: Not all of us have that mastery, though.

LAW: That's right. Language in Jamaica is a give and take. It's what we lose when we are invaded, what we modify when we are enslaved and what we restructure continuously. Language remains a necessary and major part of culture. It is the way we express ourselves and the way we can become curious about our own existence. Miss Lou has done iconic work with language: freeing people by being free, freeing people by showing them themselves. By giving the ordinary man's sound value with all of its multiplicities of meaning held in our mouths, in our bodies and in our cultural markers, Miss Lou has done much for our country. But, as I have come to learn from teaching Miss Lou's work, it is language as much as it is people. Her ability to understand who the people are and to interpret them and recreate from that is not an ordinary task. Her cultural work of taking the ordinary into something extraordinary is *neva* simple.

ISH: And that work nuh complete yet. But she brings the nation together and, powerfully, she does so using language. Would you say that makes her a nation builder?

LAW: Well, my fear is what happens if we call Miss Lou a nation builder. This movement will take her work from the ordinary individuals into the hands of the elite – by elite here, I do mean privileged as the interpretation of the language markers. The significance of her work can become lost because the value we now place on her work is in how we reduce it to its humour or elevate it to a call to codify the language.

ISH: I hear you, my friend. And as I make sense of your words, it seems that there is a way that interpreting and analysing Miss Lou's work in the classroom setting, analysing her dexterity with Patwa and the fluency with which she spoke Jamaican body language on stage can inadvertently bruk di vibe that she was trying to preserve in the first place. All this and I feel as if we've only cracked the surface of this quarrel with language.

LAW: Brush the surface, Isis.

Stitching Time Together

Meeting and Greeting in Caribbean Song

HUBERT DEVONISH

"DIS LANG TAIM": THE GREETING SONG AS WELCOME SONG

The Jamaican folksong "Dis Laang Taim Gyal Mi Neva Si Yu" was often used by the Honourable Louise Bennett-Coverley, Miss Lou, to introduce her stage performances. She described it as "the Jamaican welcome song" and would have her audience join her in singing it at the start of her shows. In spite of Miss Lou's description of the song and the use to which she put it in her performances, the song is one about greeting. To establish this point, we need to make the distinction between speech acts that welcome and speech acts that greet.

The concept of "welcome" is easiest understood by looking across languages. Germanic languages such as English and German express the concept of "welcome" with a compound word made up of two words, one similar in form and meaning to English "well" and the other to the English word "come". Thus, in German, the word equivalent to English "welcome" is *willkommen*. In the Romance languages, the forms are different but again we have units meaning "well", as in *bien,* and "come", as in *venir,* being combined, as in French *bienvenue,* to produce the meaning of "welcome".

It is important to note that the verb "come" literally means "movement to the position or place occupied by the speaker". A welcome is therefore an invitation into a space associated with or under the influence or control of the speaker. This is what is suggested if one says "Welcome to my home". Sentences such as "Welcome to your/his home", where the welcome applies to a space not under the ownership or control of the speaker, would seem extremely odd except in very special contexts.

A welcome typically involves a speaker who occupies a space and invites an approaching addressee to share the space of the speaker. This is most certainly not the case in "Dis Lang Taim". The evidence of the lyrics suggests that the song is about an encounter in public space, with the speaking protagonist greeting the addressee rather than welcoming her into a space. This greeting song was used, however, by Miss Lou as part of a performance speech act to welcome her audience to her show. What follows is a discussion of the structure of "Dis Lang Taim" and its role in stitching time together for two friends who have been separated for a long time. The concept of stitching time together in a Caribbean speech event is further explored by an examination of a somewhat similar song, "So Long", a 2019 soca song performed by the Trinidad and Tobago artiste Nadia Batson.

"DIS LANG TAIM": PERFORMING THE EXTENDED GREETING

In a situation of people meeting unexpectedly, the attention of the addressee is drawn to the speaker by the greeting speech act. In "Dis Lang Taim", this occurs in the first line of each verse and is repeated in the third line. The greeting takes the form of "Dis lang taim, gyal, mi neva si yu" (It's been a long time since I've seen you). The addressee, a female signalled by the address term "gyal", is now drawn in as a participant in the speech event.

In the fifth line of each of the three verses, however, we have what might be called an extension of the greeting. The singer/speaker exclaims, "Piiledjankruo, sidong pan chrii tap, pikaaf di blasom" (The vulture sits atop the tree picking off the blossoms). Miss Lou, at the end of her performance of the song, explains the metaphor to her audience. According to her, since the jankruo is a vulture that eats carrion, the idea that it might be seen atop a tree picking blossoms is highly unlikely and unusual. This is metaphorical exaggeration. The rarity of such an event serves to underline the once-in-a-blue-moon nature of the encounter between the two protagonists. It reinforces the message of the initial part of the greeting, that it has been a long time since the two friends have met.

Both parts of the greeting have a single focus. We can assume that a friendship takes place over a period of time and consists of a pattern of regular interaction over that time. If a considerable time passes during which that regularity is interrupted, there is arguably a rupture in the relationship. That break causes distress. This is the basis for the joy which is implied in the extended greeting performed within the song.

"DIS LANG TAIM": SETTING THE AGENDA

Time is what has separated the friends. The greeting speech act just examined establishes, by the extreme joy expressed, the pain which the separation has caused. The next speech act we might characterize as an agenda-setting one. The singer/speaker is making a set of proposals as to how the two friends might spend the time they have together. The objective is to renew the friendship. To do this, one has to resume, as if time had not passed, the interactions which were previously more frequent. The singer/speaker sets the agenda, to stitch time together again.

The first stitch involves re-establishing physical presence and contact. The line "Kom mek mi huol yu han" occurs four times in the first verse of the song and twice in the concluding section or outro, referred to by Miss Lou as "the mento" portion of the song. This matches the "Dis lang taim, gyal, mi neva si yu" of the greeting, sung six times in the song. The focus on physical touch and presence is actually described by Miss Lou in her comment on stage about the song. She explains, with reference to the rarity of the meeting, that the speaker reacts with "What an impossible thing! I never thought we would have met, my darling. Kom huol mi han" (Come and hold my hand).

The second stitch involves making up for lost time and, specifically, all the enjoyment of each other's company that had not been experienced in the period of separation. The invitation to "wiil an ton" (that is, dance holding hands while swinging around in a circle) is aimed at them heightening the excitement generated from meeting and being in each other's physical presence, against the background of long separation. The intensity of this experience in a short time span would make up for the more normal level of enjoyment extended over the time that has been lost.

In the third verse, the agenda item presented by the speaker to the addressee is to "Kom mek wi waak an taak" (Let's walk and talk). Since they have met in a public space, one not belonging to nor controlled by either of them, it is proposed that they reconnect and share each other's company by walking together through that common space. The talking which accompanies the walking is the means by which the two would catch up on the news about each other. Had they been meeting regularly, this catching up would not have been necessary. Given the large time gap since their last meeting, the talking serves as a stitch to mend the knowledge gaps, and attach friendship past to friendship present.

There is an outro or concluding component, which Miss Lou describes in performance as "the mento". For this part of the song, we get a repeat of the request to "mek wi wiil an ton" (let's spin around in dance). It is presented in the second verse as a celebration of their meeting. It here appears again, at the presumed end of the encounter between the two friends. The proposition, this time, is that they spin around in dance "til wi tombl dong" (until we fall down). The dancing here is the equivalent of "one for the road", with the falling down symbolically bringing an end to the encounter.

The pattern of meeting presented in the lyrics of "Dis Lang Taim" is one of greeting, holding hands as part of that greeting, celebrating the meeting through dance, then walking and talking, and then a final extreme celebration of the meeting by wheeling, turning and falling down. Arguably, embedded in the lyrics of the song is a Jamaican and Caribbean construct for the maintenance of close friendships of people without regular access to each other. It would be useful to see how this model holds up against other songs which cover similar subject matter.

"SO LONG": PERFORMING THE EXTENDED GREETING

The 2019 soca song from Trinidad and Tobago by Nadia Batson, "So Long", explores the same themes covered in "Dis Lang Taim". It includes extended greeting in reaction to a surprise meeting, the desire to make physical contact as part of checking that the experience is real and the use of dance as a means of celebrating that meeting. Interestingly, much that has to be inferred in "Dis Lang Taim" is explicitly stated in "So Long".

"So Long" is a song with three verses and a repeated chorus. It opens with a chorus which intersperses the verses. The greeting speech act starts the chorus that begins the song with "Is that you? Can't believe that is you!" In the verse that follows the opening chorus, we get an extension of the greeting in the form of details: "Eeh, eeh, look who? So long mi eehn really see you, Could be bout a year or two." This is a very explicit statement about the length of time since they last met. This contrasts with the line from "Dis Lang Taim", which used the "once in a blue moon" metaphor about the jankruo picking off blossoms.

Later in the verse of "So Long" we get, along the same lines, "Eeh, eeh, long time, been a while we eehn bus a lime" (It's been a while since we've hung out with each other). We then get the metaphorical exaggeration, "Ah thought yu hiding, Ah thought you went foreign" (emigrated), to emphasize the fact that this long lost friend was actually missed and longed for. What pops up next is the surprised expression, "Look how tings does happen, na, Look how tings does happen, na!" This line appears in the second verse as well.

All of the preceding are part of what we have been calling the extended greeting. It is preliminary to the substance of the discourse. It sets the stage for a proposal to do something with the opportunity provided by the chance meeting. This is what we have referred to as the agenda-setting speech act.

"SO LONG": SETTING THE AGENDA

As in "Dis Lang Taim", the agenda of "So Long" includes physical dance, physical touch and talk. A proposal to dance comes first on the agenda. In the second line of the chorus, following on from the first line greeting, we get the request to "Gi mi a wine that ah want long time" which, we are told, is to "make up for all this time". "Wine" here is a dance move involving gyration of the waist. We get background here that the singer/speaker had wished to dance with the addressee for a long time, but the period of separation prevented this. Now was the time to put a stitch in time and reconnect the friendship through the interrupted "wine". That an agenda is being set can be seen clearly by the line in the form of a question in the first verse, "Wha we go drink or wha we go do". This question is asked with a view to the two protagonists doing something to celebrate the meeting.

Instead of "walk and talk" being proposed explicitly as in "Dis Lang Taim", the singer/speaker actually speaks to the addressee in the song. In order to indicate commitment to the friendship, the singer/speaker tells the addressee in the second verse, "I aks yu fren an dem when las dey did talk to yu, so long ah eehn talk to yu" (Because I hadn't spoken to you in a long time, I asked your friends when last they had spoken to you). Even though the addressee has been out of sight, she or he has not been out of mind. The addressee is praised for looking fine, not having aged in appearance in the time since the last meeting, and looking prosperous, "like money running real nice".

Soon after that, we get the request for physical touch, to "let me hug up and squeeze yu". Whereas in "Dis Lang Taim" the request is part of the sequence at the start of the interaction, in "So Long" touching is part of the routine that marks the end. The request to touch in "So Long" is, in fact, a build up to a farewell speech act as expressed in the immediately following lines, "Ah don't want to leave yu, Ah don't know when we'll bounce up again, So let me take a little ting until then". There is an implied farewell in "Dis Lang Taim" involving wheeling and turning and falling down to close the song and, by implication, the interaction. By contrast, this closure along with the bidding of farewell appears explicitly in the lyrics of "So Long".

DISCOURSE RITUALS OF CARIBBEAN MEETING AND GREETING

The rituals of meeting as presented in Miss Lou's performance and explanation of "Dis Lang Taim" and the performance of Nadia Batson's "So Long" present discourse aimed at repairing relationships. These are relationships ruptured by the separation of the protagonists over a period of time. The discourse structure involves an exaggerated focus on the length of time of the separation and the amazing luck of the accidental meeting between protagonists. Time is set up in the discourse as the culprit. This sets the stage for the presenting of an agenda, a list of actions or activities to be undertaken in order to repair the friendship. The target of these activities is time itself. Through touching and establishing physical presence, through dancing in celebration of the meeting and through talking inclusive of the paying of compliments, the interlocutors hope to defeat the effects of time by acting as if time had not actually passed. They are proposing, through the agenda-setting phase of the discourse, to mend ruptured time and, in so doing, renew their friendship.

The Politics of Language and Identity in Jamaica

From Miss Lou to De Bumpy Head Gal

CAROLYN ALLEN

The debates about the status of Jamaican Patwa and its place in the education system, public media and the arts still rage on decades after independence.

Without question, the work of Louise Bennett-Coverley has had a significant impact on the society, allowing one to trace changes in the dominant position and social mood. The fact that the controversy surrounding the works of Joan Andrea Hutchinson, who is consciously writing as a protégé of Miss Lou, is focused on her public image – De Bumpy Head Gal – rather than on language is instructive. While many of us appreciate our "mother tongue" (especially as art and heritage), to present ourselves in the colonially denigrated image of the African mother opens a wound unhealed by the passage of time and the rhetoric of roots.

This chapter examines the public debate on the works and image of these two women writers, exploring the complexity of the relationships between the politics of language, notions of propriety and the rhetoric of national identity.

In the book *Caribbean Creolization,*[1] several writers address the question of Caribbean cultural identity and language, reflecting on their various experiences. Erna Brodber talks about a woman who was socially handicapped because she spoke a language which did not belong to the

1. Kathleen M. Balutansky and Marie-Agnès Sourieau, eds., *Caribbean Creolization Reflections on the Cultural Dynamics of Language, Literature, and Identity* (Gainesville: University Press of Florida, 1998).

community in which she lived. Merle Collins recalls growing up in the presence of two languages at odds with each other. Jean Binta Breeze, with a similar heritage, had a different personal experience. In her article "English a Co-opted Language", she notes that, for her, both languages were learned in the same way (orally) and were equally accessible. Unlike so many others, she found it "very difficult to separate the literary from the oral".[2] If any number of writers, from Mutabaruka to Derek Walcott, have all had to come to terms with the social politics of language in their native countries as individuals, the craft of writing will have sharpened their sensitivity and imposed choices.

The positions in the language debate are no doubt familiar to all of us: Can a language of oppression express the experience of the oppressed? With a limited local readership, is the writer not obliged to appropriate the international idiom? Should we discard a legitimate inheritance?

Let us consider the case of Jamaica through the experiences of Louise Bennett-Coverley and Joan Andrea Hutchinson, two writers more widely known by the names given in the title of the paper: "Miss Lou" and "Dat Bumpy Head Gal", respectively. What makes them appropriate subjects for this reflection? One might have chosen the pioneer Una Marson and any one of a number of contemporary women writers. The interest in these two derives, first, from their privileging of Jamaican Patwa, and second, from the similarities in their styles and the public perception of their artistic personalities. Not only do many people consider Joan Andrea Hutchinson today's Miss Lou, she herself publicly claims Louise Bennett as a predecessor and she benefited from her mentorship on a personal and professional level.

It was reading a poem by Miss Lou as a child which inspired Joan's interest in writing. There are also similarities in the paths their careers have taken. As actresses, both have played memorable roles in the annual Little Theatre Movement National Pantomime and appeared in films. As media personalities, they have worked with children and teenagers on television and on radio. For years, Miss Lou was host of *Ring Ding*, a

2. Jean Binta Breeze, "English a Co-opted Language", *Critical Quarterly* 35, no. 4 (1993).

programme in which children performed and Miss Lou taught songs and riddles; Joan produced for Power 106 a programme supporting students who took Caribbean Examination Council exams. Both have appeared at home and abroad as motivational speakers and cultural ambassadors.

Miss Lou's formal training was in acting and social work. As she travelled around the island she carried out extensive research into Jamaican folk customs. Joan, on the other hand, is a trained media practitioner who studied linguistics, with a view to disseminating the insights of academia via the artistic vehicle.[3] Dressed most frequently in national costume or African print with head tie, Miss Lou became a living icon, an embodiment of Jamaican folk culture. Joan, for reasons we will explore in more detail later, has refused ever to appear in "costume", resisting that image of Mother Culture. Nevertheless, it is as comedians, commenting on Jamaican society in the language of the people, that these writers are most widely seen and known.

This is not without reason. Both have held up the proverbial mirror to society so that we may take a mildly critical look at ourselves. Objective and vehicle are evident in the titles of their publications: Miss Lou's *Jamaican Humour in Dialect* and Joan's *Jamaica Kin Teet*.[4] As far as content goes, these titles are the same. They say the same thing. The phrases share a common structure: the nation comes first – this is their primary source and audience. Vehicle and mode come next – humour.

For many Jamaicans, laughter and the name Miss Lou are synonymous. Indeed, she hardly got through a conversation without it. It was her professed way of seeing things.[5] Joan admits to sharing the humorist's gift of bringing the comic to whatever she observes.[6] But for Miss Lou it went beyond the realm of individual talent. It is, in fact, a characteristic of the Jamaican sensibility and worldview, confirmed in the popular proverbs

---

3. Joan Andrea Hutchinson, personal communication, May 1998.

4. Louise Bennett, *Jamaican Humour in Dialect* (Kingston: Jamaica Press Association, 1943); Joan Andrea Hutchinson, *Jamaica Kin Teet* (Kingston: Jahro Productions, 1997).

5. "I have found a medium through which I can pretend to be laughing." Louise Bennett, "Bennett on Bennett", interview by Dennis Scott, *Caribbean Quarterly* 14, nos. 1–2 (1968): 97.

6. Hutchinson, interview.

"tek bad sinting mek joke" and "tek kin teet kibba heart bun". This is no doubt the source of the "kin teet" in Joan's cassette title. So "humour in dialect" in 1943 becomes "kin teet" in 1998.

Miss Lou's long career in creative writing and folklore studies was inspired by a line uttered by a market woman in the back seat of a tramcar: "Pread out yuhself, one dress-oman a come." The "dress-oman" was in fact only a schoolgirl, spruced up to go to the movies. It was with a poem recording that event that Louise Bennett found her voice.

> Pread out yuhself deh Liza, one
> Dress-oman dah look like seh
> She see de li space side-a we
> And waan foce herself eendeh.[7]

Bennett had been dissatisfied with her earlier writing because it had nothing to do with the life and people around her: "being interested in people and what the people were doing and the 'now' of their lives, these were [to become her] pre-occupations".[8] But there was another element in that memorable line which would also mark Miss Lou's career – its purpose, to maintain a social divide. For practical and, Miss Lou suggests, not prejudicial reasons,[9] the back benches of the tramcar were reserved for the market vendors with their load. Having none of that prejudice herself and wanting to be at the back among them, the young Louise was heading for the vacant space. But the market women would have none of it. After all, to judge by her dress, she was not one of them.

As Miss Aggy, the self-hating black mother in Trevor Rhone's *Old Story Time*, would constantly remind her son, this is a society in which "you must know your place". Thinking the women well within their rights, delighted by their ability to express themselves, and aware that few writers were paying any attention to this, Miss Lou wrote consistently from the point of view of the common (wo)man.

---

7. Quoted by Mervyn Morris, introduction to *Selected Poems*, by Louise Bennett (Kingston: Sangster's, 1982), v; from "On a Tramcar" (see *Miss Lulu Sez* [Kingston: Gleaner Company, 1949], 150–51). Still vividly recalled in January 1998 in interview with the author in Toronto, Canada.

8. Bennett, "Bennett on Bennett", 99.

9. Bennett, interview with the author.

Turning life into rhymes was not new to her. She had always entertained at home and school with her verses, and it was not long before she found a place on stage.[10] With her mother's encouragement she would accept invitations to perform without pay, despite the fact that the verses were not primarily intended for stage. Louise Bennett had always considered herself a writer. She was to learn that in this too, she was "passing her place".

The *Gleaner* repeatedly rejected her submissions. When the Jamaica Poetry League eventually invited her to participate it was to read someone else's work. She made it into the *Jamaica Independence Anthology*, but just barely in the miscellaneous/humour section at the end. And most surprising of all, she never appeared in *Focus* till the 1980s editions, edited by Mervyn Morris. These points bear further scrutiny. The *Gleaner* has dominated the Jamaican press for over one hundred years. It is a publication with a reputation for being conservative and inclined to the political right.

Miss Lou did come to have a regular column in that newspaper, but here is the story: When her poems were read on Jamaica's first radio station, it brought an invitation from a wealthy citizen to entertain his dinner guests – mostly local whites.[11] Present was the editor of the *Gleaner*, who then realized, from the response of the gathering, that this would be good business.[12]

Then there was the case of the Jamaica Poetry League. Here was an organization which grew out of a colonial institution. There was little question about where its standards and taste were shaped. J.E. Clare McFarlane, poet laureate and chairman, wrote in commentary on Claude McKay's dialect poems that Jamaican dialect was a "broken tongue with which it is impossible to build the edifice of verse possessing the perfect

10. In the January 1998 interview with the author, she recalls how her mother would warn her clients, "Mine how yu talk, she will put you ina rhyme." For an account of Miss Lou's early career, see Barbara Gloudon, "The Hon. Louise Bennett, O.J.: Fifty Years of Laughter", *Jamaica Journal* 19, no. 3 (1986): 2–10.

11. See Morris, introduction, v. Also recalled in the January 1998 interview with author.

12. Bennett, interview with the author.

symmetry of finished art".[13] It comes as no surprise then that Miss Lou's work was never considered poetry by their criteria. She was hardly unaware of this position. One notes with interest Hewitt's observation that Miss Lou herself avoided the use of the word "poem" in her early book titles, preferring the term "verses". In her interview with Dennis Scott, she stated, "I have been set apart by other creative writers a long time ago because of the language I speak and work in. From the beginning nobody recognized me as a writer . . . Up to now a lot of people don't even think I write. They say 'Oh, you just stand up and say these things!' "[14]

As for her near exclusion from the independence anthology, I can only speculate on the reasons. But by that time she had already published four books of poetry and had a weekly column in the *Gleaner*. Perhaps the difficulty was finding a place, a category for her among the conventional literary genres – Short Stories, Poems, Extracts from Novels. She appears in the final section: Miscellaneous – (Autobiography, History, Folklore, Humour).[15] Who can reasonably argue against seeing her as a folklorist and a humorist? More challenging is her invisibility to the editor(s) of *Focus*.

What is interesting about this case is the fact that the *Focus* group was very much anti–Poetry League and anti-colonial. It would not be unreasonable, I think, to consider them the literary branch of one notable wing of the island's political movement(s), calling for self-government and the empowerment of the mass of the people. Edna Manley, the editor, was after all the wife of one of the nation's founding fathers, Norman Washington Manley. Why would she, who was supportive of other anti-colonial artistic efforts, overlook Miss Lou?

In her doctoral thesis on the work of Louise Bennett and Zora Neale Hurston, Mary Jane Hewitt quotes Edna Manley's response to that question, which at first had her stumped: "To be perfectly honest, I think we

13. J.E. Clare McFarlane, *A Literature in the Making* (Kingston: Pioneer, 1956), 84.
14. Bennett, "Bennett on Bennett", 98.
15. Drama was also missing from the anthology. A.L. Hendricks and Cedric Lindo, eds, *The Independence Anthology of Jamaican Literature* (Kingston: The Arts Celebration Committee of the Ministry of Development and Welfare, 1962).

were a bit intolerant, and we didn't regard it as a serious literary effort."[16]

Admitting their error in not recognizing Miss Lou's work as a "remarkable commentary", she cites one example of a brilliant poem which had them all laughing at the onomatopoeic imitations of the sounds of new buses, precisely the kind of thing which made the work seem trite. So Bennett was seen as lightweight, not to be taken seriously, largely because of the language in which she chose to write. Moreover, some might have thought that she did not take herself seriously, since laughter and playfulness were such important elements in her style.

When asked whether this was the case, Bennett replied, "This is true. . . . Sometimes their missing of the [serious social] point is deliberate. They prefer to pretend that it's all in fun."[17] In 1967, Mervyn Morris published the first extended commentary on the poetry of Louise Bennett, arguing that she deserved to be read seriously.[18] Though it was not the focus of his discussion, Morris was aware that there was much more involved in that exercise than literary skill. First we must share the artiste's respect for and pride in the language of the material and, beyond that, consider the personae and experiences worthwhile subjects. Neither of these would have been a common attitude among the colonially educated of pre-independence Jamaica.

No reader of Caribbean literature can be unfamiliar with the impact of colonial education on the region. I hardly need to rehearse here the denigration and attempted proscription of all that was culturally alien to Europe. What we need to recall more specifically are the related attitudes to language in these territories where the official language is not commanded by the majority.

In "Creole Discourse and Social Development",[19] Lawrence Carrington gives a useful schematic, a seven-point outline of the background to

16. Mary Jane Hewitt, "A Comparative Study of the Careers of Zora Neale Hurston and Louise Bennett as Cultural Conservators" (PhD thesis, University of the West Indies, Mona, 1989).

17. Bennett, "Bennett on Bennett", 101.

18. Mervyn Morris, "On Reading Louise Bennett, Seriously", *Jamaica Journal* 1, no. 1 (December 1967) 69–75.

19. Lawrence D. Carrington, "Creole Discourse and Social Development" (Manuscript Report 212e, International Development Research Centre, December 1988), 10.

traditional attitudes towards Creole languages as inferior to the official standard. Beyond the trappings which would make the Creoles comparable to standard English and therefore more respectable – like scholarly material, dictionaries and grammars, its use in the education system, a writing system – he cites two directly sociopolitical elements: "their origins as the forms of speech produced by the group who were lowest on the social scale of the plantation society" and, the flip side, "the association of European languages with power and control of the societies".

Carrington develops on these points with a description of the social relationship between Creole and standard English, where typically (as we know), "the use of the Standard official language of the society would be characteristic of the upper classes and related aspirants while the use of the Creole would typify the lower classes", and again on the tacit social agreement on functions for each: "the Standard languages would be the vehicles of formal serious communication related to the management of the society, educational practices and public self-presentation. The Creole vernaculars would be the vehicles of folk communication, oral traditions, unofficial activity and private interaction."[20]

Against this background (which describes a regional phenomenon), it is easy to see why Miss Lou was set apart. She was indeed "passing her place", so to speak, writing in a language mostly spoken, moving the private into the public domain, elevating the informal to the formal arena – that is, if she were to be taken seriously.

As we have seen, and as Morris confirms in his article, the initial reaction of the power brokers and culture wardens was to classify the work with the language as inferior, thereby maintaining the status quo. As DeCamp observed, and it remains partially true today, "Language is an important social symbol of social status to Jamaicans, and inability to approximate the Kingston standard is a serious social and economic handicap."[21]

This inadequacy seems to have become a source of humour for the

20. Ibid., 11.

21. David DeCamp, "Social and Geographical Factors in Jamaican Dialects", in *Creole Language Studies II: Proceedings of the Conference on Creole Language Studies*, ed. R.B. Le Page (London: Macmillan, 1961), 84.

educated classes. In a dialogue outlining moments in the historical development of the Jamaican language, Charles Hyatt and Shirley Maynier-Burke, then editor of the *Jamaica Journal*, evoke the period of change when urban speakers of English would come into regular contact with speakers of rural Patwa at the market. From there, they would take away expressions, repeating them for the amusement of others at home. This, Hyatt wrote, is the source of the notion that Creole is for comedy only.[22]

All these factors contributed to the early reception of Miss Lou and, though she may not have anticipated the intensity of it, the response came from the very condition/situation which moved her to write – a love for the people and a desire to see them respected in the way she had learned to regard everyone as a child. She wrote that all her mother's clients with whom there was interaction carried the title "lady" – "the fish lady, the yam lady, the store lady, the teacher lady".[23]

Primary among the recurring themes in her work, as Hewitt and Morris have observed, are issues of national and racial identity, the use of language, topical events, and the value of Jamaica's heritage. In her prose descriptions of how the Jamaican language came into being,[24] she argued that it is no more a corruption than English is, because of all the source languages it is said to be derived from. Exposing the inherent prejudice in the distinction between "corruption" and "derivation", she gives the African etymology of selected words, substituting some knowledge for the ignorance which enables prejudices to thrive unchecked.

---

22. Charles Hyatt, "The Development of Jamaican Language: The Editor Interviews Charles Hyatt", interview by Shirley Maynier-Burke, *Jamaica Journal* 45 (May 1981): 10. This element Joan seems to exploit (not to the advantage of the persona) in poems like "White Witch", "Fraggle" and "How Mi Did fi Kno", the "belittling" by the ones of superior knowledge being the element which makes me uncomfortable and which seems to me very different in spirit from Miss Lou, where the critique often comes from a visible one of the same class (the critique is not personified in Joan's) and is usually aimed at pretentiousness, failed attempts to take on the standard and its manners, rather than gaucheness or error resulting from ignorance, which becomes amusing (only?) to those who know "better".

23. Morris, introduction, iii. Also recalled in the January 1998 interview with the author.

24. See Louise Bennett, "Jamaica Language", in *Aunty Roachy Seh*, ed. Mervyn Morris (Kingston: Sangster's, 1993), 1–3.

The language issue also received poetic treatment. Most often there was mild or at least implicit ridicule of a persona who held the local language in contempt: a mother distressed that her son has returned from abroad without acquiring a foreign accent, if nothing else; a son who is ridiculous in his pretensions to a British accent and manners, making him the laughing stock of those around; and a confrontation with "Maas Charlie", who has sworn to eradicate dialect. He is warned about the danger of inadvertently committing a crime of dialect speech and becoming the object of his own campaign of scorn.[25]

In all three cases the implicit position of sanity, a quality Morris commended highly in his first critical commentary, is that of a healthy respect for and acceptance of local speech. The listener is made to find these attitudes laughable, though in fact she may share them. And so Miss Lou works towards a change of perception.[26]

This phenomenon of, to use Carrington's words, "the emergence of recognised literary and artistic figures who use the vernacular in their works" is one of the factors which contribute to changing attitudes towards Creoles.[27] The published text gives a certain validity and some prestige. In this way, at least for the reading public, Creole begins to overcome the stigma of not being a language. Its use is no longer restricted to speech.[28] The increasing use of Creole in all literary genres, but especially in poetry, is so marked that no editor or critic can overlook it. Gradually, Creole has been "passing its place", filtering into a number of formal spheres, including the electronic media and the speaker's platform.

---

25. The poems are, respectively, "Noh Lickle Twang!", "Dry Foot Bwoy" and "Bans o' Killin". See Louise Bennett, *Jamaica Labrish* (Kinsgton: Sangster's, 1983), 209, 205, 218.

26. Here again I am reminded of my discomfort with Joan's pieces, which to me seem only to reinforce, in laughing complicity, the disempowering status quo (perhaps unconsciously and unintentionally). It seems to me, in short, a classist humour, with which the "underdog" may also laugh in order to identify with the empowered.

27. Carrington, "Creole Discourse", 12.

28. Carolyn Cooper and Hubert Devonish outline the effect of writing and print technology on the perceived prestige of different languages in their chapter "A Tale of Two States: Language, Lit/orature and the Two Jamaicas", in *The Pressures of the Text: Orality, Texts and the Telling of Tales,* ed. Stewart Brown (Edgbaston: Centre of West African Studies, University of Birmingham, 1995), 60–74.

Political movements leading up to independence and sweeping the young nation have given support to this trend. Anticolonialism, nationalism and the brand of socialism spouted during the seventies, the influence of Black Power and the growing influence of Rastafari all contributed. Akers notes that where a politician would formerly have been unable to win respect without commanding the standard, political survival today demands a facility in Creole, at least on the platform.[29] What was an advantage has become a handicap. In Carrington's words, "Deprecation of Creoles is increasingly considered to be part of an undesirable tendency of the ruling groups . . . to despise anything that is associated with the mass of the society. Reversal of that pattern has promoted the Creole languages into being markers of protest, symbols of identity and even rallying points of political change."[30]

An increased confidence in the legitimacy of the Creole can be heard in the speech of members of the public expressing their views in vox pops, giving information in on-the-spot news reports or addressing the host on any of our several radio talk shows. The presence of a microphone is much less likely to bring hypercorrection in the language of the monolingual Creole speaker.[31]

Moreover, Patwa is the language of reggae music, a powerful, highly visible vehicle for the expression of popular experience and feeling and, just as importantly, a moneymaker, an alternative road out of dispossession, a new set of heroes.

And then there is the culturo-political challenge of Rastafari, deconstructing the English standard, introducing another voice promoting Africa and its heritage. Again, poetry registers these forces in the emergence of a new form, called "dub" by many, not all, using reggae and

---

29. Glenn Alan Akers, *Phonlogical Variation in the Jamaican Continuum* (Ann Arbor, MI: Karoma, 1981), 9.

30. Carrington, "Creole Discourse", 12.

31. Perhaps, then, Joan's pieces are a sign of maturity, an ability to laugh at ourselves, co-identification among the classes, rather than an expression of implicit superiority? More a kind of "I love my people" sentiment? Still, there seems to me some politics worthy of concern in the genuine thrill of the overcrowded bus, the rural donkey, all the things which speak "underdevelopment" which anchor us in a sense of place and peoplehood, for which I have no answer, no politically correct alternative.

rasta rhythms under verses which exploit the features of oral rhetoric and privilege Creole over standard. In this changed climate, "culture" comes to refer primarily to a lifestyle, philosophy and artistic practice which is Afrocentric; just the opposite of its other meaning (to be well bred).

Acknowledgement of Miss Lou as a trailblazer comes readily from writer/performer dub poets.[32] Hyatt credits her along with her colleagues on stage and radio for opening (the) doors to Creole. Joan Andrea Hutchinson's tribute goes further:

> Now we no shame fi chat we owna language
> A[n] we dah thank yu fi it Miss Lou
> Dem a teach it clear a university
> An ongle sake a you.[33]

Though it is a slight exaggeration to give Miss Lou all the credit; there is no denying that academic research has indeed had a role to play in enhancing the status of Creole. What greater prestige than to become the object of intellectual interest? As we gain a greater understanding of the language itself, we have also been examining the historical forces which shaped our attitudes, some of which linger on, as we shall see from the experiences of Joan Andrea Hutchinson.

Earlier in the chapter, I pointed out the common areas of activity in the careers of Joan Andrea and Miss Lou. We have heard Joan crediting Miss Lou for paving the way, and we saw evidence of the change of climate in Joan's use of Creole in her album titles. Still there were negative reactions to her occasional use of Creole on air in the programme *CXC Power*, directed at teenagers preparing to sit the regional examinations. When I suggested that perhaps the educational context made listeners more sensitive to language choice, Joan disagreed, maintaining that Creole was thought inappropriate because radio is a formal medium. "Only this week, this very issue again became the focus of discussion

32. See Morris, introduction, xiv.

33. Joan Andrea Hutchinson, "Tenky Miss Lou, Tenky", side A, track 7 (audio cassette), *Dat Bumpy Head Gal* (n.d.).

on a television panel discussion about the role, function and appropriate style of the (radio) talk show host(s)."[34]

In response to the allegation/charge of being vulgar, University of the West Indies lecturer Michael Witter contended that the perception was based on his use of the Creole, to which the host had to acquiesce. This, after being commended by the president of the Press Association of Jamaica for not only bringing to the airwaves members of the society not previously heard (especially not on KLAS radio), but for speaking the language which they best understood, thereby showing himself to be an effective communicator.

The debate rages on. Significantly, no one ever questioned the right of the callers to use Creole on air. The concern was for the presenter's conduct. Witter is in fact bilingual or diglossic, commanding a fairly wide range of the Jamaican language continuum.[35] When asked why his style (meaning, essentially, his choice of language) was so different on the television discussion programme he also hosts, Witter insisted that the popularity of the medium of radio in Jamaica allowed for an informality inappropriate to the more formal medium of television.

I have included this account to demonstrate the currency of the debate, but also to introduce the controversy which led to Joan Andrea being known as Dat Bumpy Head Gal. Appearing as the host of a discussion programme on television in April 1996, Joan had her hair done in Nubian knots, traditionally known as "chiney bumps" in Jamaica.[36] This brought reactions from the viewing public, among them one woman who was offended in the extreme that this black, ugly and unkempt creature, unfit

34. *On the Record*, CVM Television, 17 May [c. 1998], host Cliff Hughes; panelists Michael Witter, Barbara Gloudon and Garnett Roper.

35. Discussing the Jamaican language situation as a continuum, DeCamp observes that each speaker "represents not a single point but a span on this continuum, for he is usually able to adjust his speech upward or downward for some distance on it". "Social and Geographical", 82.

36. Before its recent emergence as a fashionable style, "chiney bumps" was the way children's hair would be combed right after washing. No doubt, some people see it as the counterpart of curlers, which proper ladies of class do not expose outside the domestic domain. Joan had actually started wearing this style while abroad. At the time of the television appearance, it was not yet popular in Jamaica.

for public view, could have been allowed to invade her living room. The terms of abuse are recalled in the title piece of Joan's first compilation:

> You seh me hairstyle disgusting, chakkachakka an tan bad
> An favour sinting out a street
> An seh me shoulda shame fi lef me house tan so
> An me smile caw me feeling sweet
>
> Yu see the truth is me no fraid a me owna self
> Me not afraid of me
> An when me look ina de mirror
> Me like de smaddy weh me see a look pon me

The matter soon mushroomed into a public controversy. Shortly after, in that very slot on television, the topic of discussion was black identity and self-perception. On that occasion we heard primarily from the "converted" about how liberating and self-affirming it was when they came to recognize beauty in their natural black features. There was also support in the press (one writer going as far as suggesting that some people should not be allowed the services of a telephone).

More telling was the commentary of Ted Dwyer who reported on a social work experiment which revealed that, among a group of black women, none of them wanted their child to be black. This meant that "the black child was already 'rejected' in the womb".[37] Joan was, in fact, called to her hairdresser's one day for a face-to-face discussion with just one such woman: she had married a man who could lighten the complexion of her children and she told them constantly they were not black. She was in distress that day because the hairdresser was unable to restore her weave and she could not allow her husband to see her natural hair; in about eight years of marriage, he never had. As Dwyer observes, for those offended people, the television set is a mirror "on which they vicariously see Joan Collins of *Dynasty* as themselves".

To be confronted there with the image of their blackness, especially one reminiscent of the gollywog and picaninny, is deeply repulsive and brings a visceral reaction. These are women who have internalized the "black

37. Ted Dwyer, "Comments: Rejected from the Womb", *Jamaica Herald*, 8 May 1996.

is bad" notion that Miss Lou had heard around her but found unacceptable even from childhood, thanks in part to her mother's intervention.[38]

Have we strayed from the question of language? No, not very far, for the rejected image is precisely that of the creator of Creole. The response makes it clear that the association of blackness with illiteracy and low social (and moral?) status has not disappeared. In the speech section of our annual festival of performing arts competitions there is a consistent trend for performers of pieces in standard to be well groomed and dressed up, while the unkempt or poverty-stricken look is chosen for dialect pieces.

We have come full circle to Miss Lou on the tramcar. What did the designer who offered to dress Joan for the stage propose? Voluminous skirts, puff sleeves, bright florals, a basket of fruit on her head; in short, a larger-than-life stylized market woman. This seems the logical choice for the performer who uses Creole. But Joan would have none of it. For this would only perpetuate the stereotype, confirming the notion that Creole is not good enough for any serious discourse, relegating the speaker of Creole on stage, to use Joan's words, to the level of the buffoon.

Still, although she dresses "wrong" – that is, in outfits suited for the office or a (semi-)formal evening event, Western style – Creole, humour and of course the "bumpy head" have become hallmarks of Joan's style and stage persona. Her stint on a television social commentary slot in the late 1990s was short-lived. For the station, it was not funny enough. One viewer agreed, chastising Joan for trying to appear middle class and intelligent, which was not the real her. (No comment.)[39]

In her 1968 interview with Dennis Scott,[40] Louise Bennett resisted the label of "professional entertainer of the middle-classes": "I think I speak to all Jamaica. In a performance . . . a large cross section of the community, from the Governor-General to the man in the street, can

38. See Morris, introduction, iii. Miss Lou credited her mother with pointing out the fallacy of that notion to her (interview with the author).

39. Daughter of a police superintendent and a nurse and living in Russell Heights, one of the prestigious suburban residential areas of St Andrew, Joan attended a leading high school and has a university degree. We must assume the gentleman is unaware of her background.

40. Bennett, "Bennett on Bennett", 100–101.

react to the line and the situations I present. So I can't feel that I belong to any class." Why then, Scott asks, did it take so long for her work to be regarded as "respectable"? Her reply: "Because for too long, it was considered not respectable to use the dialect. Because there was a social stigma attached to the kind of person who used the dialect habitually." Miss Lou speaks in the past tense here. Clearly she had seen some changes. And yet, three years later there would be controversy again over the dangerous effects of her dialect commentary on radio.[41] Periodically we rehearse the debate(s): language, hair and blackness. Though the weight of opinion shifts fairly steadily, we are still struggling to fully un-denigrate ourselves.

41. Morris, introduction, xiii.

Celebrating Miss Lou's Historical Record

A Canadian Perspective

VIVIAN LEWIS

Growing up in the Western traditions of anglophone Canada, I had no idea what a significant impact Miss Lou would have on my professional and personal life.

Little did I know that I would find myself travelling to Jamaica multiple times – to be present at the commemoration of the magnificent Miss Lou statue in Gordon Town Square in 2018 and to return to witness the renaming of that same awe-inspiring space as Miss Lou Square a year later.

Little did I imagine that I would have the opportunity to meet several extraordinary members of the large Jamaican Canadian community, many of whom had fond memories of seeing Miss Lou perform, or that I would one day be up on stage competing for the much-sought title of "honorary Jamaican" at a Jamaican Canadian Association Boonoonoonoos Luncheon. It has been a remarkable journey for which I am eternally grateful.

I have the great honour of serving as McMaster's university librarian. McMaster, located in Hamilton, Ontario, is the proud steward of the portion of Miss Lou's archival record gathered during the last decade of her life in Canada. The first and primary accrual was donated to the university library in 2010 by her estate's co-executors: the former citizen judge Pamela Appelt and Fabian Coverley, Miss Lou's son. The second accrual was made in 2015 by writer Neil Armstrong.

Miss Lou's archive at McMaster sits alongside the papers of some of the world's great writers, like Farley Mowat and Austin Clarke, of musicians like Bruce Cockburn, and of great social commentators like

Bertrand Russell. The collection includes 8.5 linear metres of Miss Lou's legal, financial, personal and professional documents, writings, awards, photographs, and sound recordings. Significant portions of the collection have been digitized and are now freely available to scholars wherever they are as part of the university library's digital archive.

The presence of Miss Lou's material has made an indelible mark on the university. The library played a role in celebrations marking both the fiftieth and fifty-fifth anniversaries of Jamaica's independence. In 2017, we had the great honour of welcoming the Most Honourable Juliet Holness (member of the House of Representatives and wife of Prime Minister Andrew Holness) to campus, where she took part in a tour of the Miss Lou Archive, accompanied by dignitaries from Jamaica and the Jamaican Canadian community, including Her Excellency Janice Miller, the high commissioner of Jamaica to Canada, Judge Pamela Appelt, and Howard Shearer, chief executive at Hitachi Canada and former member of McMaster's Board of Governors. Other Jamaican dignitaries have toured the archive, including the Honourable Olivia Grange, minister of culture, gender, entertainment and sport.

In September 2019, we hosted the Canadian celebration of the one hundredth anniversary of Miss Lou's birth (in partnership with Harbourfront Centre and the Jamaican Canadian Association) in the beautifully appointed Miss Lou's Room at Harbourfront. Along the way, the McMaster's university library has built a rich partnership with the National Library of Jamaica to ensure that scholars who start in one collection can easily find their way to the other.

The partnership makes good sense. Our esteemed colleagues at the National Library of Jamaica hold the records assembled during the considerably longer portion of Miss Lou's life in Jamaica (along with the records of her dear husband, Eric Coverley) while McMaster holds the more modest run of collections from her later life in Canada.

Together, McMaster University Library and the National Library of Jamaica work to support and promote Miss Lou's historical record for scholars wherever they are. The two organizations have placed links to each other's collections on their respective websites. I like to think that Miss Lou's digital presence, linked between the two organizations and the two countries, brings us all closer together and that Miss Lou would have been pleased with this result. Miss Lou routinely reminded her friends that Jamaica existed wherever she was, whether that be on the island or in some other colder and less sunny part of the world.

Each one of McMaster's archival collections is significant, but Miss Lou's collection is particularly unique since it touches on so many distinct areas of human endeavour. Miss Lou wasn't simply an actress, a poet, a musician. She was a linguist and a social critic of incredible talent and influence. Her work was deceptively complex. She masked blistering commentary about race and class in the guise of laughter. As noted in the Toronto *City News* report shortly after her death, Miss Lou was "the only poet who has really hit the truth about her society in her own language". It is a tremendous honour, but also an impossible task, to provide a global perspective on Miss Lou's contributions. Impossible because Miss Lou's contributions are so vast, so far-reaching and so embedded in the global understanding of Caribbean culture and language. She honed her craft in concert halls, recording studios and classrooms around the world. As noted by Mervyn Morris and others, she recognized early on that the Jamaican oral tradition was something to be proud of. Its uses had to be defended and celebrated.

I have seen countless musical groups, poets and academics recite her work, and always with the awe and respect owing to an international icon. I have witnessed young Jamaicans, both in Jamaica and in Canada, interpreting Miss Lou's work in new ways, through interpretive dance and dub poetry, and through derivative works of their own creation.

Of course, the official recognitions and awards Miss Lou received during her lifetime from around the world tell part of the story. In 1988, her composition "You're Going Home Now" won a nomination from the Academy of Canadian Cinema and Television for best original song. In 1998, she received an honorary doctorate from York University in Toronto. Sadly, Miss Lou was not able to receive her last honour: the Jamaican consulate in Toronto was scheduled to present her with a significant recognition a few days after she passed away.

There was an outpouring of commendations on the occasion of Miss Lou's passing. The *Guardian* in the United Kingdom described her as "a patriot" whose work "cleared the way for others by demonstrating that Jamaican Patwa could be a medium of significant art". That same article referred to her as the "Mother of Jamaican Culture", "larger than life, earthy, humorous, warm, good natured, highly creative, and full of wisdom". She was described as the champion of dialect verse and the godmother of performance poetry. The London *Times* described her as a "cultural icon on par, among her own people, with Bob Marley, one of many artists she influenced through her poetry in the island's patois". Miss Lou's impact is felt not just in the artistic community but in the classroom. The first time I heard of Miss Lou in Canada was when I was in university in the mid-1980s. My English literature professor asked us to reflect on a selection of poems from various parts of the world and one of those poems was Miss Lou's "Colonization in Reverse", her brilliant take on the immigration of Jamaicans to the United Kingdom in the 1950s and 1960s. Our professor described that poem as a perfect example of contemporary social criticism wrapped in the guise of humour. Miss Lou was artfully slamming pretension, social arrogance, colour/class hierarchy – but with laughter rather than overt condemnation.

That same experience plays out in classrooms across the globe, where Miss Lou's work continues to be studied. At McMaster, we have entire classes of English and cultural studies students coming into the archive to access Miss Lou's collections. The impact on young people – regardless of where they were born – is truly inspirational, but not at all surprising.

Miss Lou's work is well represented in research libraries across the world. A quick review of WorldCat ("the world's largest library catalog") reveals hundreds of libraries holding copies of *Jamaican Labrish*, arguably Miss Lou's most popular book. Her work is well covered in peer-reviewed journal articles, scholarly books, videos, music CDs and children's picture books. Over one hundred theses/dissertations have been written on Miss Lou's contributions to Jamaican culture and the literary and musical record of the West Indies.

Thank you to the many Jamaican nationals (some of them proud and well-accomplished McMaster University alumni) who have welcomed me into their circles with great hospitality and grace. Thank you to the many inspiring Jamaican leaders for their guidance and engagement in archival collections in Jamaica and beyond. Thank you as well to our wonderful partners at the National Library of Jamaica – especially the extraordinary national librarian and chief executive officer, Beverley Lashley for her generosity and assistance as we work together to carry Miss Lou's legacy forward for the next generation of readers and listeners.

Miss Lou's contributions are vast, far-reaching, and deeply embedded in the global understanding of Caribbean culture and language.

Jamma Language Ketch a University

THE UWI MONA LIBRARY

The One Hundred Days of Celebration series of events organized by the Institute for Gender and Development Studies at the University of the West Indies (UWI), held from September to December 2019, provided an opportunity for partnership between the institute and the UWI Mona Library through the launch of an exhibition *A Class Act: Celebrating Louise Bennett-Coverley*.

MISS LOU AND ACADEMIA

> Thank God mi live fi see me and me jamma language ketch a university.
> —*Miss Lou*

Louise Bennett-Coverley's impact has transcended time and space. Scholarly discourse continues on her body of work some fourteen years after her death. Her passion for the Jamaican dialect, poetry and storytelling attracted academic attention from as early as 1942, when her first collection, *Dialect Verses*, was published. It was therefore important that the library's exhibition acknowledged the magnitude of research interrogating this national griot's work.

The West Indies and Special Collections (WISC) of the Mona Library has been collecting evidence of Miss Lou's influence from as early as 1987. The WISC supports scholarly communication through the use of the collection and has been facilitating class visits so students can explore Miss Lou and discuss the different ways she impacted scholarship.

OVERVIEW OF THE EXHIBITION

In conceptualizing *A Class Act*, the library sought to highlight the influence of Miss Lou's writing, broadcasting and teaching on present-day scholars at the UWI and beyond. The exhibition presented items that revealed Miss Lou's commitment to preserving Jamaican Patwa as well as a montage of short videos including interviews and performances that was created by the National Library of Jamaica. These features evoked feelings of nostalgia and awe.

LAUNCH OF THE EXHIBITION

> Jamaica needed Louise Bennett when her talents emerged. . . . It became the lifelong project of Louise Bennett, working in a variety of modes, to increase the recognition of these elements, and to share her infectious pleasure in the lore and practices of most Jamaicans.
>
> —*Mervyn Morris*

A Class Act was launched in the Multifunctional Room of the Main Library at the Mona campus on 23 October 2019. The event featured contributions from a creative writer, a librarian, a poet laureate and a student performer before the viewing of the exhibition. We are grateful to Professor Opal Adisa Palmer, Professor Mervyn Morris, Mrs Francis Salmon and Mr Delroy McGregor, who shared their experiences of researching and being inspired by Miss Lou. The exhibition ran from 23 October 2019 to 23 March 2020 in the Catalogue Hall of the Main Library.

Archiving the Life and Works of a Phenomenal Woman

The Honourable Louise Bennett-Coverley

THE NATIONAL LIBRARY OF JAMAICA
Chantal Cousins, Geraldine Goulbourne, Drusilla Grant, Kaffilee Moore, Keisha Myers and Chantelle Richardson

The National Library of Jamaica (NLJ), an agency of the Ministry of Culture, Gender, Entertainment and Sport, is the premier institution for collecting, preserving and providing access to information on Jamaica's history and culture. The library primarily houses print, audio-visual and digital materials published in Jamaica, by Jamaicans and about Jamaica, and ensures that these materials are preserved as best as possible for the use and benefit of future generations.

THE NATIONAL LIBRARY OF JAMAICA'S ROLE IN PRESERVING MISS LOU'S CULTURAL LEGACY

In accordance with its mandate of cultural preservation, the NLJ is proud to house the national archive of the late Louise Bennett-Coverley. In 1994, the NLJ was given access to control and retain custody of the Coverley Collection by way of gift from the Honourable Mrs Louise Bennett-Coverley and Mr Eric Coverley. The deed of gift was formalized in 2018 between the NLJ and the estate of Louise Bennett-Coverley (per its duly appointed executors, Pamela Appelt and Fabian Coverley). The Honourable Olivia Grange, minister of culture, gender, entertainment and sport, signed the deed of gift under which the collection was turned over to the NLJ.

Upon delivery to the NLJ in 1994, the collection was stored in over one hundred boxes. The contents of the collection comprise a mixture of works by Miss Lou and Eric Coverley. Based on its size, the collection was restructured and different archives for Miss Lou and Eric Coverley were created. Visiting archivist Rosemarie Dodd, a Jamaican residing in the United Kingdom, volunteered to organize and assess the collection. She found that the majority of works were in good condition with only a few items in need of repair. The staff of the Preservation and Conservation Branch of the NLJ was assigned to advance preservation and conservation work and later placed the items in acid-free boxes and folders to prevent yellowing and brittleness. The management, organization and preservation of the Coverley Collection is an ongoing project, and the NLJ is working diligently and is committed to ensuring that both archives are preserved for future access and posterity.

THE MISS LOU ARCHIVES

The Honourable Louise Bennett-Coverley Archives (MS 2177) are currently housed in the Special Collections Branch at the NLJ and can be accessed for study and research. The intellectual property rights to her archive rest with her estate. Requests for permission to copy, distribute, perform, broadcast and make adaptations of the works must be made to her estate through the National Library of Jamaica. The collection consists of forty-six boxes organized into ten main series, which are further divided into sub-series for easy access. The main series are described here.

Series 1: Correspondences from 1943–1988

This series contains personal and professional correspondence or letters relating to Louise Bennett-Coverley and Eric Coverley. All letters that were sent to and received by the couple, whether separately or jointly, can be found within this series.

Series 2: Legal and Financial Documents 1950–1988

This series contains copies of the Coverleys' birth and marriage certificates as well as contracts and royalties that contain correspondence and other documents relating to the Gleaner Company Limited and Island Records Limited.

Series 3: Writing and Performance 1950–1988

This series contains prose, poetry, songs, research material and papers by other writers. The series is further divided into several subseries, such as Anancy, language and culture, pantomime and plays, poems, radio, *Ring Ding*, stories, television, film and video, and other writings.

Series 4: Writing and Performance 1944–1987

This series contains published and printed material by and about Louise Bennett-Coverley, theatre programmes in which she was featured, memorabilia collected by the Coverleys and various documents on Jamaica.

Series 5: Personal and Professional Documents 1936–1988

This series contains Louise Bennett-Coverley's résumés, interviews and writings. The series is divided into a number of sub-series, such as biographies, honours and tributes, diaries, lists and notes, travel and health matters, religious pamphlets, programmes, and drawings by Eric Coverley.

Series 6: Academic and Related Papers 1964–1981

This series contains academic documents and other papers relating to information about Jamaica.

Series 7: Artefacts

Series 7 consists of Louise Bennett-Coverley's purse containing Jamaican coins, a Universal Negro Improvement Association award plaque and an Association of Computational Linguistics Cultural Award plaque, and a filing cabinet that previously housed most of the files from the collection.

Series 8: Photographic and Audio-Visual Materials

This series contains photographs, negatives, and audio and video tapes about Louise Bennett-Coverley and Eric Coverley. It includes photographs of the couple's wedding, photographs of friends and family, and photographs of Jamaican scenes.

Series 9: Eric Coverley's Papers

This series contains fourteen boxes of Eric Coverley's papers.

Series 10: Books and Periodicals

This series contains pamphlets, books and serials used by and given to Eric and Louise Bennett-Coverley at various times throughout their lives.

McMASTER UNIVERSITY COLLECTION

In addition to the Honourable Louise Bennett-Coverley Archive at the NLJ, there is also an archive at the McMaster University Library in Ontario, Canada, called the Miss Lou Archives. As described by the McMaster University Library, the collection has nearly nine metres of textual, graphic and audio-visual materials, reflecting the life of Louise Bennett-Coverley as a writer, performer and promoter of Jamaican culture.

The collection includes correspondence, legal and financial documents, writings, published and printed materials, personal and professional documents, awards, photographs, and more. The collection "Louise Bennett Coverley fonds" reflects objects collected by the McMaster University Library from 1941 to 2008. The collection was acquired in April 2010 from Judge Pamela Appelt and Fabian Coverley, executors of Louise Bennett-Coverley's estate; an addition to the collection was donated in 2015 by journalist and long-time friend Neil Armstrong. Additional data can be obtained from the website https://archives.mcmaster.ca/index.php/louise-bennett-coverley-fonds.

ACCESSING THE ARCHIVES

By housing the nation's treasures, the NLJ has ensured that visitors to the library have access to all its collections. In order to access the library's resources, a registration process is required. Those wishing to access the collection for research, publication and exhibition purposes must produce a valid identification (driver's licence, voter's ID or a student identification card). Registration grants those over the age of fourteen access to the library.

Enquires about the Coverley Collection can be done via email or telephone or by visiting the NLJ. According to a deed of gift signed between the NLJ and the estate of Louise Bennett-Coverley, the collection is to be made accessible in ways that allow for public consultation and for "study and research, and use in educational and cultural publications, subject to the library's existing rules governing access to its collections and in accordance with the terms of the agreement". However, if someone wishes to use the materials for publication, exhibition or any other commercial activity, written permission must be sought from the estate.

Another means of accessing work done on and about Miss Lou is through the NLJ's website. This webpage allows access to a plethora of poems by many of Jamaica's outstanding poets. General searches for books and pamphlets can also be done via the NLJ's WorldCAT-Local page, https://nlj.on.worldcat.org/discovery. Another point of access is NLJ's Poetry Index, which can also be accessed via the website.

A few of the photographs in the NLJ's collection are included here.

Louise Bennett, September 1932

Louise Bennett and Eric Coverley

Louise Bennett with Eric Coverley and two others on her wedding day, 30 May 1954

Miss Lou

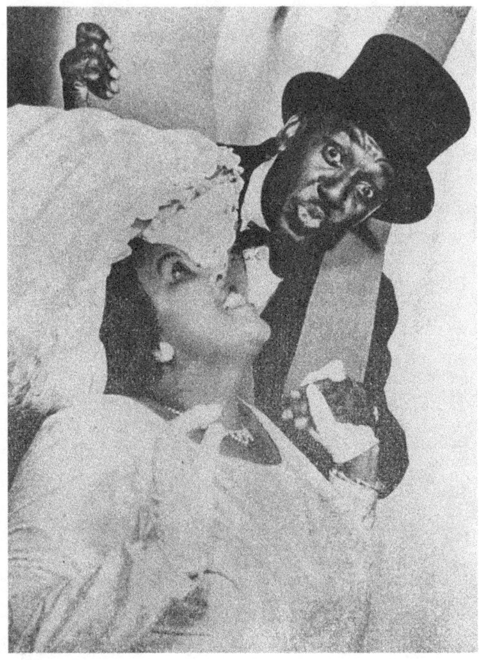

Miss Lou and Ranny Williams, in a scene from the LTM Pantomime *Bredda Buck*, 1965

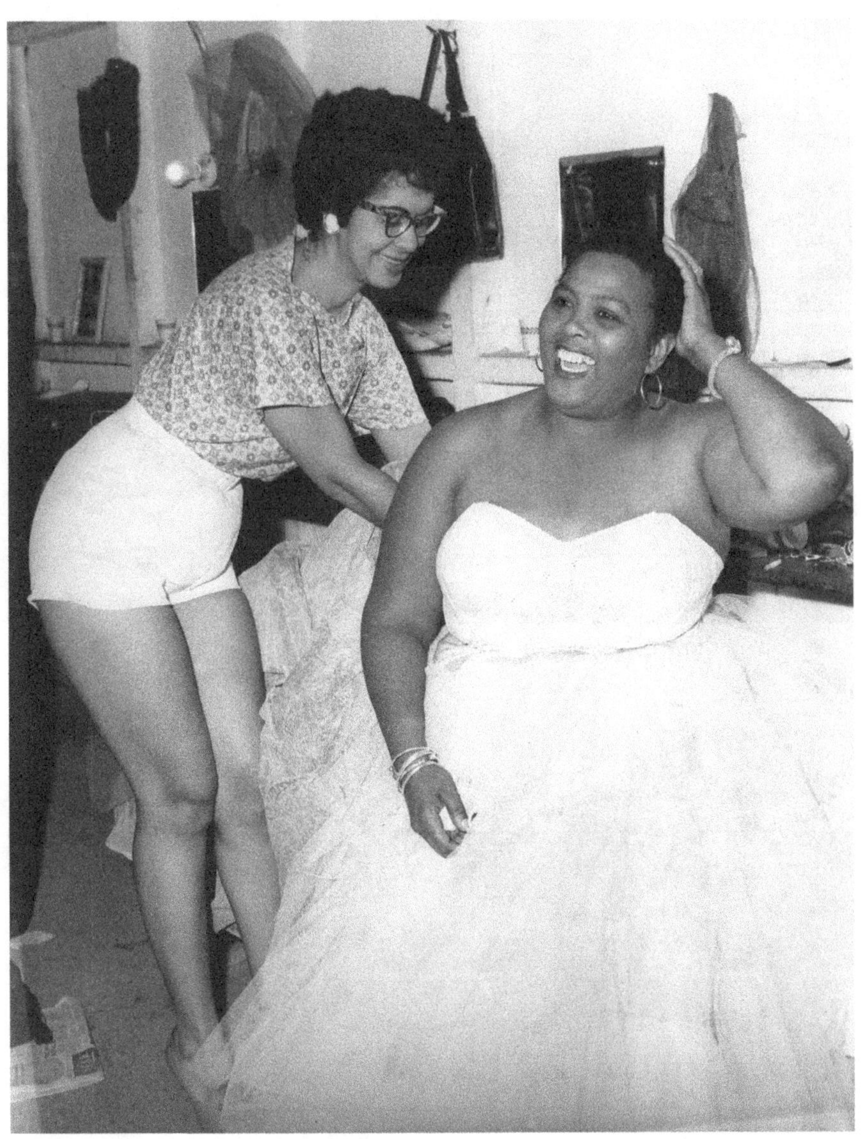

Miss Lou getting ready for a show

Miss Lou on the set of *Ring Ding*

Miss Lou reading in the comfort of her home

Contributors

OPAL PALMER ADISA is the outgoing university director of the Institute for Gender and Development Studies – Regional Coordinating Office, the University of the West Indies, Mona, Jamaica. An award-winning writer of twenty published books, she is a cultural activist and a gender specialist.

CAROLYN ALLEN has lectured in literature at the Mona and Cave Hill campuses of the University of the West Indies, and taught part-time at the Edna Manley College of the Visual and Performing Arts.

LILLIAN ALLEN is a professor of creative writing at OCAD University, Toronto, Canada. She is an internationally acclaimed poet and playwright and a Canadian Juno award–winning recording artist.

CHRISTOPHER ALLEN is a poet from Clarendon, Jamaica, whose work explores religion, language and loss. In 2019, he received the Poet Laureate of Jamaica: Louise Bennett-Coverley Prize for Poetry.

PAMELA APPELT served for eleven years as judge of the Court of Canadian Citizenship. In 2008, she was honoured by the Government of Jamaica with the Order of Distinction for dedicated service to the Jamaican diaspora in Canada.

NEIL ARMSTRONG is a journalist who has worked in radio, print media and television.

SIHLE ATKINSON is a writer and foreign language educator.

DALEA BEAN is a historian, gender scholar and the graduate coordinator at the Institute for Gender and Development Studies, Regional Coordinating Office, the University of the West Indies, Mona, Jamaica.

FARIKA BERHANE is a pan-African writer and journalist with major works on the Jamaican language.

MARGARET RECKORD BERNAL is an arts communicator, poet and Jamaican heritage specialist. She has been active in the fields of cultural documentation, academic research and community development.

AMINA BLACKWOOD MEEKS is a writer, director, performer and custodian of Jamaica's oral tradition. She is the director of the Culture in Education Programme in the Ministry of Education, Jamaica, and founder of Ntukuma, the Storytelling Foundation of Jamaica.

ANDRENE BONNER is the author of four non-fiction books about student resilience and the parent-teacher partnership. Her work of fiction, *No Life in Olympic Gardens,* won the Tamarind Festival of Caribbean Literature's 2009 Lorna Goodison Award for Transformative Literature.

JEAN "BINTA" BREEZE was a Jamaican dub poet and storyteller. She was an honorary creative-writing fellow at the School of English, University of Leicester, and was appointed a Member of the Order of the British Empire in 2012 for services to literature.

MAXINE J. BROWN is a media specialist, events planner and short-story writer.

FRANKLYN HORACE CAMPBELL is a bass musician, songwriter and producer, and has been the leader of the Fab 5 band for the last fifty years.

GRACE CARTER-HENRY LYONS is the musical director for the Heritage Singers, based in Toronto.

QUEWANA COLLMAN is an Excelsior High student who aspires to become a journalist and an actress.

MEL COOKE is a fellow of the Calabash International Literary Trust and the author of the 2008 poetry collection *11/9*.

CAROLYN COOPER is professor emerita and former head, Department of Literatures in English, and a former director of the Institute of Caribbean Studies, the University of the West Indies, Mona, Jamaica.

CHANTAL COUSINS works at the National Library of Jamaica and is an active member of the Library and Information Association of Jamaica.

FABIAN COVERLEY is chief executive officer, Coverley Holdings Inc., and director/consultant, International Management Agencies Inc., in Markham, Ontario.

VIVIAN CRAWFORD is the executive director of the Institute of Jamaica and former pro-chancellor of the University of Technology, Kingston, Jamaica.

KEMAR CUMMINGS is a graduate of the University of the West Indies, Mona, Jamaica, and a poet.

FAITH D'AGUILAR is a singer who has toured with Byron Lee and the Dragonaires and performed with many local and foreign artists. As an actress, she appeared in pantomime with Miss Lou.

NORMA DARBY is the director emerita and founder of the Jamaican Folk Revue, a Florida-based cultural group, and founder of the Louise Bennett-Coverley Heritage Council.

RAUL A. DAVIS is a language interpreter and translator.

SUSAN LYCETT DAVIS, aka Dr Sue, is a professor emerita, Nova Southeastern University, Fort Lauderdale, Florida, and an HR/organizational leadership consultant.

KWAME DAWES is the author of numerous books of poetry, fiction, criticism and essays. He is director of the African Poetry Book Fund and co-founder of the Calabash International Literary Festival in Jamaica.

HUBERT DEVONISH is a professor emeritus of linguistics, the University of the West Indies, Mona, Jamaica, and former coordinator of the Jamaican Language Unit.

ASHLI-ANN DOUGLAS is a PhD candidate, educational researcher, social media content creator, and poet with a passion for the creative arts and educational equity.

ERIC DOUGLAS was a producer/director at the Jamaica Broadcasting Corporation, where he worked with Miss Lou on *Ring Ding*. He is the author of *A Look in the Mirror* and *Torn and other Stories*.

FAE ELLINGTON is a communication and media consultant, veteran media personality, journalist, actress, teacher, trainer and speaking coach. She celebrates fifty years in theatre in 2021.

DAVIA ELLIS is a poet who empowers her secondary and tertiary students and audiences through fashion therapy, guided meditation, music, drama and life-skills training.

OWEN BLAKKA ELLIS is a professional actor and writer and a top comedic entertainer in the Caribbean. He is a senior lecturer in the School of Arts Management and Humanities, Edna Manley College of the Visual and Performing Arts, Kingston, Jamaica.

LINDA GAMBRILL's close friendship with Miss Lou inspired her to write a series of children's books about a girl who was also named Beenybud. She was one of the editors of *Skywritings*, Air Jamaica's in-flight magazine.

BARBARA GLOUDON is a journalist, author, playwright and theatre chair. She worked as an editor at the Gleaner Company for several years and hosted a radio talk show on RJR for thirty years.

LORNA GOODISON has published numerous poetry collections, a short-story collection and the memoir *From Harvey River: A Memoir of My Mother and Her People*. She is a former poet laureate of Jamaica and a painter.

GERALDINE GOULBOURNE is a librarian at the National Library of Jamaica. She has authored the PEP civics column for the *Jamaica Observer*.

OLIVIA "BABSY" GRANGE is Jamaica's minister of culture, entertainment, gender and sport and a reggae enthusiast. She is a founding member of the Jamaica Association of Composers, Authors and Publishers.

DRUSILLA GRANT is a librarian/research officer at the National Library of Jamaica.

EMILE GRANT is a metallurgist working in Ontario, Canada.

COURTNEY GREAVES, aka "Little Miss Lou", is a Jamaican poet, philanthropist and child rights advocate.

TEJAN GREEN WASZAK is the co-author of the poetry collection *We Were Us* and co-editor of *The Idea of the Human Anthology*. She is a lecturer and course co-director in the University Writing Program, Columbia University, New York.

SEAN C. HARRISON is a Jamaican singer and writer and has published six poetry chapbooks.

MARLON HENRY is a high school teacher in Portmore, Jamaica. He is also a poet, songwriter, actor and creator of various forms of content for social media.

BONGO HERMAN is a Jamaican drummer, percussionist and singer who has been in the music business since the early 1960s. He is a tour guide at the Bob Marley Museum in Kingston, Jamaica.

NADIA L. HOHN is the author of seven books for young people. She is completing an MFA in creative writing at the University of Guelph-Humber.

MICHAEL HOLGATE is the head of the Philip Sherlock Centre for the Creative Arts at the University of the West Indies, Mona, Jamaica, and artistic director of the ASHE Company.

JULIET HOLNESS is a member of the House of Representatives in Jamaica. She is a motivational speaker, real estate owner and chartered accountant.

DONNA P. HOPE is professor of culture, gender and society and former head of the Institute of Caribbean Studies, the University of the West Indies, Mona, Jamaica.

RUTH HOWARD is a writer and performer with a passion for the creative arts.

JOAN ANDREA HUTCHINSON is an author, cultural educator, motivational speaker, storyteller and actress.

PAUL KEENS-DOUGLAS, aka Mr Tim Tim, is one of the most eloquent and best-known raconteurs and social commentators in the English-speaking Caribbean. His books include *Tanti at de Oval, Savannah Ghost* and *Role Call.*

DEANNE KENNEDY is a Barbadian writer, poet, visual artist, craftsperson, and storyteller.

LOLITA KNIBB PHILLIPS is a graduate of York University, Toronto, Canada.

LINTON KWESI JOHNSON is a UK-based Jamaican poet and recording artiste. In 2002 he became the second living poet, and the only black poet, to be published in the Penguin Modern Classics series.

BEVERLEY LASHLEY is the national librarian at the National Library of Jamaica.

EASTON LEE is a communications professional and a former announcer at the Jamaica Broadcasting Corporation.

JESSICA C. LEWIS is the head of the West Indies and Special Collections at the University of the West Indies, Mona, Jamaica.

VIVIAN LEWIS is university librarian at McMaster University, Hamilton, Canada.

ANN-MARGARET LIM is a poet and the author of *Kingston Buttercup* and *The Festival of Wild Orchid.*

JEAN LOWRIE-CHIN is a communications consultant, seniors advocate, author and newspaper columnist. She is the founder and managing director of PRO Communications Limited.

SHIRLEY MASSEY is a poet and the author of *Countri Labrish: A Collection of Jamaican Patois Poems.*

DELROY McGREGOR is a writer and a student at the University of the West Indies, Mona, Jamaica.

MELISSA McKENZIE teaches English language and literature at Old Harbour High School, Jamaica.

ALEXANDRIA MILLER is a writer and historian and the US editor of *BASHY* magazine. She is working towards a PhD in Africana studies at Brown University, Providence, Rhode Island.

KEI MILLER is a professor of English at the University of Miami, Florida. He is the author of numerous works of poetry, fiction and essays.

KALIAH WHAYNETTE MINTO is a grade four student of the Albion Primary and Junior High school. She is actively involved in the culture club and the peer-counselling group.

ALMA MOCKYEN is known for her contribution to the arts in Jamaica, as a radio, television and stage personality. She is the author of *Rewind*, a historical account of radio broadcasting in Jamaica.

KAFFIELEE MOORE is a senior library assistant at the National Library of Jamaica.

SCHONTAL MOORE is a lecturer in language and literature education and the Graduate Studies coordinator for the School of Education at the University of the West Indies, Mona, Jamaica.

PAMELA MORDECAI is a poet, novelist, short-story writer, scholar and anthologist. She has been a teacher, a TV host, a businesswoman and an editor, and has published poems and stories for children and adults.

MERVYN MORRIS is a professor emeritus of the University of the West Indies, Mona, Jamaica. He is a former poet laureate of Jamaica and has written extensively of the life and work of Miss Lou.

MUTABARUKA is a Rastafari dub poet, actor and host of two popular radio programmes, *The Cutting Edge* and *Steppin' Razor.*

KEISHA MYERS is a librarian at the National Library of Jamaica.

CURTIS MYRIE is a veteran sports and features journalist, television producer and marketer.

AJAMU NANGWAYA is a lecturer in the Institute of Caribbean Studies at the University of the West Indies, Mona, Jamaica.

CHERRY NATURAL is a performance dub poet and martial artist. Her most recent work is the album *Self Mastery* (2021).

LILIETH H. NELSON is a poet, singer, entrepreneur and science educator.

KEVIN A. ORMSBY is the artistic director of KasheDance and teaches in the Faculty of Dance Performance at Centennial College, Toronto, Ontario.

PERCIVAL JAMES PATTERSON is a former prime minister of Jamaica. He is the founder of HeisConsults and the author of *My Political Journey: Jamaica's Sixth Prime Minister.*

VELMA POLLARD is a retired lecturer in language education at the University of the West Indies, Mona, Jamaica. She has published numerous works of poetry, fiction and non-fiction.

PATRICIA REID-WAUGH is a retired chartered accountant and author *Retirement: A New Adventure.*

CHANTELLE RICHARDSON is a librarian at the National Library of Jamaica.

TOMMY RICKETTS is a filmmaker, actor and musician. He co-founded the Poetry Society of Jamaica and is its current president.

LINCOLN ROBINSON served as press secretary to former prime minister Portia Simpson Miller and as the director of communications in the Office of the Prime Minister, Jamaica.

ANNIKA SIMONE ROWE is a poet, entrepreneur and social activist. She is the founder of the non-profit organization Uncommon Arts, which serves inner-city communities.

OLIVER SAMUELS is a comedian and actor, often described as the Jamaican "King of Comedy". He was the star of Jamaica Broadcasting Corporation's television series *Oliver at Large.*

ALECIA MARIA SAWYERS is a Jamaican educator, author and freelance editor. She is a fellow of the Calabash Writer's Workshop.

LASANA M. SEKOU has published over twenty books of poetry, monologues and short stories.

ISIS SEMAJ-HALL is the Riddim Writer, a disruptive dub doctor with a creative practice that is nurtured by sound. She is a co-founder and editor of *PREE: Caribbean Writing.*

JAYNA SHIELDS

JEAN SMALL is an actress, director, playwright, puppeteer, storyteller, poet and educator.

AISHA SMITH is pursuing a master's in teaching at the University of the West Indies, Mona, Jamaica.

MALACHI SMITH is a fellow of the Mitchener Caribbean Writers Institute at the University of Miami, Florida, and a founding member of Poets in Unity.

PAULINE STONE MYRIE is a public relations consultant, actress and producer.

CHRISTINE SWABY works for the City of Evanston, Illinois.

SHELLEY SYKES-COLEY is a poet and the author of *Chat 'Bout! An Anthology of Jamaican Conversations.*

LISA GAYE TAYLOR is a poet and a graduate of the University of the West Indies, Mona, Jamaica.

fabian m. thomas is a performing arts specialist and adjunct lecturer at the University of the West Indies and the Mico University, Kingston, Jamaica, and the author of *New Thought, New Words.*

LISA TOMLINSON is a researcher, author and lecturer at the University of the West Indies, Mona, in the Institute of Caribbean Studies.

ANTONIA VALAIRE is a poet, Christian, and award-winning author of *Pearls among Stones, Black Gold* and *Out from Babylon System: Liberation of Mind.* As a spoken-word artist, she has been nominated for an International Reggae and World Music Award.

KLIVE WALKER is an author, music historian and cultural critic. He is the author of *Dubwise: Reasoning from the Reggae Underground.*

L.A. WANLISS is a teacher and is the CEO of L.A. Wanliss Editing and Consultancy. She is completing her MFA in creative writing at the University of the West Indies, St Augustine, Trinidad and Tobago.

DONNA AZA WEIR-SOLEY is the author of *Eroticism, Spirituality and Resistance in Black Women's Writings* and the poetry collections *First Rain* and *The Woman Who Knew.* She is current president of the Association of Caribbean Women Writers and Scholars.

MARJORIE WHYLIE is an acclaimed pianist, percussionist, educator and composer. She is the former musical director of Jamaica's National Dance Theatre Company and orchestra leader with the National Pantomime Movement.

SONIA S. WILLIAMS is a writer, director, performance artist, educator and researcher in African Caribbean culture.

LATTECHA WILLOCKS is a multidisciplinary Jamaican artist, designer and writer.

JEAN WILSON is a writer and communication consultant and former journalist for *Daily Gleaner* and the *Daily News* in Jamaica. She is the author of *No More "Smalling Up" of Me.*

BERNADETTE WORRELL-JOHNSON is a librarian in the West Indies and Special Collections, the University of the West Indies, Mona, Jamaica.

BEVERLEY ELAINE WRIGHT is a doctor with over thirty years of service in the public health sector.